Struggles before *Brown*

D0145661

2008

OCT

HU

Advancing the Sociological Imagination

A Series from Paradigm Publishers

Edited by Bernard Phillips and Harold Kincaid

Goffman Unbound! A New Paradigm for Social Science
By Thomas J. Scheff (2006)

The Invisible Crisis of Contemporary Society: Reconstructing Sociology's Fundamental Assumptions
By Bernard Phillips and Louis C. Johnston (2007)

Understanding Terrorism: Building on the Sociolotgical Imagination
Edited by Bernard Phillips (2007)

Struggles before Brown: *Early Civil Rights Protests and Their Significance Today*
By Jean Van Delinder (2008)

STRUGGLES BEFORE *BROWN*

EARLY CIVIL RIGHTS PROTESTS AND THEIR SIGNIFICANCE TODAY

Jean Van Delinder

Paradigm Publishers
Boulder • London

Published in the United States by Paradigm Publishers, 3360 Mitchell Lane Suite E, Boulder, CO 80301 USA.
Paradigm Publishers is the trade name of Birkenkamp & Company, LLC,
Dean Birkenkamp, president and publisher.

Library of Congress Cataloging-in-Publication Data

Van Delinder, Jean, 1956–
  Struggles before Brown : early civil rights protests
and their significance today / Jean
Van Delinder.
     p. cm.—(Advancing the sociological imagination)
  Includes bibliographical references and index.
  ISBN 978-1-59451-458-6 (hardcover : alk. paper)
  ISBN 978-1-59451-459-3 (pbk. : alk. paper)
    1. African Americans—Civil rights—History. 2. Civil rights movements—United
States—History. 3. Kansas—Race relations—History. 4. Oklahoma—Race relations—
History. I. Title.
  E185.61.V29 2008
  323.1196'073—dc22

                                                                              2007045741
Printed and bound in the United States of America on acid-free paper that meets the standards of the American National Standard for Permanence of Paper for Printed Library Materials.

Designed and typeset by Straight Creek Bookmakers
11 10 09 08   2 3 4 5

This book is dedicated to those who shared their stories.

Contents

Acknowledgments

I would like to thank my series editors, Bernie Phillips and Harold Kincaid, who provided encouragement, guidance, and support through the early stages and drafts. Special thanks to Dan Krier for his unfailing generosity in giving me critical feedback along with keen insights. Thanks to Jack Weller who always understood what I was trying to accomplish. I also appreciate previous critical feedback from Bob Antonio, Joane Nagel, and Norm Yetman. To David Norman Smith for his key advice and vital support. I would like to acknowledge the institutional support from Oklahoma State University for sabbatical and summer ASR grants and encouragement from my department heads Chuck Edgley and Patricia Bell. Thanks to Helen Clements who could always find a needed article or citation at the last minute and to Tim Rives, National Archives-Central Plains Region, the staff at the Kansas State Historical Society, the Johnson County Museum, the Oklahoma State Historical Society, and the Oklahoma Territorial Museum. I especially want to acknowledge previous advice and support from Cheryl Brown Henderson and the Brown Foundation, Topeka, Kansas; Deborah Dandridge, Kansas Collection, Spencer Research Library, University of Kansas; and Pat Michaelis, Kansas State Historical Society. Finally, thank you to my husband, Brad, who has provided unfailing support to this project for many years.

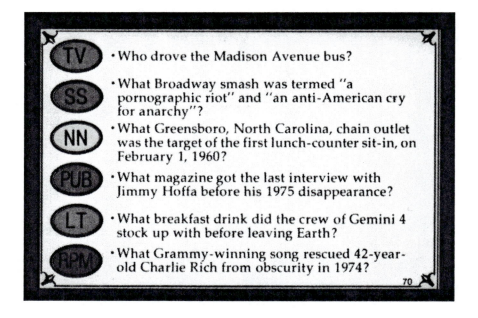

- **TV** · Who drove the Madison Avenue bus?

- **SS** · What Broadway smash was termed "a pornographic riot" and "an anti-American cry for anarchy"?

- **NN** · What Greensboro, North Carolina, chain outlet was the target of the first lunch-counter sit-in, on February 1, 1960?

- **PUB** · What magazine got the last interview with Jimmy Hoffa before his 1975 disappearance?

- **LT** · What breakfast drink did the crew of Gemini 4 stock up with before leaving Earth?

- **RPM** · What Grammy-winning song rescued 42-year-old Charlie Rich from obscurity in 1974?

70

Baby Boomer

- **TV** Ralph Kramden
- **SS** *Hair*
- **NN** Woolworth's
- **PUB** *Playboy*
- **LT** *Tang*
- **RPM** *Behind Closed Doors*

70

Trivial Pursuit® and related proprietary rights are owned by Horn Abbot Ltd. Used with permission.

PART I

Overview

Lunch counter sit-in at Katz Drug Store, August 26, 1958, in Oklahoma City (courtesy of the Oklahoma State Historical Society).

1

Introduction

The success of any great moral enterprise does not depend upon numbers.

—*William Lloyd Garrison, abolitionist editor* [1]

The recent fiftieth anniversary of the 1954 *Brown v. Board of Education of Topeka* landmark Supreme Court decision against school segregation brings to mind some puzzling questions: Why Kansas? Why and how did this nonslaveholding state located on the western border of the South have a system of racial segregation in the first place? The 1954 *Brown* case was the culmination of a legal strategy challenging the constitutionality of school segregation begun in the 1930s by the National Association for the Advancement of Colored People (NAACP) and carried through by the New York-based NAACP Legal Defense and Educational Fund (LDF). School segregation became legal after the 1896 *Plessy v. Ferguson* judgment "separate but equal" was not a violation of the Constitution. After 1896, all public facilities, including public schools, were subject to segregation. Though school segregation was common in Southern states, it also occurred in other places—such as Kansas. Obviously, racism is not endemic to the South. It is troubling that in the nine states of the former Confederacy there was a coercive line of separation—that is, a fixed line between blacks and whites, called a "color line," which was codified by law and sustained by social custom. Writing several years after the abolition of slavery, Frederick Douglass (1881) and W. E. B. Du-Bois (1901) used the term to symbolize how racial prejudice vindicated blacks' ongoing economic and political inequality as well as beliefs about their social and moral inferiority. The color line's presence, then, is not

3

completely illogical given the terrible history of slavery in the nine states of the former Confederacy. But why did the color line exist in border states such as Kansas, where slavery never existed? What effect, if any, did this have on subsequent challenges to change it? These are some of the questions that come to mind while we, as Americans, are still trying to come to terms with the institution of racial segregation fifty years after it was declared unconstitutional by the *Brown v. Board* decision.

These questions open us up to the enormous complexity of human behavior. To obtain answers, they call on us to probe nothing less than the forces deriving from social structure, from culture, from the agency of individuals, and from the momentary phenomena occurring within particular situations. My response is to come forward with a methodology—the Web and Part/Whole Approach (Phillips 2001; Phillips, Kincaid, and Scheff, 2002; Phillips, ed. 2007; Phillips and Johnston 2007)—which builds on the broad orientation of C. Wright Mills's *The Sociological Imagination* (1959). It is a methodology that follows the scientific ideal of opening up to such a wide range of forces, assuming that they are all relevant to these questions. By so doing, I am also invoking a methodology that bridges sociology's many specialized and subspecialized areas, one that can address not only diverse social movements but also the diversity of substantive and applied problems throughout the social sciences.

This book approaches civil rights protest not as a uniquely southern problem, but as an American problem. How can we as Americans reconcile our cherished cultural values of liberty, equality, and freedom with the legal sanction of slavery and the later institution of racial segregation? We all know that slavery in the South was terminated during the Civil War and that the Southern civil rights movement during the 1950s and '60s eventually removed racial segregation; this book does not attempt to address those questions. What it does address, though, is how racial segregation was challenged in areas where racial separation was not built on the ruins of slavery. Seventeen states (Texas, Oklahoma, Missouri, Arkansas, Louisiana, Mississippi, Alabama, South Carolina, Georgia, Florida, North Carolina, Tennessee, Kentucky, Virginia, West Virginia, Maryland, and Delaware) enacted strict segregation acts physically separating the races in most public facilities such as schools, restaurants, and restrooms (White 1994, 15). Four states (Kansas, Arizona, New Mexico, and Wyoming) had more permissive segregation statutes in that racially mixed public facilities were not specifically prohibited. This book concerns itself with two border states, Kansas and Oklahoma, both situated next to each other but wedged between the South and the West, representing a mix of the South, North, and West. The ambivalence of Northern and Western attitudes toward racial exclusion is reflected in the limited, permissive segregation experienced in Kansas, while Oklahoma had the more hegemonic, pervasive *de jure* segregation found in the Southern regions. Although legitimated by different legal statutes, the color line in Topeka, Kansas, and Guthrie, Oklahoma, is nevertheless very different than in Birmingham, Alabama, or Greenwood, Mississippi. This book seeks to answers to questions such as "What is the regional variance in challenges to the color line?" Though Oklahoma shared *de jure* segregation with its southern neighbors, its civil rights protest is rarely included as "significant." Campaigns for racial justice in Oklahoma include lunch counter sit-in protests against restaurants refusing to serve African Americans in the late 1950s. The first nonviolent occupation of lunch counters was thought to have occurred in Greensboro, North Carolina, in February 1960. This raises another question this book seeks to answer: Why have the non-Southern challenges to racial segregation become obscured by the better known ones of the civil rights movement?

Prior to the 1954 *Brown* case in Topeka, Kansas, there were eleven other challenges to Kansas school segregation reviewed by the Kansas State Supreme Court between 1881 and 1949 (Wilson 1994). As discussed in the succeeding chapters, these suits all involved plaintiffs who were suing local school districts on behalf of their minor children in order to obtain equal access to a school system funded by their tax dollars.

Similarly, in early twentieth century Guthrie, Oklahoma, African Americans used their legal status as tax payers to protest having to pay for a new public library they could not use (Van Delinder 2002). Like school segregation, lack of access to public libraries was just another obstacle African Americans faced in Oklahoma where "the minority educational system suffered abysmally" (Robbins 2000, 38). This challenge was also gendered because as a cultural institution, libraries were a public space where women could go unattended by a male companion. It should come as no surprise that this challenge is led by an African American woman, Judith Carter Horton, who had come to Oklahoma Territory seeking work as a teacher after earning a degree at Oberlin College in 1891. Standing just four feet ten inches, Horton overshadows others by her determination to obtain racial justice. In the late 1950s, this time twenty miles south of Guthrie, in Oklahoma City, another African American woman, Clara Luper, organized lunch counter sit-ins using young people, ranging in age from six to fifteen (Reese 2003, 328). The image of NAACP Youth Council children occupying seats customarily reserved exclusively for white adults aroused sympathy for the injustice of racial segregation and also made it difficult for the police to use force when evicting them for trespassing. Luper's strategy would later be used in Greensboro, North Carolina, in February 1960, which is usually credited as the "start" of the student sit-in movement.

Though many of these episodes are not unknown to civil rights scholars, they have been shunted to the side in many civil rights narratives because they "did not have a mass base" (Morris 1984, 193). Civil rights scholars have assessed these early protests, sit-ins, public boycotts, and school desegregation attempts as lacking in organizational structure and not relevant to the political process model of black insurgency (McAdam 1982; Morris 1984). These incidents are not unknown; they are just forgotten.

Studying these neglected protests makes possible an enhanced understanding of civil rights activism, as well as demonstrates the general utility of examining the way individual action is carried out within specific social situations. As Maines (2001, 3) reminds us, "[H]uman behavior must occur somewhere, and if that behavior is overtly social then it occurs with someone in a cultural, institutional, gendered, national, racial, economic, and/or historical context." As with Maines, this book takes into account these multiple aspects of social behavior in analyzing social action.

This book discusses "forgotten" civil rights protest, that is, those borderline areas of the civil rights movement, both geographically and theoretically, which have been unappreciated, understudied, and thrust to the side in the overall narrative of the civil rights movement. Studying this type of protest helps to illustrate how individuals embedded in specific situations are also linked to social structure without forgetting that individuals and society are inseparable.

The "Master Narrative" and Civil Rights Protest

One problem in studying forgotten civil rights protest is the lack of a coherent framework connecting the foundational but seemingly disparate situational protests of the earlier era with the better-known mass mobilizations in the later era. One obstacle to making this connection is the predominance of the historical narrative or "'Master Narrative' of the civil rights movement" (Payne and Green 2003, 1–9). This "dominant narrative" (Hall 2005, 1234) is an idealized version of the civil rights movement as a series of protests progressing gradually against Southern oppression, the fateful intervention of charismatic leaders—such as Martin Luther King, Jr.—providing inspiration for mass activism. According to the Master Narrative, these events caused the federal government to realize that racial prejudice and discrimination was a national dilemma and was morally wrong in the context of American democratic values (Payne and Green 2003, 143).

The narrative of this book posits the 1954 *Brown v. Board of Education of Topeka* landmark Supreme Court decision as the inspiration for the sudden appearance of radicalized protest, thus consigning pre-*Brown* protest as less essential to understanding the civil rights movement. This post-*Brown* dominance obscures the activism behind this landmark decision in places like Topeka, Kansas. The Master Narrative also only considers civil rights protest as mass protests against the Southern comprehensive "tripartite system of domination" used to control blacks "economically, politically, and personally" (Morris 1984, 1).

This study takes issue with the way civil rights protest is characterized in the Master Narrative, since it renders invisible the struggles of ordinary people. The Master Narrative simplifies and ignores many types of social action by ignoring the complicated relationships between agency, culture, social structure, and situations in social movements. When focusing on the civil rights movement, the Master Narrative posits the 1954 *Brown v. Board of Education of Topeka* landmark Supreme Court decision as the single most important agent of change and the inspiration for the sudden appearance of radicalized protest. It emphasizes the types of protest supporting racial integration—the objective goal of the civil rights movement. It frames the discourse on civil rights protest by focusing on spectacular events and trivializes activism occurring on its edge. Challenging this Master Narrative brings human agency back into focus by examining the stories of "ordinary people" who by undertaking "everyday resistance" brought about social change.

From Master Narrative to Border Campaign: Employing Ideal Types

The study links the agency of ordinary people to social action through the conversion of the Master Narrative into an ideal type that is contrasted with a second ideal type, Border Campaign. After Weber, ideal types are heuristic constructs incorporating subjective meaning (agency to social action) to empirical realities. This is accomplished by dividing structure into institutions (political and economic) and culture (ideas and belief systems). Unlike the one-dimensional and specific concepts employed by the Master Narrative, ideal types are multidimensional and general in nature. Ideal types help to maintain conceptual uniformity when confronted with cases of data heterogeneity and nonlinear causality (Weber 1964).

In this study, the Master Narrative ideal type represents the conventional understanding of social movements in general and the typical narrative understanding of the civil rights movement in particular. This ideal type emphasizes homogeneity of data, that is, a linear causality of action that is instrumentally rational; agency is referred to in terms of "oversocialized" or exceptional individuals who concert their efforts through structural, political, and economic institutions. This type focuses on social movements utilizing formal organizations and charismatic leadership directed toward specific, material goals. So, as the conventional understanding of social movements, the Master Narrative obscures social action that is not spectacular. As a narrative, the Master Narrative emphasizes linkages between significant historical events in the story of the civil rights movement.

In contrast to the Master Narrative there is the second ideal type: Border Campaign. This ideal type emphasizes heterogeneity of data, a nonlinear causality of action that is value-rational rather than instrumentally rational—action that is understood in terms of individual and subjective values rather than generalized, objective goals. Border Campaign complicates the ways in which agency and identity are operationalized within social movements. Assuming that neither agency nor structure is totally consistent, the Border Campaign type emphasizes their interplay; this helps to differentiate a wider range of associations between groups of actors (the degree of social interaction) from either the orderly or contradictory part of the social structure (the degree of system integration) (Archer 1996). In this way, the Border Campaign assumes that a dynamic and oftentimes even contradictory relationship exists between agency and structure in social movements. It takes into account incongruities underlying ideas embedded in cultural systems and their causal consensus or influence on people's actions (sociocultural interaction).

The Border Campaign ideal type complicates our understanding of the cultural dynamics of racial segregation. It emphasizes discrete units of civil rights protest directed toward subjective (value-rational) intermediary goals consistent with a specific time and place. It brings into focus those types of actions that help to create a better immediate reality while knowing they are not going to fundamentally transform the overall structure of racial injustice. For example, in the early twentieth century African Americans in Kansas were more likely to agitate in support of racial segregation as a way to gain control of their children's education by insisting that only black teachers be employed in segregated schools. The Master Narrative casts aside this type of protest as not being consistent with the goal of integration, a long-term objective of the civil rights movement. When this same data is analyzed by the Border Campaign, this type of protest comes into focus as being characteristic of a specific region and time; integration threatened the power of black status groups benefiting from segregation such as teachers, doctors, lawyers, and other professionals whose livelihood rested on the black community not having access to goods and services in the white community.

Border Campaign focuses on generalities between the disparate actions in social movements without surrendering their distinctiveness. It is also a way of studying forgotten civil rights action apart from the goals that evolved later in the broader civil rights movement. More generally, it provides a way to study social movements as long-term aggregates of discrete protest units rather than viewed in relationship to higher-level (i.e., more abstract) goals. Whereas the later civil rights movement challenged everything related to segregation, including its ideological foundations, forgotten civil rights protest had a much more limited repertoire of action focusing on short-term goals related to a specific time and place.

In summary, comparing Master Narrative to Border Campaign brings into focus the following: (1) how actions of individuals are disparate; (2) how distinct actions coalesce into collective action; and, finally (3) how action is mediated by ideas embedded in cultural systems, highlighting the dynamic interplay between agency and structure. By paying closer attention to how it intersects varying dimensions of agency and structure, action is no longer one-dimensional and static. In effect, the Master Narrative works as a social movement "master frame" that is fixed by an "overarching ideational and interpretive anchoring of subsequent interpretations" (Snow and Benford 1992, 144). The Master Narrative inhibits how events are interpreted and eventually written as social movement narratives, constraining them as being largely a political mass-based movement between two groups of observable antagonists: African Americans and white racists. Through comparison of the Master Narrative and Border Campaign ideal types we can come to a better understanding of forgotten civil rights activism as outlined below:

- Though the origin of national school desegregation is situated in Topeka, Kansas, near the geographical center of the United States, there has been little attention given to the community-level actions that brought about racial desegregation in that city. What is the relationship of school desegregation in Kansas to other challenges of school segregation elsewhere? Why has this activism been forgotten? What was the relationship of this pre-*Brown* school desegregation era to the later mass mobilizations of the post-*Brown* era?
- Sit-ins began in Wichita, Kansas, on July 19, 1958, and a month later in Oklahoma City, Oklahoma. Without external support, the local NAACP Youth Councils in Wichita and Oklahoma City disrupted lunch counters after negotiations to integrate them broke down. Local youth councils were recognized for their efforts to at the fifty-first conference of the NAACP, held in 1960, which the Greensboro youths attended. In Oklahoma City, the sit-ins would continue as forgotten civil rights protest until July 1964. Why has this precursor to the 1960 student sit-in movement been overlooked? What can we learn about the difficulties in sustaining protest that is applicable to other social movements?
- The birth of mass mobilizations in Montgomery and Birmingham, Alabama, in 1955 and 1963, respectively, represent the mixture of a preexisting protest tradition that coexisted with the mass mobilization protest tradition. The dramatic events surrounding the Montgomery Bus Boycott and the near-riots in Birmingham eight years later have eclipsed the agency of Jo Ann Robinson and the contributions of the Women's Political Council organized in Montgomery in 1946 and the efforts of labor activist E. D. Nixon in Birmingham dating back to the 1930s. Both Robinson and Nixon continued their efforts during the

mass-mobilization era, but the significance of their agency has been obscured by the importance of charismatic leadership outlined in the Master Narrative. What can we learn about the contributions of other types of leadership not specified in the Master Narrative?

All of these "border" episodes are striking testaments to the power of marginal civil rights protests. Certainly not all of them were "mass mobilizations" in any strict sense concerned with the large-scale organization of people and resources to take action against racial segregation. How then might they be understood? The thesis is that, for all the understandable interest, focusing only on the dramatic "mass mobilization" aspects of the civil rights movement stands as an obstacle to recognizing the full range of *civil rights* tensions between the established social order of racial segregation and the protest campaigns challenging it. These tensions are particularly disparate in the pre–mass mobilization era, roughly the first half of the twentieth century. The heterogeneity of these pre- or early civil rights actions have rendered them relatively invisible as protest, since they did not fall under established sets of rules used to study the civil rights movement. The purpose here is to describe the alternative approach that this book takes to exploring those tensions, to better understand not only the early civil rights era, but also the mass mobilization era of the civil rights movement in general.

By dating significant civil rights protest to the mid-1950s, the Master Narrative of the civil rights movement obscures how by the middle of the twentieth century racial segregation was being directly challenged by "ordinary people" in American society. That these struggles are largely lost from view is partially due to a few primarily symbolic national racial initiatives occurring at this time that are often mentioned as important "precursors" to the modern civil rights movement (Dalifume 1968). Even before the United States officially entered World War II in December 1941, the March on Washington Movement (MOWM) was being organized as a national collective protest against racial segregation in the military and by discriminatory hiring practices by civilian defense contractors. Organized by the national labor leader A. Philip Randolph, head of the Brotherhood of Sleeping Car Porters, the MOWM was conceived as a mass demonstration against the hypocrisy of racial inequality, especially in a democracy gearing up to fight a war to eliminate tyranny and oppression. This looming political embarrassment was circumvented when President Franklin Delano Roosevelt signed Executive Order No. 8802, forbidding racial discrimination by civilian defense contractors.[2]

Though the MOWM was a nonevent since it did not actually occur, it was to be an important model for future civil rights mass mobilizations captured by the Master Narrative of the modern civil rights era (Dalifume

1968). It also provided a model for analyzing the role of the federal government in handling racial contention by trying to defuse it and thereby avoid a national crisis, yet at the same time keeping change to a minimum (Lawson 1998, 4). This is illustrated by President Harry S. Truman's official desegregation of the peacetime army in 1948, which had already seen black and white Americans fighting side by side in World War II. That same year, under the guise of states' rights, racial issues split the Democratic Party, threatening Truman's reelection. Clearly, well before the mid-1950s, the issue of race had emerged in American political consciousness; everywhere, people were being forced to choose sides.

But the national debate over racial justice is not just a matter of "black and white" or "for" or "against" racial equality; it was complicated by political, economic, and social considerations including individual determinism, states' rights, the role of the federal government in local affairs, funding of public schools, employment opportunities, job protections, and questions of who lived next door to you, where your children would attend school, and who would be their friends. By the end of the 1940s, the ideology of racial equality was slowly emerging as a broad cultural goal in American society. However, given the permeation of "separate but equal" or "Jim Crow" segregation, codified either by law or custom, the institutional means to achieve the cultural goal of racial equality was severely limited. What was the gap between cultural goals and institutional means in the early civil rights era? How was this gap narrowed by the first national victory for more racial inclusion—school desegregation culminating in the *Brown* decision? Though the Master Narrative of modern civil rights gives it "Big Event" status, it also trivializes it by exhaustively studying it as a watershed moment, largely ignoring how its slow progression to national significance was sustained through the everyday resistance of ordinary people.

Border Campaign, Ideal Types, and Interpretive Analysis

This book examines these and other questions posed by the Border Campaign and left unanswered by the Master Narrative. To assist us in this problem, I have identified three crucial categories that remain uncomplicated in Master Narrative that Border Campaign seeks to answer about social movements: (1) human agency; (2) the social relationship between agency and structure; and, (3) the mediating role of cultural systems (beliefs, values, and language). The Master Narrative reduces these relationships to a simpler form, conflating them into a single person, leader, or event; this is in contrast to the Border Campaign, which complicates the relationships by analytically separating agency from structure as being mediated by cultural belief systems. Each of these categories will be discussed in more detail below, but first it is necessary to get behind the singularities of the Master Narrative, which treats social movements in terms of overarching conceptualizations or as "big events," oversimplifying their relationship to preexisting protest traditions. In each case, we posit how we use Border Campaign as an alternative to Master Narrative in studying forgotten civil rights action.

The Neglected Centrality of Border Protests

As a sensitizing measure of the problematic nature of the civil rights Master Narrative, we now review some key points contained in the Master Narrative of the civil rights movement: the 1954 *Brown* decision (school desegregation), the 1960 student sit-in movement, and the Montgomery and Birmingham mass mobilizations.

- Topeka, Kansas, is the home of the landmark 1954 Supreme Court case *Brown v. Board of Education*. This case began in September of 1950, when Oliver Brown took his young daughter Linda by the hand and walked her the short distance from their house to Sumner Elementary School in an attempt to enroll her for the coming term. Although the Brown family lived near the school, and Linda was the correct age to attend elementary school, she was not eligible to attend Sumner because of her race. Instead, Oliver Brown was directed to return his daughter to the Monroe School, almost twenty blocks away. It was the school designated for African Americans living in that particular neighborhood. Oliver Brown sought to redress the injustice of segregated schools in Topeka and the rest of the nation by managing to convince twelve other parents to join him in a lawsuit, eventually enlisting the aid of the national NAACP.
- The sit-in movement started on February 1, 1960, in Greensboro, North Carolina, by four college students. The actions of these students ignited the sit-in movement and the birth of the Student Nonviolent Coordinator Committee (SNCC).
- The mass mobilizations of Montgomery and Birmingham, Alabama are characteristic of civil rights protest and offer a benchmark of what the civil rights movement is all about.

In the Master Narrative, the watershed event is the 1954 *Brown v. Board* case and is used as a demarcation point in the civil rights movement (Bloom 1987; Blumberg 1984; Branch 1988; Chafe 1980; Dalifume 1968; Greenberg 1994; Klarman 1994, 2004; Kluger 1976; Lawson 1991). In the Border Campaign, the actions leading up to the *Brown* case, rather than the *Brown* case itself, are thrust into the foreground. Much of the material discussed in the subsequent chapters focuses on the Midwest, not the South, as an overlooked site of racial unrest by the Master Narrative. Two of the cases—Montgomery and Birmingham—are "familiar geographical signposts of civil rights demonstrations" that "derive their greatest importance as places that molded the critical national debate on ending racial discrimination" (Lawson 1998, 4). However, like the antecedents of the *Brown* decision, the contributory events in Montgomery and Birmingham have been subsumed into the singularity of the Master Narrative. Rigid conceptions of what constitutes "civil rights protest" have rendered the Midwest cases imperceptible or, if noticed at all, to be dismissed as borderline; the Southern cases don't always clearly belong to one of two categories of civil rights protest. What can we learn from these "borderline" cases? What is a Border Campaign?

By studying forgotten civil rights activism, we expand our understanding of the regional variation of civil rights activism. This analysis draws on the voluminous literature on the origins, history, and significance of the civil rights movement.[3] This literature depicts the South as the only location with a "race problem." Since rigid conceptions of what constitutes "civil rights protest" have rendered non-Southern cases imperceptible or, if noticed at all, to be dismissed as borderline, the Southern cases are usually judged as indistinguishable. Defining the civil rights movement exclusively in terms of a single region (the South) in a single time period (late 1950s and '60s), sociologists have constructed oversimplified explanations that miss the significance of space, timing, and cultural differences in collective action. The case studies discussed in this book (school desegregation, sit-ins, and boycotts) occurred in border state communities that anticipated national events such as the 1954 *Brown* case and the 1960 student sit-in movement. This borderland region is a place where race relations were defined more ambiguously than they were in the South.

For example, the Kansas color line was more permeable, reflecting its moral ambiguity toward monitoring race by incorporating a mix of social practices that were sometimes surprisingly racially inclusive as well as more conventionally exclusive (Kluger 1975, 371). The decision to segregate public education was left up to local school boards in cities that had a population of at least fifteen thousand.[4] If a local community decided to segregate their schools, as Topeka did, only segregated elementary schools were permitted by law.[5] Marginality also created uncertainty in knowing where and how the color line was drawn. For instance, one white woman growing up in Topeka in the 1940s was never quite sure when to invite her African American school friends to her social functions.[6] Though she interacted with them daily at school, she felt pressured to confine her interracial school relationships to the school building itself.

It is tempting to assume Kansas's permissive segregation statutes meant it was more progressive in terms of racial equality. However, the specificity of limiting segregation to certain cities was also related to its cost to taxpayers: racial segregation was only implemented where its tax base could subsidize the cost of separate school facilities. At the time of the 1954 *Brown* case, only four Kansas cities could afford the price: Kansas City, Manhattan, Wichita, and Topeka (Wilson 1995). Of course, the law did not deter smaller communities from trying to segregate its schools, and illegal or *de facto* segregation did emerge in the smaller towns of Salina, Ottawa, and Merriam. As discussed in Chapter Two, Ottawa and Salina would discover the hidden costs in trying to circumvent the state segregation law along with African Americans mobilized to challenge illegal segregation.[7]

Historically Situated Activism

The cases discussed in this book do not provide a comprehensive historical analysis of school desegregation, nor is it an attempt to write a revisionist history. Rather, the main purpose is to contribute to the conceptual understanding of the relationship between social action and its social contexts. By better understanding these forgotten civil rights protests, fought in regions bordering the South, we can also better understand and explain other social movements and thereby contribute to the theoretical understanding of the relationship between culture, social structure, individual action, and specific historical context. This will also help to deepen the understanding of the relationship between social action and its social location within communities and within a social movement.

The empirical data in this monograph draws on historical research on the early civil rights movement in Kansas and Oklahoma. The civil rights movement in these places manifested a different type of historically situated activism that has been overlooked. Instead of focusing primarily on charismatic leadership or the political resources provided by the institutional structures of black churches and activist organizations, I ask this: What were the indigenous patterns of accommodation and paternalism that had to be broken before change could occur? Which forces paved the way for protest? Who led the forces of resistance? How did both sides use the same ideals of American freedom and liberty to either justify the inclusion or exclusion of a whole class of citizens on the basis of race?

The approach of this book is to take into account the multiplicity of audiences toward which protest is directed. The Master Narrative assumes that civil rights protest is only undertaken by African Americans against racist whites. The Border Campaign questions this intended audience by considering there are more spectators such as nonsympathetic blacks and sympathetic whites. For example, throughout the early civil rights era, there were whites and blacks who were responsible for initiating challenges and those who resisted. Both blacks and whites perceived existing race relations as unjust and were willing to participate in programs to fight segregation. But there were those from both sides of the color line, who, for different reasons, either sought to preserve segregation or kept racial integration to a minimum.

Examining the neglected centrality of border protests provides a useful way to study social movements by connecting structure and agency through incorporating cultural values. This alternative is inspired by C. Wright Mills's idea that social scholarship or research should not limit itself to just one methodological or theoretical problem (1959, 143). Instead, Mills suggests a framework based on understanding the interconnection between the "coordinate points" of biography, history, and social structure. Mills understood that the inclusion of more than one "orienting point" offers a more comprehensive approach to understanding the complex problems of social change in modern society.

Ideal Types

Once again, ideal types are useful to understand better the contributions of individuals within a specific historical location. The ideal type approach used here is a way to organize disparate, historical data without simplifying it and creating monocausal explanations, which is one problem with the existing literature on the civil rights movement. In this study, the Master Narrative represents the aforementioned singularity of the civil rights literature that "view[s] activists only as harbingers of change—colorful, politically impotent, socially isolated idealists and malcontents who play only fleeting roles in the drama of American political history" (Carson 1986, 19-20). The Master Narrative also evaluates social movement outcomes and goals of social movements by examining the effects of national interventions over local initiatives. This is in contrast with the Border Campaign ideal type that contains a multiplicity of protest narratives, as well as the numerous social movement theories used to explain them.

In the Border Campaign ideal type, *Border Campaign* refers to an historical context and a unit of analysis of social movements. In this book, *Border* calls attention to historical contexts that mix significant segregated and integrated institutions and ideologies, in contrast to a Southern segregationist hegemony (Harding 1984). In places like Kansas, permissive segregation shapes actions that both challenge and preserve the color line; these contradictory actions draw further attention to particular social locations in which challenges and defenses were attempted.

Campaign refers to social action directed toward social change and the primacy of action in comprising social movements (Marwell and Oliver 1984). The Border Campaign ideal type provides a model of civil rights activism that incorporates borderline areas where racial segregation was less pernicious and protests less cohesive. In this way, the Border Campaign ideal type helps us to understand "what happened?" from a variety of perspectives. It also allows us a way to discuss civil rights activism with the understanding that our questions might have many possible answers. Utilizing an ideal type methodological approach helps to amplify tendencies observed in forgotten civil rights protest that took place outside the glare of national media attention and apart from the mass mobilizations of the civil rights movement subsequent to *Brown*.

Analysis of historical events is integral to understanding the unfolding of social action in terms of the local situation, particularly forgotten civil rights protest. This is done by focusing on the connection between meaning and action using ideal types. As a methodology, ideal types model the relationship between interpretation of meaning (cultural values) and analysis of various courses of action.

As outlined in Figure 1.1, rather than ranking meaning and action, an ideal type gives meaning and action equal weight. In this way meaning (cultural values) becomes a conceptual exposition tool for the analysis of the courses of action, the subject of the substantive analysis. Ideal types help to account for the multiplicity of standpoints in any social situation as well as to further distinguish between different strands of collective action. Ideal types are useful in identifying regularities in actions (i.e., frequencies) that aid in describing previously incomparable social actions in a systematic manner.[8]

Figure 1.1 Ideal Type Framework: Meaning and Action

Meaning — Cultural Values — Action

Ideal types are used to analyze both meaning and action without isolating one from the other (Weber 1949, 55). Since they are "intermediary concepts," they do not replicate social phenomena. Instead, they "assist research rather than trying to capture it" or extract it from its context (Kalberg 1994, 85). Rather than seeking "to capture overarching differentiation, universalization, or grand-scale evolutionary processes," ideal types offer a way to "conceptualize patterned orientations of meaningful action" without devising yet another abstract theory to explain them (84).

For example, the Border Campaign ideal type can be employed to view the color line in the following overlapping ways:

- as a type of hegemonic domination that varies according to specific historical geographical situations; and
- as the target of social actions using different claims of legitimacy are informed, *but not subsumed*, by the concept; the concept orients the analyst to important dimensions within the case and prompts the analyst to sometimes look for aspects of the case not indicated by the concept to draw that feature into significance.

This ideal type approach provides a way to shift away from a focus on the interpretation of meaning (conceptual exposition) to include an analysis of the courses of action, which is the subject of the case studies in the remaining chapters of the book. In the discussion of these forgotten civil rights cases, prominence is given to the different geographical and ideological configurations of the color line, ranging from exclusive to permissive. How open or closed these practices were not only shapes everyday social practices related to race, but also shapes how they are defended and attacked. As an historical artifact, its contours were shaped by competing claims for legitimacy made by its challengers and defenders. As a type of domination, the color line is integral to understanding and analyzing the courses of action undertaken in forgotten civil rights activism.

Culturally, the color line provides a focal point to better understand the heterogeneity of racial practices: as an historical "artifact" situated in a specific time and place. The color line can also be conceptualized more generally as a social phenomenon of the nature of institutional practices related to race across different time periods and in different geographical regions. Therefore, as illustrated by the empirical case studies in this book, nineteenth-century civil rights actions are oriented toward reconfiguring the color line, not destroying it. Challenges to racial customs were more covert and indirect. Certain regions tolerated some practices and challenges while others did not.

Once again, ideal types assist us in seeing the relationship between social action and value orientations, without collapsing action into structure or subsuming value orientations under goals. Weber's definition of social action is "both failure to act and passive acquiescence" that "may be oriented to the past, present, or expected future behavior of others" (1978, 22). Using this approach, we can examine how social actions directed toward the injustices of racial segregation were sustained at three different levels: individual, community, and structural. This approach emphasizes how these different levels of society can be simultaneously captured by the interrelated concepts of agency, social action, and cultural values within an ideal type. Additionally, this approach is pertinent to studying social movements in general since it emphasizes the link between meaning and action, rather than trying to distinguish one from the other. This approach is diagramed in Figure 1.2. On the left are the different levels of analysis ranging from the concrete level of individual action toward the more abstract level of social structure. In parentheses are the interrelated concepts of agency, social action, and cultural values. This diagram illustrates how the complexities of social action directed toward racial injustice can be examined without conflating and/or prioritizing one level over another.

This focus on "social action" is also related to uncovering the overlooked importance of value orientations in social movements. The narratives in this book are constructed using a web orientation "where no

---

Figure 1.2 Ideal Type Linkages Between Meaning and Action

Structure   (cultural values)
|
Community   (social action)
|
Individual   (agency)

---

proposition is seen in isolation from all others" (Phillips 2001, xii), in order to emphasize the nexus between meaning and action, analyzing them as indistinguishable from the subjective meanings in which they are identified and situated. Theory and method are integrated into the ideal types, each given equal weight, without prioritizing one over the other, nor is meaning prioritized over action or action over meaning.

Agency and Value-Rational Action

Though many of the challenges discussed in this book have been forgotten, reexamining them provides us with new insights for understanding social movements in general by bringing into focus the imperceptible actions and of ordinary people. As Morris (2000, 452) points out, social movement theory continues to slight the fundamental role that human agency plays in social movements. The overlooked contribution of human agency in the social movement literature is due to the emphasis placed on objective goals based on important assumed rationality of the actors. This type of social action is what Weber (1978, 24) characterized as instrumentally rational social action where primacy is given to the actor's "own rationally pursued and calculated ends." In this way, those actions are discounted that cannot be explained in terms of an actor's means-end calculations in relationship to the broader goals of a social movement. This tends to reduce the significance of individual social action within a particular historical situation.

Drawing on Weber's typology of value-rational social action, which places human agency, in all its complexity, at the center of collective action, this approach also emphasizes the importance of persons who, according to Weber (1978, 24–25) engage in "actions ... regardless of possible cost to themselves, act to put into practice their convictions of what seems to them to be required by duty, honor, the pursuit of beauty, a religious call, personal loyalty, or the importance of some 'cause' no matter in what it consists." Value-rational action is further differentiated from "instrumentally rational" action, which focuses on how "the end, the means, and the secondary results are all rationally taken into account and weighed" (26). Emphasizing value-rational action also provides a way to give equal weight to both challengers and defenders of segregation from both sides of the color line, without extracting the meaning of these actions from their historical context. In this way, individual action can be isolated by placing undue emphasis on organizations and leadership.

To further aid in capturing the border region's temporal and spatial limitations, the Border Campaign ideal type links analysis of subjective meanings related to biography (social action and agency) with that of structural forms (organizations, groups, institutions). By being sensitive to the breadth of civil rights activism, we can extract the situational context or momentary scene from the historical processes of forgotten civil rights activism without diminishing its importance to social action. At the same time, the ideal type provides salient points of comparison with better known civil rights episodes.

Civil rights campaigns were mounted on numerous fronts in places such as Montgomery and Birmingham, Alabama. The Master Narrative focuses on the contributions of charismatic leaders—Reverend Martin Luther King, Jr.—while obscuring the preprotest tradition of King's predecessor, Reverend Vernon Johns, and contributions of community activists Jo Ann Robinson and E. D. Nixon. In Birmingham, there was a concerted effort by white elites to remove the director of public safety, Bull Connor; even though their efforts where successful, King took advantage of Connor's remaining weeks in office as a lame duck to launch the Birmingham confrontations (Branch 1988). Birmingham will be forever etched into the American civil rights framework for its brutal repression of innocent bystanders while the lengthy, behind-the-scene negotiations to reconcile protests with differences is largely obscured and forgotten (Van Delinder 1992). The contrast of the Master Narrative with Border Campaign provides insight into the complicated vocabularies of social action contained in social movements.

As illustrated in Figure 1.3, the contrasts offered between the Master Narrative and the Border Campaign are as established tendencies along a continuum from closed or fixed categories to more fluid and variable. The Master Narrative's singularity is based on rational social action directed toward material goals—in this case desegregation. Each ideal type has its own internal logic of action. In the Master Narrative, it is instrumentally rational action directed toward formal goals—in this case segregation. This is in contrast to the Border Campaign's underlying logic that is value-rational, action that is not exclusively rational in terms of perceived ends or goals but makes sense in terms of discrete units of action. This broader conceptualization of action not only captures efforts directed toward a material goal like desegregation but also includes efforts when "racial justice" means sustaining segregation rather than dismantling it. While the Master Narrative assumes social movements are determined almost

Figure 1.3 Contrasts Between Master Narrative and Border Campaign

FORMAL	INFORMAL
Master Narrative Tendencies	*Border Campaign Tendencies*
Formal Organization—	Informal Organization—
Social Movement	Campaign
Charismatic Leadership	Mediating Leadership—
	Unaffiliated Agency
Confrontational Tactics	Mixture of tactics—Negotiation
Underlying Logic	*Underlying Logic*
Instrumental Action	Value-Rational Agency
and Long-term Goals	and Short-term goals

exclusively by their long-term goals, the Border Campaign also considers more intermediary goals.

Social Action and Racial Segregation

Davies (1962, 1971) argues that rising expectations and feelings of relative deprivation occurred in places where there was less than absolute hopelessness and poverty, bringing social change in a positive direction. Nationally, the growing race consciousness among African Americans after WWI resulted in sporadic civil rights protests in the 1930s, and accelerated even more after WWII. In Kansas, civil rights activism was initially targeted at forcing whites to acknowledge that color lines existed. These contradictory practices encouraged potential civil rights activists in more clearly defined segregated settings to develop their own "revolution of rising expectations" directed at the cultural value of equality they observed within integrated settings. It also created space for the minority of whites who sought interracial contacts in the belief that integration would uplift individual and community values through full inclusion. Finally, it helps us understand why *Brown* took place in Kansas and not the South. Building on Davies (1962, 1971) and a literature in the study of revolutions helps us to better understand the significance of "rising expectations" and social action in terms of the civil rights movement. This book limits its discussion to forgotten civil rights protest in the border states of Kansas and Oklahoma, offering a contrast to better known Southern civil rights protest.

The spatial and temporal dimensions of the border campaign ideal type helps to provide a way to discuss why the geographical location of Kansas, with its limited legal segregation and relatively equal schools, became a national focal point for school desegregation—and not Virginia,

South Carolina, or Mississippi. The latter, as well as other locations in the South, had much worse schools and were places where people faced extreme poverty, resulting in them being much more hopeless about the prospects of change.

Overview of the Book

Borders and the Civil Rights Movement: Incorporating Kansas and Oklahoma

As border states, Kansas and Oklahoma provide a contrast to the southern states featured in the Master Narrative. Both states were important to national legislation to end school segregation: the 1954 *Brown* case in Kansas and two cases in Oklahoma targeting segregation in higher education (*Sipuel v. Oklahoma State Regents for Higher Education,* 1948[9]; *McLaurin v. Oklahoma State Regents for Higher Education,* 1950[10]). However, the focus of this study is on early civil rights activism overlooked by the Master Narrative. In Kansas, the center of attention will be on attempts at school desegregation in local communities. The focal points in Oklahoma will be on how black citizens in Guthrie circumvented an all-white library and the late 1950s sit-ins staged in Oklahoma City. The type of civil rights protest in both of these states has been eclipsed by the importance of the 1954 *Brown* case and the 1960 student sit-in movement that started in Greensboro, North Carolina. Kansas and Oklahoma are also important because as border states they had different stakes in maintaining racial segregation.

Since the type of civil rights protest that erupted in Kansas and Oklahoma is more subdued than in the South, it has been largely overlooked and forgotten. Why is civil rights protest more subdued in this region? This is partly due to the association of "civil rights protest" with key, dramatic confrontations. What about less spectacular ones? Is it possible there is a common characteristic of both these outcomes? Since both types of events involve social action challenging racial segregation, this study uses the following as a common denominator of civil rights protest: social actions targeting the color line. As we will see in later chapters, these social actions were sometimes multidirectional in that both whites and blacks rose to confront challenges to the color line, especially if attacks threatened their respective power relationships and legitimacy. It is also important to realize that racial segregation was not one institution but many, as evidenced in the previous discussion of the regional variations in segregation laws. Though it was sustained by a single ideology (white supremacy), segregation was built on a set of competing traditions or value orientations toward liberty, equality, and freedom. The importance of these cultural values to the configuration of the color line is discussed in later chapters.

Intersection of Biography, History, Social Structure, and Culture

Each chapter in this book demonstrates the utility of studying social movements by linking objective abstractions of structure (social and individual) with the subjective, everyday lived reality of the momentary situation. Using empirical data obtained from oral history interviews and other primary sources, the book uses C. Wright Mills's framework to highlight the importance of biography, history, and social structure as a way to better understand abstract social forces and broad social change. Each chapter also uses Weber's definition of value-rational social action as the basis for understanding the importance of individual action (agency) and its relevance to culture in capturing the momentary scene in social movements. The conceptualization of agency is taken from Archer's (1996, 72–100) analytical dualism approach to culture and agency. Archer argues that a dualist approach separates culture into cultural system and sociocultural levels. The cultural system is the plane of logical relationships and "has an objective existence and autonomous relations amongst its components (theories, beliefs, values arguments, or more strictly between the propositional formulations of them) in the sense that these are independent of anyone's claim to know" (107). The sociocultural level refers to causal relationships between groups and individuals. This "two-fold relationship with human agency" takes into account "conditional effects (on people) ... [and] ... the logical consequences (of people) on the [cultural] system" (143).

Using this conceptualization of culture and adding it to Mills's "intersection of biography and history" provides a more systematic way of linking the individual with social structure that is bidirectional: people both influence and are influenced by social structure. Mills's original method of linking the individual with social structure is somewhat limited since his critique was primarily directed at the need for sociology to develop a human "psychology ... that is sociologically grounded and historically relevant" (1959, 143). Though inclusion of "a psychology of man" into sociological studies was innovative in his time, Mills's approach can be made more relevant by including this dualist notion of culture and cultural values as another "orienting point" in addition to biography, history, and society. Phillips's recent work (2001, 82–83; see also Phillips, Kincaid, and Scheff 2002; Phillips, ed. 2007; Phillips and Johnston 2007) defines culture as a "powerful structure" of value orientations. As Phillips points out, in *Weber's The Protestant Ethic and the Spirit of Capitalism* ([1905] 1958), cultural values were crucial to building "the bridge" between economic and religious institutions by "channeling the individual's enormous motivation for attaining religious salvation into a work ethic" (82).

Each chapter also emphasizes the relevance of how cultural values played an important, but unappreciated, role in creating a sense of injustice toward racial segregation in a democratic society. Since cultural values are "invisible and internal forces" (Williams 2004) they are largely ignored in contemporary sociological studies, especially in studies of early civil rights activism. Using the Web and Part/Whole Approach, this study uses predominant American cultural values such as liberty, freedom, and equality to situate discussion of the historical processes of racial segregation by highlighting the role of human agency and its linkage to social structure.

American Cultural Values of Liberty

This understanding of American cultural values in the context of a voluntary society is also suggested by Fischer's (1989, 9) definition of "modern" and use of William Graham Sumner's "folkways" as "distinctive customs" shaped by "the normative structure of values, customs and meanings." Though Fischer identifies twenty-seven folkways related to the cultural origins of American society, this book focuses on just one of them—"Freedom Ways"—and its expression as four regional variations of "liberty" that were eventually transferred to places like Kansas and Oklahoma (8–9). These differing notions of liberty would be important to the development of competing ideologies of racial segregation, ranging from inclusion to exclusion. Kansas was influenced by its New England settlers who brought with them the Puritan notion of "ordered liberty," a complicated understanding of liberty in terms of public, or mutual, obligations that could either be collective or individual. "One person's 'liberty' in this sense became another's restraint." Liberty was also conceived of in terms of "soul liberty" or strict adherence to religious dictates that was tempered by a collective obligation (collective conscience) to individual liberty in terms of the importance to "protect individual members from the tyranny of circumstance" (199, 201–205; Fischer 2004, 24). This notion of liberty conflicted with a southern notion of liberty as "hegemonic" or "liberty-as-hierarchy" consistent with the contradictions of owning slaves (Fischer 1989, 410–418; Fischer 2004, 24). Both of these notions of liberty were tempered by the Quaker idea of "reciprocal liberty that embraced all humanity" (Fischer 1989, 595–603). Finally, Oklahoma was heavily influenced by its predominance of backcountry settlers, a fiercely independent group of Scottish-Irish origins. They brought with them a fourth notion of liberty as "natural liberty," which "did not recognize the right of dissent or disagreement," had a low tolerance for deviance from cultural norms, and suppressed opposition with violence (781). The coming chapters will further discuss the significance of these cultural understandings of liberty and their resonance in constructing ideologies of race.

Borders of the Civil Rights Movement: Kansas and Oklahoma

The chapters in Part II discuss some forgotten civil rights episodes using the theoretical and methodological framework outlined in this chapter. Chapter 2 discusses early challenges to school segregation in Kansas. Chapter 3 discusses Guthrie, Oklahoma. These two case studies of nineteenth and early twentieth-century tributary civil rights protest signal the emergence of cultural goals and the development of institutionalized means to achieve social change. Chapter 4 discusses the intersection between the gendered radicalism of white women and challenges to illegal segregation in Merriam, Kansas. Chapter 5 discusses the complex issues of legal segregation *behind* the 1954 *Brown* case in Topeka, Kansas. Chapter 6 discusses the significance of the Oklahoma City sit-ins as precursor to the organizational tactics employed in their more famous counterparts in Greensboro, North Carolina, in February, 1960.

Finally, Part III discusses "Implications for the Analysis of Social Movements." In Chapter 7, the case studies analyzed in Part II are considered in light of the current debates in social movement literature. These debates center around two competing theoretical paradigms: structural and cultural (Goodwin and Jasper 2004). The structural model or "political process" theory prioritizes structures of power, economics, formal organizations, and social networks as crucial resources that have been extracted out of empirical research. This approach has dominated social movement theory for the past several decades (McAdam 1982; McCarthy and Zald 1977; Meyer 1993; Staggenborg 1991; Tarrow 1983; and Tilly 1978, 1995). The cultural side favors less abstract explanations, focusing more on the micro-level social interaction of individuals and interpretation of subjective meanings (Kurzman 1994; Morris 1984; Polletta 1997; Snow and Benford 1992). Finally, the implications of this research are presented for the analysis of social movements and, in particular, the study of new social movements. These implications are methodological no less than theoretical, and they include the potential of the Web and Part/Whole Approach for the study of social movements (Phillips 2001; Phillips, Kincaid, and Scheff 2002; Phillips, ed. 2007; Phillips and Johnston 2007). Chapter 8 provides a summary and conclusion to this study by suggesting ways to rethink master narrative, particularly the Master Narrative of the civil rights movement. The chapter provides a brief reconsideration of the benchmark civil rights campaign in Birmingham, Alabama, using the Border Campaign type, while also providing suggestions for future directions for social movement research using the Web and Part/Whole Approach. The overall purpose of this task is to expand our understanding of social movement action in general, and the early civil rights movement in particular.

Notes

1. William Lloyd Garrison. 1968. *Selections From the Writings and Speeches of William Lloyd Garrison, With an Appendix.* New York: Negro Universities Press (reprint of 1852 edition), 153.

2. This order also established the Fair Employment Practices Committee (FEPC) as a regulatory agency to investigate charges of racial discrimination.

3. Studies on the civil rights movement include studies with a "top down" approach, asking questions about how national organizations brought change into local communities (Lawson 1991). The second type focuses on in-depth discussions of the local community such as William Chafe's *Civilities and Civil Rights* (1980) on Greensboro, North Carolina; David Colburn's *Racial Change and Community Crisis* (1985) on St. Augustine, Florida; and Robert Norell's *Reaping the Whirlwind* (1985) on Tuskegee, Alabama. The third type includes interactive studies connecting local and national issues related to social and political factors. Contributing to this latter approach are sociologists Doug McAdam, *Political Process and the Development of Black Insurgency* (1982); Aldon Morris, *The Origins of the Civil Rights Movement: Black Communities Organizing for Change* (1984). See also Killian (1984), White (1964), Smith and Killian (1958), Meier and Rudwick (1973), Killian and Smith (1960), and Oberschall (1973, 1989).

4. Part Two of the Brief for Appellants in Nos. 1, 2, and 4 and for Respondents in No. 10 on Rearguement (November 16, 1953) states that "Kansas, a loyal border state, had adopted a policy of permissive segregation whereby boards of education were authorized, but not required, to establish separate schools (Kansas Laws 1862, c 46, Art 4, Sec. 3.18; Kansas Laws 1864, c. 67, Sec. 4; Kansas Laws 1865, c. 46, Sec. 1)." U.S. Supreme Court, *School Segregation Cases* (1953), p. 179. See also Paul Wilson (1995) for a sound, legal analysis and concise summary of Kansas's "permissive segregation" policy.

5. High schools were integrated (grades nine through twelve), however there were exceptions to this practice (Carper 1978; Woods 1983; Van Delinder 1994). There was one segregated high school in Kansas City, Kansas—Sumner High School (Vandever 1971, 46). In 1905, a special law was passed to allow the African American community in Kansas City, Kansas, to open its own high school (Kluger, 371). For a more detailed discussion of these exceptions see the next chapter.

6. Anonymous White Female Respondent interview with author, Topeka, Kansas. July 17, 1994.

7. Challenges to Kansas's legal and illegal segregation are more thoroughly analyzed in Chapter Two, along with a discussion of the challenges to school segregation in Ottawa and Merriam. These communities brought successful lawsuits that were reviewed by the Kansas State Supreme Court in 1881 and 1949, respectively. The *Webb* case files are located at the Kansas State Archives, Kansas State Historical Society, Topeka, Kansas. The *Brown* case in Topeka was never reviewed by the Kansas State Supreme Court. It was filed in the (then) 10th Federal District Court in Topeka. The ruling of this lower federal court was then appealed to the United States Supreme Court. The *Brown* case files are located at the National Archives–Kansas City Branch, Kansas City, Missouri. See Van Delinder 2004 for a discussion of these holdings.

8. For example, the ideal types of legitimate domination that are the basis of some of Weber's most perceptive structural analyses are linked to particular subjective meanings that identify the patterns of action under examination.

9. 332 U.S. 631.

10. 339 U.S. 637.

PART II

Forgotten Civil Rights Activism

Rural schools were often integrated in the early twentieth century. This picture of Wilder School was taken in 1907. This school was located in Johnson County, just west of South Park, an African American enclave (courtesy of the Johnson County Museum, Kansas).

2

Before *Brown:* Protest and School Segregation in Kansas, 1880–1941

The border state of Kansas provides an environment to analyze racial segregation practices in a geographical area that had no prehistory of slavery. It is much easier to understand why the Deep South maintained and justified a system of segregation with its preexisting institution of slavery—one oppressive practice was built on the ruins of the other. But it is much more difficult to understand why racial segregation, though limited, became the "status quo" in places like Topeka, Kansas, which had no history of African American enslavement.

Kansas's ideas about racial equality were initially influenced by the 1854 Kansas-Nebraska Act's popular sovereignty clause, which attracted settlers competing to make it slave or free (Foner and Garraty 1991, 609). Kansas and Nebraska Territory's proximity to slave-holding Missouri also made it a haven for runaway slaves (Taylor 1998, 94–97). As a border state between north, south, east, and west, Kansas's color line was shaped by competing ideologies of racial consciousness: the equal opportunity of racial integration versus the relative autonomy of racial segregation. These contending beliefs about racial control were mediated by opposing cultural values of liberty (ordered, hierarchical, reciprocal, and natural) along with the presence of Native Americans, another colonized and strictly controlled racial group.

The New England abolitionists journeying to Kansas in hopes of creating a "free state," brought Puritan notions of freedom and cultural values supporting a collective obligation to protect individuals from tyranny (Fischer 1989, 202). In trying to transplant their New England culture, these immigrants founded Lawrence and Topeka, Kansas, which also were stops along the Underground Railroad "that extended from Western Missouri . . . through Nebraska Territory, Iowa, Chicago, and finally to Canada" in the 1850s (Taylor 1998, 95).[1] Their Puritan notions of ordered, structured liberty would later complement the shared, reciprocated liberty of northern Quakers who came to Kansas just before and during the 1879 Black Exodus.

Competing with these ideologies sympathetic of racial inclusion were settlers imbued with opposing tendencies, possessing the hierarchal and natural liberty in accord with proslavery ideals. Many proslavery immigrants crossed over the border from Missouri, a slave state created by the rancorous Missouri Compromise.[2] Others drawn to Kansas were border ruffians, primarily poor whites of Scottish-Irish descent, and though obviously not slave-owners nor particularly in favor of slavery, they were part of a rootless Southern backcountry underclass or rural proletariat ever in search of "elbow room" (Fischer 1989, 756). Descendants of emigrants originally from the British borderlands between Scotland and England, these settlers' culture was shaped by "incessant violence" (626). As in their native country as well as in the backcountry of the Appalachian highlands in Tennessee, these new inhabitants carried with them a "tradition of retributive folk justice"—a system of highly personal politics that lent itself to vigilantism (766). The backcountry cultural values of liberty were highly individualistic with little regard for imposed order and little tolerance for weakness.[3] These values were also compatible with ambivalent sentiments about slavery and acceptance of blacks. The settlers helped fuel the ensuing lawlessness and violence between pro-Union (Jayhawkers and Redlegs) and the pro-Confederate (Bushwackers) guerilla during the border wars of the 1850s as well as during the Civil War (Goodrich 1991).

Kansas's racial ideologies were also tempered by its frontier environment of "openness and freedom," prevailing attitudes against Native Americans being "capable of learning the white man's ways," and general lack of desire to adapt to the Anglo culture (Woods 1983, 197). First, the mythology of the American West as a crucible "with its alleged emphasis on rugged individualism, enterprise, and pragmatism, allow[ing] human beings to work out their destinies regardless of race" has primarily focused on white European immigrants (Woods 1983, 182; Taylor 1998, 17-23). Second, "the extreme prejudice against the Indian that prevailed in Kansas . . . may have also worked to the black man's advantage" (Woods 1983, 197). The "fluidity and individuality of the frontier" working against Native Americans provided the possibility for African Americans "to be seen, within limits, as a distinct personality rather than a preconceived stereotype" (197).

From the other side of the color line, African Americans also wrestled with competing ideologies of race consciousness. Drawn to a "free" Kansas via the Underground Railroad in the 1850s, the black population was still relatively small (151 "free" and 192 "enslaved"); by the time of statehood in 1861 the free population had grown to 625 and the slave population had diminished down to two (Carper 1978, 255). At the end of the Civil War in 1865 the black population in Kansas rose to more than twelve thousand, and a steady migration increased the black population to 17,108 by 1870 (Taylor 1998, 94–95). Fifty-six percent of the black population was concentrated in the eastern portion of the state, close to Lawrence, Kansas City, and Topeka (97). The end of Reconstruction, in 1879, brought another wave of black immigrants, and by 1880 Kansas had 43, 107 black residents (Carper 1978, 255). This significant increase of black settlers fueled debate over their voting rights and access to public education (255).

The ambivalence of the old Free-Soilers toward African Americans was overcome by the realization that "one way to retain power in Kansas was to make use of the black vote. Once committed to voting rights for blacks, this element found it difficult to oppose the Negro's civil rights in other areas" (Woods 1983, 196). Unlike the South, Kansas "had not experienced the 'trauma' of Reconstruction; there was no debt to settle with Negroes, carpetbaggers, and scalawags." The political motivation to use the black vote to defeat challenges from Democrats and Populists, combined with the lack of "any genuine fear of black political and economic domination," provided an opportunity for permissive segregation statutes (196).

It should come as no surprise, then, that activism in 1880s Topeka, Kansas, was organized by members of the black elite who supported segregation in principle but challenged it when it worked against their own self-interest. The majority of these protests and lawsuits were directed against segregated schools, as the competing interests of individuals to gain inclusion to segregated schools on behalf of their children was countered by group-level interest in sustaining the indignity segregation in an effort to maintain autonomy from white authority.

The "Black Bourgeoisie" and Racial Segregation

In studying these early civil rights actions we see how the interests of black status groups—the clergy, teachers, lawyers, doctors, and undertakers—seemingly work more toward supporting segregation than challenging it (Frazier 1957). However, upon closer examination of the historical record, we see that initial challenges to segregation arose from this same small, closed group of professionals whose livelihood was tied to maintaining segregation by offering their services exclusively to the black community. Why would black lawyers and ministers seemingly work against their own self-interests? The Master Narrative defines civil rights activism as a mass movement led by "new" leaders who rejected segregation, neglecting other types of actions. What happened in Kansas prior to the *Brown* case was not a mass movement, nor was it always directed against segregation; sometimes it seemed to sustain it. The revolutionary potential of the black elite has also been overlooked by the Master Narrative. In addition, the contour of this border state activism is obscured when measured against the mass mobilizations in the South.

This chapter examines the limitations of the Master Narrative in understanding early challenges by the black elite to segregated schools. The Master Narrative conceptualizes racial segregation as a set of fixed practices with little movement for maneuvering on either side in the color line. Border Campaign, on the other hand, conceptualizes racial segregation as emergent, mediated by competing cultural values of freedom and liberty. This more nuanced understanding of social interaction and cultural ideology provides an insight into the linkage between agency and structure. In the Master Narrative and social movements' literature, the issue of agency has been shunted to the side in favor of studying structural and organizational processes as expressed in the resource mobilization and political process models. These theorists prioritize structures of power, economics, formal organizations, and social networks. This approach has dominated social movement theory for the past several decades (most notably McAdam 1982; McCarthy and Zald 1977; Meyer 1993; Staggenborg 1991; Tarrow 1983; and Tilly 1978, 1995).

Recently, scholars have become interested in learning more about how "individual social psychological processes" are related "to collective processes (Johnston and Klandermans 1996, 11) by considering how culture—ideas, ideology, language—figures in mobilizations in addition to structural issues. Renewed interest in culture has led scholars to draw from the vocabulary of symbolic interactionism, focusing on "identities, meanings, and emotions" (Kurzman 1994; Morris 1984; Polletta 1997; Snow and Benford 1992, 2004, vii). Goffman (1974) is particularly important since his idea of "framing" is frequently used as a way to focus on human agency and interpretation (Snow and Benford 1992), which has increased our understanding of motivations for mobilization, i.e., injustice, agency, and identity. However, one shortcoming of the framing perspective, much like the resource mobilization approaches it critiques, is that the question of culture is usually considered from a "traditional social movement" perspective—or factors located within social movements (i.e., movement-centric)—rather than to include a contextual understanding of the broader society (Williams 2004, 94–95).

Beginning with this broader conceptualization of culture, I propose to better understand how personal troubles become public issues in order to more clearly explain collective action and/or social movements. How can linkages of agency and structure in social movements be better understood through the insertion of culture? Why is culture another important domain of society to be considered in conjunction with other social structures arising from political and economic institutions when studying social movements? By analyzing racial segregation as a set of emergent social practices, defining racial boundaries embedded in a specific regional culture helps to better understand these crucial linkages between agency, structure, and culture. Using the lens of the Border Campaign provides an alternative understanding and appreciation for the heterogeneity of actions involved in any social movement.

"Along the Color Line"

The Crisis, a publication of the National Association for the Advancement of Colored People (NAACP), had for many years a regular column called "Along the Color Line." The column contained various accounts of challenges and infractions against racial segregation. Sometimes the news was minor and sometimes it was of monumental importance. Items mentioned ranged from reporting the football scores of the leading segregated college teams to attempts to establish integrated public accommodations in a major city. The column header featured an illustration of a pair of surveyors, one hunched over his equipment scrutinizing the horizon while the other stood some distance away providing a fixed point on the horizon in order to draw a straight line.

This image provides us a visual representation of segregation—that though the color line was drawn using some fixed point on the horizon, something would happen that would cause it to shift, necessitating the surveyors to come out once again and redraw a line using a different point of orientation. Like the two surveyors, a person's perspective changed depending on which point they stood and where they aimed. The color line itself was not always straight; it had spatial and temporal dimensions in addition to an ideology or hegemony of "proper" or "improper" racial etiquette. As it was continuously being crossed in both directions, it was also continuously being redrawn and reconfigured.

The infinite patience of these surveyors show that social change is an interactive process demonstrating that while no single event is earth shattering in itself, taken together and cumulatively, multiple events can bring about social change. Though many of the stories in "Along the Color Line" were not significant—like the winning seasons of segregated college football teams—underlying all of them was the hope that at some point in the future they would develop into something of more interest and importance, perhaps even to reshape the contours of the color line. For the war against the color line was not always a large battle, but often a series of skirmishes along the border.

School Segregation in Kansas, 1861–1879

The limited degree to which to Kansas did practice racial separation revolved around its schools. The belief that education was the crucible for black citizenship is reflected in contemporary ideologies of white paternalism and moral uplift; "[s]chooling was touted frequently as a prerequisite for participating in the American Dream" (Carper 1978, 255–259). Kansas's school segregation statutes were permissive, leaving the decision to segregate public education an option for local school boards in cities that had a population of at least fifteen thousand (Wilson 1995). If a local community decided to segregate its schools, as Topeka did, only segregated elementary schools were permitted by law.

Kansas's competing cultural values related to personal and collective liberty underlie the shifts back and forth between integration and segregation in successive school legislation. Challenges to school segregation resulted in modifications to the school segregation laws in 1867 and 1879 because instead of mandating a uniform system of segregated schools, the original constitution of 1861 left that determination up to local school districts and local custom (29). This left a small window of opportunity for African American elites to have some legal basis from which to challenge the constitutionality of segregated schools in their own communities. It also gave them the right to appeal to the local board of education to review its policy of segregation if it did not conform to state statutes. In the Knox family, the parents of two school-age children requested this in Independence, Kansas, in 1880, and in Topeka the local NAACP chapter did this on behalf of all African American children in 1948, before pursuing the actions that resulted in the *Brown* case. In just over sixty years, the interests of the black elites had expanded beyond petitioning on behalf of selected individuals, usually their own children, to include all school-age children.

The paradoxical role Kansas would come to play in outlawing national school segregation is illustrated by events in 1867; it ratified the Fourteenth Amendment the same year it passed a law that empowered its larger cities to segregate schools (37). The equal protection clause of the Fourteenth Amendment was the basis upon which "separate but equal" was later found to be unconstitutional in *Brown*.[4] The 1867 statute that permitted school segregation did not specify separate schools; it simply denied African Americans admission to its public schools. Later that same year, this exclusionary action was tempered by a more inclusive policy that fined school boards and threatened them with imprisonment if they denied eligible children to enroll, regardless of race (37). If a school district decided to segregate its schools, it would have to be able to afford the cost of "separate, but equal." It could not simply deny children an education because of their race, especially if their parents paid local taxes.

This directive was circumvented by closing public schools and opening private ones instead, a similar response to the *Brown* case nearly a century later. This practice to circumvent integration was noted in the 1867 Annual Report of the Kansas State Superintendent[5]: "It is a notorious fact that in many districts of the State, the public schools have been broken up and discontinued the moment that an attempt was made to force colored children into such schools with white children, and that in such districts the schools have been discontinued entirely, or replaced by subscription schools."

Three years later, in 1870, a bill was defeated that would have "required racially separate schools."[6] The bill's sponsors rationalized their actions by arguing "equality of opportunity for African American students could be assured only in separate African American schools subject to the same standards and supervision as other schools. It was contended that in mixed schools discrimination was inevitable" (37). Once again, the rationalization for segregation was similar to the arguments used in the twentieth century against desegregation: the fear of integration meant that African Americans would not be treated fairly.

Although after 1867 segregated schools were lawful in any community that its school district could afford to fund, the implementation of a uniform system of segregated schools remained unresolved. There was another effort toward integration in 1874 when the Kansas legislature passed a civil rights act prohibiting discrimination "on account of race, color, or previous condition of servitude" applying to "schools and public institutions on all levels, to common carriers, and to places of public accommodation and entertainment licensed by municipalities" (38). There could be several factors related to this legislation, both regional and national, but one significant demographic change was that in the first part of the 1870s, the African American population decreased in Kansas, while its white population increased (Athearn 1978; Painter 1986, 146). This suggests that a decrease in the African American population contributed to a decrease in funding for segregated schools. Consistent with this interpretation, a significant increase in the African American population after 1877 was followed by a significant reversal regarding segregated schooling—the 1879 law once again made it constitutional for some cities to segregate their schools.

The Political Impact of the "Exoduster" Movement

Another demographic change to Kansas's population occurred in the late 1870s and illustrates how color line boundaries were constantly renegotiated. The end of Reconstruction, the Compromise of 1877, and the subsequent withdrawal of federal troops out of the South, accelerated the migration of African Americans to the North and West. This mass "Black Exodus" to Kansas of former slaves or freedmen were called "Exodusters" and this migration was the first significant African American migration after the Civil War (Athearn 1978; Painter 1986). This migration had such a dramatic impact that the United States Senate formed a special committee to investigate "the causes of the removal of the Negroes from the Southern States to the Northern States."[7]

The response to these refugees provides insight into Kansas's ideology of limited racial segregation or what Woods (1983, 197) terms the "doctrine of parallel development." This approach to race relations was not founded on genetic inferiority but rather common humanity constructed on the grounds of an assumed capacity "for intellectual development, moral growth, and material advancement" (197). Though there were "natural differences between the two races," whites had a moral obligation to "provide their black brethren with an education and moral guidance," but it was up to the individual to "pull themselves up by the bootstraps" (197–198). The development of this ideology of limited racial inclusion is reflected in the earlier discussion of freedom ways. The Puritan cultural values of liberty and social obligations were tempered somewhat by the Quaker's practice of reciprocal liberty in that the notion of common humanity was extended to African Americans.

The impact of the Exodust Movement had a significant effect on Topeka and would significantly change race relations for decades to come. Topeka's black population grew from 7,272 in 1875 to 15,528 in 1880 (Cox 1982, 201). The immigrants overwhelmed existing local relief capacities, and institutions on both sides of the color line were established to coordinate aid for the refugees. For example, the African American mission parish of St. Michael's Episcopal Church in Tennesseetown, a predominately African American part of Topeka, was established at the time of the Exoduster Movement. These refugees also heightened racial tensions as the mutual obligations for parallel development were severely strained. In his testimony before the U.S. Senate Committee, M. Bosworth, a resident of Topeka and a member of the Kansas Freedmen's Relief Association of Topeka, estimated that between eight thousand and ten thousand African Americans arrived in Topeka during 1879. Though many refugees passed through to other points in Kansas, thousands stayed or eventually returned to Topeka. Bosworth described the condition of the immigrants as "in about as dilapidated condition as you can imagine; occasionally one of them has a little money; occasionally one is very well clothed.... Generally, they come very thinly clad and very poorly provided to stand our winter climate."[8]

Bosworth went on to remark that the flow of refugees included whites as well as African Americans. When asked if these immigrants, of either race, were a public nuisance by being reduced to "roaming the streets," Bosworth replied, "Well, we have idlers—African American and white—in our country. If a man should go to Topeka for the purpose of finding Negroes loafing around the streets he would find examples of it, when another man went for with the purpose of finding whites ... [he] ... would find them too."[9]

What seemed to concern the Voorhees committee more than the destitute circumstances of the Exodusters was any possible political motivation behind their actions. The political dimensions of the Exoduster Movement revolved around the fear that the immigrants might be Republicans.[10] Their suspicions were increased by the fact that the Republican Kansas governor, John St. John, and other political officials, including a United States district court judge, formed a relief organization that was later reorganized into the Kansas Freedmen's Relief Association. The Senate Committee feared that these immigrant relief societies, such as the Freedmen's Relief Association, were politically motivated to encourage migration to Kansas in order to control future political elections. St. John was accused of creating more Republican votes in Kansas by encouraging the Exodusters to come to Kansas since he was instrumental in providing them food, shelter, and clothing. St. John defended his actions to the Senate committee by providing the following information: "I make the prediction that the present year [1880] will bring at least 100,000 ... [former slaves] ... northward. They must find a resting place somewhere. Kansas has never done anything to encourage the colored people to leave the South. We have simply, in dealing with this question, done as we believed God would have us do. It is not a political question; it rises above politics."[11]

St. John's actions disturbed the equilibrium of the color line. Locally, some Topekans were also suspicious of the governor's possible political motivations and tried to prevent St. John from helping the Exodusters. For example, when St. John granted permission to build a temporary barracks for the refugees on the fairgrounds in Topeka, some local businessmen objected, and the barracks were torn down. Within six weeks of their construction, St. John had them rebuilt in North Topeka, which was outside of the city limits. [12] Other forms of organized resistance to the arrival of the Exodusters and to St. John's policy of "Kansas ... [being] ... open to receive everybody" arose where "... the arrival of ... [a] boat-load ... [of Exodusters] ... a military company was sent to prevent them from landing".[13] St. John responded with an impassioned speech stating "Kansas was a free State, and he would welcome to the broad acres of Kansas anybody who had a mind to come, African American, white, or anybody who wished to come; that they should find a home in free Kansas."[14]

Also accused of being politically motivated in giving assistance to the homeless immigrants were two Quaker women, Elizabeth Comstock and Laura Haviland. Though neither lady testified in person before the Senate committee, they did provide written testimony. In Comstock's correspondence of January 27, 1880, that is part of the findings of the committee, she writes "Our number of refugees in this city fluctuates very much.... The poor creatures arrive now at the rate of 600 weekly.... Yesterday 120 arrived.... It is estimated that 20,000 are now in the State. Topeka, our headquarters, is very much crowded, resulting in sickness and death."[15]

Because they could not appear personally before the U.S. committee, Comstock and Haviland could not be cross-examined. So, instead, Mr. Bosworth had to answer for the two ladies and justify their actions as not being politically motivated. When asked, "Is Mrs. Comstock connected with the association or working on her own hook as a general correspondent?" Bosworth replied that Comstock was "there in the interest of charity and humanity."[16]

Criticism also came from the other side of the color line. Self-consciousness about threats to their elite status, African American businessmen spoke out against giving aid to the refugees. The Topeka chapter of the National Conference of Colored Men published an article in the Topeka *Colored Citizen* in June of 1879 stating that the "sudden influx of an unorganized" group of destitute African Americans would be detrimental to race relations in Kansas. The same article, however, noted that white immigrants far outnumbered the African Americans, but even though whites were more numerous, any negative impact on the city would be blamed on the former slaves. Topeka's black bourgeoisie realized that, to date, they did not "constitute enough of a political or economic threat to warrant total ostracism" (Woods 1983, 197). The dramatic increase in black immigrants meant that the fears of the black elite would be realized with renewed attempts to control the black population.

Restructuring of Public Schools after 1879 and Legal Challenges in Ottawa and Independence

A consequential and direct response to the Exoduster Movement was a modification made to the color line in an 1879 law permitting segregation only in elementary schools located in settlements with a population of more than fifteen thousand, which it termed "cities of the first class." In 1879, there were three cities that were large enough to segregate: Leavenworth, Atchison, and Topeka. In comparison, by 1952, after the *Brown* litigation had begun, there were twelve cities of the first class but only half had segregation—Coffeyville, Fort Scott, Kansas City, Leavenworth, Parsons, and Salina. Of the remaining six, one never exercised its option to segregate (Hutchinson), one had partial segregation (Lawrence), two had voluntarily terminated segregation (Pittsburg and Wichita), and two had begun to implement desegregation (Atchison and Topeka) (Wilson 1995, 29–39).

Legal challenges to the color line began in 1881, two years after the state segregation law was changed. These challenges were initiated on behalf of single plaintiffs or siblings, and were successful. In Ottawa (*The Board of Education of Ottawa v. Elijah Tinnon,* 1881) and Independence (*Knox v. Board of Education,* 1891) cases were brought forth by the single plaintiffs' suing on the grounds of passing a white school while traveling to a segregated school. In a statement dated May 19, 1880, the Ottawa Board of Education's Committee on Building and Grounds announced that because of overcrowding in Ottawa's schools, "colored children of school age" would now be assigned to a smaller wooden building across the street from the main school. Elijah Tinnon objected to his son being assigned to a segregated school that was noticeably inferior and petitioned the local school board to admit his son. In a decision reported in the 1881 July term of the Kansas Supreme Court, William Wheeler, principal of public schools in Ottawa, was ordered to admit Leslie Tinnon "to the white school house, second grade."

In Independence, nearly a decade later, the parents of Bertha and Lilly Knox also objected to their children having to pass by a white school in order to attend an inferior and segregated school. The Knoxes pointed out that since Independence's population was under fifteen thousand it was not a city of the first class, rather it was considered a city of the second class and therefore had not legal grounds by which to segregate its school. The Kansas Supreme Court ordered that the Knox children be admitted to the white school.

Meanwhile, in Topeka, attorney James Guy initiated activism resulting in a strategic "accommodation" to the color line. Guy demanded that Topeka employ only African American teachers in Topeka's segregated schools. White teachers had been hired when segregated schools began in 1876, and this practice continued until Guy challenged it in the early 1890s (Cox 1982). Pressure from Guy and other African Americans in the community resulted in the exclusive hiring of African American teachers for the segregated schools after 1894.

The employment of black teachers in segregated schools was an important occupation that the black bourgeoisie would try to protect. Racial segregation offered an opportunity for this small elite to advance the race by acting as role models. This ideology of self-sufficiency is reflected in Guy's own words in an article in the *Times-Observer* on May 28, 1892: "We should not attempt to be in places that we are not wanted. We should recognize our differences and need to establish race pride and confidence."

Black Topekans were trying to gain control of the quality of instruction in their schools. By hiring teachers of their own race, they hoped to improve the quality of teaching in the African American schools. When the school board agreed to hire only African American teachers to teach in the segregated schools, the African American community had gained some control over its children's education, even though black children still had to contend with the stigma of attending separate schools.

Although Cox (1982) states that this "reinforced segregation" was a blow to the African American community, not all African Americans felt this way about segregated schools: some thought of this as an opportunity. For example, teacher and civil rights activist Septima Clark worked hard to get African American teachers hired in South Carolina's public schools twenty years later. Clark felt that African American students "were just at the mercy of the white teachers, who often didn't care anything about them" (Wigginton 1991, 18). Clark eventually gathered twenty-two thousand signatures stating that African Americans wanted teachers of their own race employed in the public schools. Finally, in 1920, a few African American teachers were hired in Charleston. Because of state segregation laws, there was not any legal way that teachers of different races could teach in the same school, just as there was no legal way for children of different races to attend the same schools. Any policy that stipulated that only African American teachers could be hired in African American schools would mean that the local school board would have to fire whites in order to maintain segregation. The introduction of African American teachers in South Carolina's segregated schools was gradual and occurred much later than in Kansas. These and other attempts to employ African American teachers would be dismantled by school desegregation in the 1950s.

Real Estate Speculation and Race: Topeka, 1890–1910

Challenges to the color line also occurred as the city limits of Topeka expanded to incorporate rural communities in outlying areas that had already established their own informal, yet distinctive patterns of integration and segregation. Each annexation created new fault lines along the color line as its practices were renegotiated as part of the confrontations between real estate developers, city government officials, the board of education, and parents of school-age children. The sociology literature tends to focus on the post–World War II period, but urban sprawl occurred in previous eras—it just wasn't as spectacular.

The *Reynolds* case (1890) was an important confrontation over the configuration of the color line in neighborhood schools between real estate developers, city government officials, the Topeka Board of Education, and African American parents. William Reynolds, an attorney, objected to his son being forced to attend a segregated school several blocks away while Lowman Hill Elementary was close by. The segregated school, Buchanan Elementary, is described by the plaintiff as "unsanitary, inconvenient, and, undesirable ... a veritable cesspool."[17] The school board defended its segregation policy because of parallel development: African American children and white children had "somewhat different intellectual requirements."[18]

Reynolds lived with his son in an area of Topeka called Lowman Hill, which was originally designated as an outlying area under the jurisdiction of the county school district and annexed by the city in 1890. Lowman Hill had "been a mixed school for both races, and was continued as such by the Board of Education until the year 1900. The reason for this was that the Board of Education was financially unable to provide separate schools." After the Lowman Hill district was incorporated into the Topeka school district, segregation was not implemented until after the old Lowman Hill School burned down on July 20, 1900, six weeks before classes were scheduled to begin for the fall term. The school board was forced to quickly find temporary school facilities for 175 white and 35 African American children. Though a building referred to as Campbell Court was found to serve as a temporary school, it was not large enough accommodate all the students. The school board decided it was easier to transfer the thirty-five African American students to segregated Buchanan School, eight blocks away, rather than transfer the 175 white students to Clay Elementary School, which was thirteen blocks away. Meanwhile, plans were being developed to build a new Lowman Hill School.[19]

Reynolds was outraged that his son was forced to travel several blocks to a segregated school. The father petitioned the school board to live up to its promise that his son would attend the new Lowman School. The school board denied they had made any promises about the new school being integrated, arguing that the two schools were separate but equal, in compliance with *Plessy v. Ferguson* (1896).

Not all the black parents agreed with Reynolds's petition, and several other African American families living in the Lowman Hill area petitioned the superintendent to provide a closer segregated school for their children to attend instead of Buchanan. "After this decision, a committee waited upon the Superintendent asking him to provide a building in the Lowman Hill locality and the committee was told that the Board would be glad to provide such a building if one could be found." The other black parents disagreed with Reynolds on the issue of integrated schools. "All these committees of colored people which called upon the Superintendent during this time expressed themselves in favor of separate schools. It was school accommodations in their immediate vicinity they desired, and not the mixing of schools."[20] At the beginning of fall term in 1902, the school superintendent found a building at Tenth and Spruce streets to serve as a temporary school building for the African American children. Though Reynolds lost this important challenge to segregation, his son and the other children were able to attend school closer to their neighborhood. The Reynolds case illustrates how the expansion of Topeka's boundaries made it more cost effective to fund segregated schools and provided opportunities to control and contain African Americans into the next century.

Challenges to Topeka's Racial Status Quo, 1910–1930

The founding of the Topeka chapter of the NAACP in 1913 provided an organizational structure from which to launch challenges to segregation. Prior to *Brown,* eleven desegregation lawsuits reached the Kansas Supreme Court. Four of the eleven desegregation court cases involved the Topeka Board of Education, and three of these four lawsuits were filed after the Topeka NAACP chapter was formed.[21]

The *Rich* (1928), *Wright* (1929), and, *Foster* (1929) cases were almost concurrent challenges to the color line in Topeka in the late 1920s. They involved plaintiffs who had lived in outlying areas that were now incorporated into the city of Topeka. These three cases were all instigated during a time when the school board was acting in ways that increased segregation. Oral history interviews revealed a system of informal integration instituted at the discretion of individual principals: the superintendent and the school board tolerated this practice until the late 1920s. Former teacher and long-time Topeka resident, El. Dorothy Scott, remembered that, as a child in the late 1920s, she

> could have gone to Highland Park, and that was all white.... They would have had to accept me ... oh now there was a time in Topeka where African American children went to white schools.... They went to Sumner. They didn't go to ... [segregated] ... Buchanan School. They do tell this story that some of the African American principals wanted the African American schools so that some of the African American women and men could get jobs. Now you could go to the white schools but they didn't hire the African American teachers. That's where the rub came ... and then as they began to plead for some schools where they might hire some African American teachers; we got our African American schools. They said that the African American principals tried to hold onto that. But before that time, I could have gone down to a [white] school called Parkdale, where I later taught.[22]

Both *Rich* (1928) and *Wright* (1929) involved African American plaintiff's petitioning to attend Randolph Elementary School. In September of 1928, Mrs. Maude Rich tried to enroll her three children in the Randolph School that was five blocks from her home. School Superintendent A. J. Stout ordered Blanche, age twelve, Richard, age eight, and Yvette, age five, to attend the segregated Buchanan School that was twenty blocks away from their home. Mrs. Rich stated, "As her cause of action that she lived within five blocks of Randolph ... and that some colored students were permitted to enter Randolph.... Mrs. Rich declared the board's ruling arbitrary."[23] The Topeka Board of Education did not deny Mrs. Rich's claim that African Americans had been attending Randolph School prior to

1928. Superintendent Stout admitted that two African American families were attending classes at Randolph in the present term. His reason for this, however, was that both of the families had lived in the area before it had been annexed by Topeka, and the Rich family was new to the area.

When the rural school was closed, all pupils were placed into the Randolph School, including the children in the two African American families, who had been attending the white school. Stout said that in permitting a few African Americans to attend Randolph, "[p]erhaps we have been wrong in doing that but those children grew up with the school. I understand that the Rich family has just moved into the neighborhood. If this case goes to court and it becomes a matter of throwing all the schools open or excluding these older pupils from Randolph, I suppose we will have to take them out of the school." Superintendent Stout was willing to modify the color line on a case-by-case basis, with people he knew, but he would not go so far as to "throw all the schools open."

The limited flexibility demonstrated by Superintendent Stout was the privilege William Reynolds had wanted for his son when Lohman Hill was annexed in 1890. The willingness of Superintendent Stout and the school board to negotiate outside the legal boundaries of segregation stopped far short of changing the general effects of the segregation policy. In the 1920s and '30s, there was an apparent tightening of exclusion of instances of African Americans from white schools, as indicated by these cases.

The growing population of Topeka, partially due to its annexation of outlying areas populated by African Americans, increased the number of African Americans living nearer white schools. The school board handled this on a case-by-case basis, as indicated by the court cases. However, by the late 1920s, the number of instances of African Americans being allowed to attend white schools outside the legal boundaries of segregation had increased enough to capture the attention of both African Americans and whites. When there were only a few African Americans in a white school, they were tolerated; but when that number threatened to substantially increase, it would substantially challenge the status quo. It also jeopardized the economic justification for maintaining segregated schools.

On the other side of the color line African Americans wanted their children to attend neighborhood schools. But attempts to circumvent segregated schools contained a hidden economic threat: fewer pupils meant less demand for African American teachers. The enforcement of segregation protected the continued employment of African American teachers in the segregated schools.

After 1929, segregation began to be uniformly enforced. Wilhelmina Wright was transferred to segregated Buchanan School after having attended the white Randolph School. Though a court case was filed to prevent her transfer to Buchanan School in 1929, she lost the case as well as the subsequent appeal to the Kansas State Supreme Court. Even though she lived within a few blocks of Randolph School, the court ordered her to attend Buchanan as "[n]o contention is made that the Buchanan school is not as good as a school and as well equipped in every way as is the Randolph school." Since the school district provided "transportation to and from the Buchanan school without expense to her or to her parents [and] ... [t]here is no contention that this transportation is not adequate, appropriate, or sufficient."[24]

That same year, Howard K. Foster tried to enroll his children into the new Gage School that had opened in September. The Fosters lived outside of Topeka's city limits, and his children had previously attended an integrated school, in this case the *old* Gage School. When the new school opened, Foster was told that his children would have to ride a bus to the segregated Buchanan Elementary School. Foster filed a lawsuit against the Topeka Board of Education and Superintendent A. J. Stout. In a decision written by Judge Whitcomb, Second Division, District Court, it was determined that the school board had no authority to hire buses in order to segregate children living in outlying districts. Since the Fosters lived in Mission Township, an outlying district from Topeka, they were allowed to attend the new Gage School at 8th and Prospect avenues.

As long as the Fosters remained outside the boundary of the city, they could attend the Gage School. Once their area was annexed by the city, the Foster children were subject to segregation. According to the *Topeka Kansas Capital* dated October 14, 1929, a mass meeting attended by more than three hundred people was held at Calvary Baptist Church to discuss the Foster lawsuit and the recent actions of the school board toward segregation. Other than this mass meeting, no activism is noted in the written historical sources.

Challenges to Contingencies

High School Segregation

The ongoing legal battles in Topeka revolved around segregation contingencies not addressed in the Kansas State constitution, which was written in 1861 as public schools began to develop junior high schools separate from elementary schools (which were covered under segregation statutes) and high schools (which were exempt), except for Sumner High School in Kansas City, Kansas. (The lack of specificity about secondary school segregation was perhaps due to the small number of the population that continued on to high school in the nineteenth century.) Sumner High School was established in 1905 after a special act of the legislature changed the 1879 statute allowing segregation of a secondary school in this one instance. Support for this legislation came from both sides of the color line, illustrating how African American and white leaders sometimes cooperated to promote segregation (Vandever 1971, 46). Since the African American population in Kansas City, Kansas, was concentrated north of the downtown area along Minnesota and State avenues, Sumner High School was located in the general vicinity of the highest black population (Kluger 1975, 371). Soon after Sumner High School opened in 1905, an African American plaintiff sued to attend the nearby white high school rather than have to journey to Sumner in 1906. The Kansas State Supreme Court denied the plaintiff's plea in *Richardson v. Board of Education of Kansas City, Kansas* (1906).[25] The existence of Sumner High School would later play a role in challenges to illegal school segregation in the 1940s, as discussed in Chapter Four.

Boswell Junior High: The Graham Case, 1940–1941

The shift toward a junior high curriculum brought another challenge to Topeka's segregated schools with the *Graham* case in 1940–1941. When the segregation statutes were first written in 1861 and later modified in 1879, junior high schools did not exist. The subsequent redefinition of state segregation statutes after 1940 was in response to an innovation in the institutional structure of public education accompanied by the rapidly increasing enrollments in secondary and postsecondary institutions.

When Topeka adopted the junior high system, it implemented a different educational curriculum for seventh and eighth grade students based on race. White students were provided with a 6-3-3 system, which consisted of six years of elementary or grade school, three years of junior high school, and three years of senior high school. Black children were under the 8-1-3 plan. This meant that now African American children in Topeka remained in segregated schools through the eighth grade, choosing either to enter an integrated ninth grade at Boswell Junior High or remain in a segregated class by electing to attend Roosevelt Junior High. White children who left elementary school after sixth grade and attended junior high school were consequently introduced to a much more specialized curriculum.

The case that desegregated the junior high schools in Topeka was again filed on behalf of a single plaintiff, Oaland Graham, though newspaper accounts state a group of citizens supported the case.[26] Before trying to enroll in Boswell Junior High School, Graham had attended Buchanan Elementary School. Graham's uncle, Ulysses A. Graham, rather than Graham's mother, appeared on behalf of the plaintiff. Interestingly, the senior Graham was an employee at Merchants National Bank where the president of the board of education of Topeka, A. H. Saville, was the cashier. Because of his position with the school board, Saville is named as a codefendant along with School Superintendent A. J. Stout.

On January 26, 1940, Graham, accompanied by his uncle, tried to enroll in seventh grade classes at Boswell Junior High. He was refused admittance based on his race. Graham had just graduated from the sixth grade at Buchanan Elementary School and desired to start junior high in January rather than waiting until September. The "normal" sequence of schooling for African Americans was that after finishing the eighth grade at Buchanan Elementary School they either went to Boswell for ninth grade or to Roosevelt Junior High for one year. Roosevelt was further away than Boswell, and it was also segregated. After the ninth grade, all students, regardless of race, went to Topeka High School for the tenth through twelfth grades.

Graham's challenge to the color line in Topeka arose from the change in educational segregation in Topeka. On March 20, 1925, the junior high system was adopted in Topeka through the Laws of 1925, Chapter 240. Though the school district could lawfully segregate elementary school and not its high school, Kansas's law did not specifically say whether junior highs were elementary schools. One way to determine the dividing line between elementary and high school grades would be to challenge it legally. Prior to *Graham,* the practice followed by African American children in Topeka was to remain in segregated schools through the eighth grade, choosing either to enter an integrated ninth grade at Boswell or remain in a segregated class by electing to attend Roosevelt Junior High.

Graham's lawsuit also challenged the assumption that the course of instruction at Buchanan Elementary was equal to that at Boswell Junior High. Boswell was built for the express purpose of being a junior high, and contained many more classrooms than the elementary schools, allowing for specialized teaching. In the segregated schools, one instructor taught most of the subjects. At Buchanan School, Miss Mamie L. Williams, an outstanding African American teacher, taught a wide variety of math and English courses. At Boswell Junior High different instructors taught all these subjects. In the testimony provided by witnesses in the *Graham* case, the home economics teacher at Buchanan, Miss Ruth Ridley, reported that though her students were well prepared when they graduated from the eighth grade, they did not have the modern sewing and cooking rooms that Boswell did. But it was her opinion that there was no real difference between the two schools. Mr. J. B. Holland, who was principal of Boswell, reported that the quality of instruction and the well-preparedness for his students to go on to high school was equal to those who attended the integrated school.

The only witness to express dissatisfaction with the course of instruction at the segregated school was Daniel S. Sawyer, a serviceman for the city water department. Though he testified that the schools were the same as far as he could tell, he also remarked that Buchanan seldom failed students. If a student did not "pass" a grade, they were obliged to go to summer school, where they did remedial work that sometimes did and sometimes didn't bring them up to par with the other students. Regardless of their "actual" improvements, at the end of the summer students were promoted to the next higher grade.

Graham won his case; the junior highs in Topeka were legally desegregated. However, the effect was uncertain—the desegregation did not include the teaching and administrative staff. For example, after the *Graham* case, eight African American teachers lost their jobs due to the integration of the junior highs. The assumption that the curriculum was not equal to the white schools reflected poorly on the high dedication and exemplary training of the black teachers, which many of them resented and rightly so. At two of the four segregated schools in Topeka, more of the teachers held master's degrees than at any of the white grade schools.

Conclusion: Tentative Beginnings

Kansas's permissive segregation allowed school segregation in its more densely populated "first class" cities with a population of more than fifteen thousand (Wilson 1995, 39). The expansion of Topeka's city limits during the first part of the twentieth century resulted in some African Americans being moved from integrated rural county schools to segregated city grade schools. This shift in boundaries also shifted color line practices. Those African Americans who were caught between pressures to preserve segregation within Topeka's city limits brought the resulting challenges to the color line and the informal tradition of integration to which they were accustomed outside of the city limits. It also saw the gradual elimination of white and black elites circumventing state laws by allowing a few select children to continue attending nonsegregated schools.

Since enforcement of segregated schools in Kansas was not uniform, and individual exceptions were permitted, early court cases asked for limited, individual exceptions to the policy of segregation. It was not until the 1954 *Brown* case that the petition for the rights of a specific individual would shift to those of a group. Though the 1903 *Reynolds* decision would later be significant as a precedent contributing to successful challenges to *illegal* segregation in cities not of the "first class." The court's decision affirmed the illegality of segregated schools outside of cities of the first class, even as it denied *Reynolds's* challenge in Topeka. William Reynolds's challenge to the color line in Topeka was against a practice sanctioned by state law, even though his attorneys argued that the establishment of separate schools based on race was a violation of the Fourteenth Amendment to the Constitution. The *Brown* attorneys would use a similar argument in 1951, in their initial challenge to segregation in Topeka, Kansas.[27]

Insights from the Border Campaign in Understanding Social Action Antecedents

The Border Campaign aids in understanding antecedents of social action directed against racial segregation by focusing on the role of cultural values shaping how people in specific historical situations attempt to cultivate power through the selection of "the strategies for the exercise of the power at its disposal" (Turner and Killian 1972, 289). Given the limitations of nineteenth-century Kansas, situating action in terms of the historical context is also important because it helps us contextualize how groups select their "main power objective" and "strategies" of protest. In nineteenth-century Kansas, groups favored power objectives aimed at maintaining the racial status quo. Segregation represented the autonomy of blacks to shape their own schools and use them as institutions by which to garner racial pride and uplift their race in the midst of racial prejudice. Later, during the mass mobilization era of the civil rights movement, these strategies were displaced with ones that sought change. The Master Narrative emphasizes the importance of the cultivation and use of power, causing the role of cultural values as historically situated to be overlooked or forgotten. In early civil rights struggles, cultural values are important to understanding how the principal strategies used in the exercise of power are influenced by ideas and beliefs about race: not only in terms of black and white, but also of other racial groups such as Native Americans.

Also, in order to appreciate the heterogeneity of these forgotten struggles, it is important to consider how cultural values, in this case competing ideologies of liberty and freedom, link agency with social structure. Next, it is also important to distinguish between organizational structure and social actions. As Lofland points out, it is easy to "conflate aspects of organizations and their resources with aspects of forms of *action*" (1969, 9). By distinguishing between *organizations* and *actions* in terms of their bargaining tactics, we extend our understanding of protest on a continuum, ranging from polite persuasion to violent disruptions. This distinction between different dimensions of collective behavior in forgotten civil rights protest brings to light the relevance of loosening the coupling of organization and action as suggested by Lofland (258). This gives us a clearer conception of what is involved, by contrast, in the tight coupling of organizational form and action of mass mobilizations in places like Montgomery and Birmingham, Alabama.

The Border Campaign aids in focusing on the polite/persuasion end of the continuum as being more characteristic of forgotten civil rights protest before the 1954 *Brown* decision. Given the dominance of racial segregation, either *de jure* or *de facto,* it is not surprising that the tactics of polite/persuasion were more likely to be used; further, this type of civil rights protest can be distinguished from the mass mobilization type of civil rights protest more likely to incorporate some form of violence, characteristic after there was no longer a legal sanction for segregation after 1955.

As the civil rights movement matured after 1960, there was a shift in how the authorities defined protest, choosing to define public gatherings as needing intervention, that is, needing to be stopped or interfered with. For example, at the first sit-in staged at a drug store lunch counter in 1958, in Wichita, Kansas, participant Ronald Walters (1993, 22) remembered that when the police arrived "they looked around, and an officer said, 'I don't see any disturbance taking place.'" This definition of the situation would change rapidly as the civil rights movement developed, particularly by the time sit-ins were staged in the early 1960s.

Lofland reminds us it is important to "sharpen our perception of some basic units of human association or organization, irrespective of their relevance to collective behavior." Turning to Goffman, we can break this down even further, to understand better the dramaturgical implications of early civil rights protest by studying segregation as an interaction order or a type of organizational behavior. Due to the lack of institutional and structural resources provided in mass mobilizations, it is important to look at the structure of social interactions and how segregation was organizationally, structurally, and socially sustained in order to fully understand how it all became unraveled. Although studies of the mass mobilization era provide us with a wide variety of empirical evidence to study the dynamics and strategies or protest, it does not help us understand this earlier period because we need to shift focus to the structure of maintenance rather than the structure of change. Political opportunities and local movement center models only provide a partial picture of how this change came about.

The types of civil rights protest in which African Americans participated in the 1880s were very different from that of the 1950s. In the 1880s, particularly in Topeka, Kansas, African Americans were protesting the lack of local control over their segregated schools and demanded that teachers of their own race be hired instead of whites. In the 1950s, African Americans were challenging the entire institution of school segregation. Though the actions in the 1880s and the 1950s were fundamentally different, since one reinforced segregated schools and the other was a direct challenge to it, both types of actions qualify as "protest." By focusing on the material goal of desegregation, sociologists have studied the civil rights movement by its outcomes rather than its motivating factors. Since the outcome of protest in the nineteenth century reinforced segregation, the significance of such actions have been overlooked in the overall historical understanding of the civil rights movement, which resulted in desegregation.

The Border Campaign analyzes collective action in relationship to its historical context and not exclusively by its goals, as in the Master Narrative. In this way, the Border Campaign discloses something previously unknown about the role of agency in civil rights protest, as well as protest in general. Outcomes change and are specifically related to local and historical contexts. By generalizing the outcomes, sociologists have limited their understanding of the origins of the civil rights movement to those collective actions specifically directed against segregation.

By conceptualizing action upon a continuum ranging from persuasion, bargaining, and coercion (Turner and Killian 1972, 291), the Border Campaign recognizes the nuances in the exercise of power. These different types of strategies "are distinguished by the manner in which the movement attempts to influence the actions of the target group." Though there is overlap between these different types of strategies, the variety of racial exclusion found in forgotten civil rights activism means challenges are more likely to involve "persuasion" rather than "coercion." Defining persuasion as "the use of strictly symbolic manipulation without substantial rewards or punishments under the control of the movement," by "identify[ing] the proposed course of action with values held by the target group" (Turner and Killian, 292). If the target groups' dominant values are racial separation rather than racial equality, why is it so surprising that petitioners would have the same values? In the early civil rights movement the value of racial equality was not yet fully developed by either whites or blacks. With racial equality still embryonic, the power dynamics are more likely to be directed toward modifying segregation rather than eliminating it. Unsurprisingly, as the ideal of racial equality began to replace the one of racial separation, this led to a shift in strategy away from persuasion toward coercion. The Master Narrative's emphasis on racial equality obscures the way in which racial separation was sometimes used for black empowerment and self-sufficiency. The Master Narrative's conceptualization of protest and lack of attention paid to the local situation contributes to a lack of attention paid to the role of agency.

The Role of Elites in Facilitating Social Movements

Frazier's (1957) critical analysis of the black middle class as inhibiting rather than facilitating social change obscures the role elites played in challenges to the color line. The black middle class was not homogenous, as demonstrated by the actions of the black attorneys and business leaders in Kansas. Examining their actions within the historical context reasserts their agency and highlights their unappreciated role in laying the groundwork for challenging racial segregation. Focusing only on the dramatic "mass mobilization" aspects of the civil rights movement is an obstacle to recognizing the full range of *civil rights* tension between the established social order (racial segregation) and countercultural challenges to it. Highlighting the actions of the black middle class as pertaining to the interaction order of race (Goffman 1983, 14) also helps explore the tensions between structure and agency during any type of social change.

The cost benefit of racial segregation to ensuring the need for black professionals to service the black community is accompanied by the rising expectations of the black middle class to enjoy the benefits of consumer society. Though segregation provided financial security for the small black elite (Frazier 1957) it also inhibited them from full inclusion in American society, and their professional aspirations were limited by racial boundaries. As demonstrated by the plaintiffs in the early challenges to segregation in Kansas, individuals petitioning for privileged access to white schools conflicted with the stability of their own status group. School segregation was costly and integration meant the loss of jobs for black teachers and administrators. It was the black middle class that had the knowledge and tools to challenge segregation; the rising tide of economic prosperity fueled their determination to improve their lives. The tension between wanting to enjoy the fruits of consumerism as individuals conflicted with their communal desire to uplift the race. Like most Americans, the black middle class was trying to reconcile the contradiction between the desires of the individual with what is best for the community.

The heterogeneity of these early civil rights actions has rendered them relatively invisible in studying civil rights protest. They are perceptible only as face-to-face interaction and rarely include large groups or masses of people; this places them outside the set of "established rules" used to study the civil rights movement. Face-to-face interaction is often neglected in the two dominant and competing theoretical models in contemporary social movement theory. Political process theorists prioritize structures of power, economics, formal organizations, and social networks in creating social change. This approach has dominated social movement theory for the past several decades (most notably McAdam 1982; McCarthy and Zald 1977; Staggenborg 1991; Tarrow 1994; and Tilly 1978). Recently, cultural constructionist theorists have emerged—partially drawing on symbolic interactionism—using frames, identities, meanings, and emotions in the building of social movements (Kurzman 1996; Morris 1984; Snow and Benford 1992).

Each of these perspectives has begun a collaborative discourse, claiming to bring in the relevance of agency, emotions, and culture into the structure in the study of social movements without sacrificing the significance of either agency or structure (Goodwin and Jasper 2004). However, attempts to do this have resulted in retaining the primacy of structure over agency by concentrating on the structure of social action relationships as they coalesce in terms of institutions (organizations) and groups. In essence, this means treating face-to-face relationships as "effects … as indicators, expressions, or symptoms of social structures such as relationships, age grades, gender, ethnic minorities, social classes" rather than as "data in their terms" (Goffman 1974, 2).

In suggesting an alternative way to study face-to-face interaction as data, it is fruitful to conceptualize the effects of racial segregation as "situational" rather than "merely situated." Using Blumer's concept of "joint action" to help capture how individual or separate lines of action coalesce, eventually merging into "strips of action" (Goffman 1974) works to sensitize us as to how "individuals may orient their action on different premises," leaving open the possibility that even commonly defined joint actions can lead to a variety of courses or outcomes. This also helps to conceptualize groups as dynamic rather than static, thus arriving at an expanded definition of group action as being created and structured through the process of the building up of joint actions or strips of action, creating a vast number of social actions occurring at any given moment. This approach will help us to better understand racial segregation not only as it was constructed during the civil rights movement but also as it is now in contemporary society.

By incorporating Goffman's interaction order, the Border Campaign overcomes a limitation of the political process model, which synthesizes theory directed toward an abstract universality often overlooking the significance of unique or unusual events. The Border Campaign also avoids the constructionist path of prioritizing cultural context over structure. Instead it suggests a middle ground, prioritizing face-to-face interaction to better understand the processes and structures specific to the interaction order, and, ultimately to create social change.

The situated effects of segregation are best illustrated by imagery of the color line, that is, a boundary line drawn between black and white, wherein persons overstepping over it from either side faced either formal (legal) or informal (social) consequences. In places like Mississippi or Alabama where legal racial segregation was more exclusive, infractions were more likely to be policed by the state; in other places, like Kansas, infractions of the color line were less likely to be policed by the state, but social censure carried out through face-to-face social interaction could be just as humiliating as being arrested for sitting on the wrong seat on the bus or drinking water from the wrong drinking fountain.

Permissive segregation of public spaces shaped actions to challenge and preserve the color line as well as the selection of appropriate social locations in which these challenges and defenses were attempted. As these challenges increased, they created conditions in which different racial practices were valued, enabling new and different negotiations resulting in multiple definitions of the situation to emerge. This increased the opportunity for competing claims of legitimacy for power over the negotiated order of segregation. Using Hallet's (2003, 141) symbolic approach further illuminates how in Border Campaigns, "audiences value certain practices and imbue negotiators with legitimacy, and then how legitimacy is deployed as the symbolic power to define the situation and relevant meanings." Thus, in Kansas, though social change was incremental, it gradually evolved due to the lack of segregation in most public spaces. This lack of a uniform system of segregation provided the space for desegregation protest to formulate, gain legitimacy, and eventually employ an increased range of tactics challenging the color line.

Finally, in the twentieth century, actions oriented toward civil society predominate due to the social actor's bestowal of meaning. Like the pragmatists, we acknowledge that ideas influence social action, but we do not reify them as being real forces in social life. By only examining social structure we are left with a partial picture; it is also important to examine belief systems (culture) that are manifested in a certain type of structure. In the next chapter, we examine the interaction of agency, structure, and culture in the actions of women attempting to gain access to civil society and its public institutions from both sides of the color line.

Notes

1. In the mid-1850s pro-abolitionist settlers founded several towns, including Manhattan, Lawrence, and Topeka. These villages were established to promote not only pro-abolitionist settlement—and thus assuring a free-state vote on the referendum of slavery—but also to generate economic opportunities to become self-sufficient. Manhattan, Lawrence, and Topeka were all located strategically on rivers, which were the primary mode of transportation for cargo as well as people. These settlements became targets for pro-slavery factions who lived nearby in Missouri, a slave state. Lawrence was the recipient of numerous attacks by the notorious William Quantrill, a renegade Confederate officer who finally burned most of the town in 1863 and succeeded in killing most of the males older than the age of twelve.

2. The Missouri Compromise allowed Congress to expand slavery beyond the original thirteen colonies, setting the precedent for slavery to expand into the West. See Foner and Garraty (1991) 737.

3. Fischer notes that during the Revolutionary War "the backcountry regiments . . . made much trouble for George Washington. . . . They were difficult men to lead. The social attitudes of a Fairfax gentleman [i.e., Washington] did not sit well with them, and they were utterly defiant of discipline and order. Washington grew so angry with them that he ordered some to be tried for mutiny and threatened with capital punishment. The backcountry men responded by coming close to a full-blown insurrection" (Fischer 2004, 24).

4. The validity of this argument is still being debated by attorneys fifty years after *Brown*. In an article in the *Southern Illinois University Law Journal,* Michael J. Berry argues that school desegregation cases were incorrectly decided on the Fourteenth Amendment (due process), but rather were in violation of the Fifth Amendment (individual rights) (No. 20, Fall 1995, 53–73). One of the cases *was* decided based on the Fifth Amendment, *Bolling v. Sharpe,* the Washington, DC, case. Since Washington, DC, is not a state, it never ratified the Fourteenth Amendment. Indeed, according to the oral arguments before the Supreme Court in the *Brown* case, the 39th Congress in 1866 enacted laws "to implement and expedite the administration of the segregated system of public schools" in Washington, DC (791).

5. Annual Report State Superintendent of Public Instruction (1867), 72.

6. House Bill 219 (1870).

7. See "Report and Testimony of the Select Committee of the United States Senate to Investigate the Causes of the Removal of the Negroes from the Southern States to the Northern States." U.S. Congress, Senate Report 693, 46th Congress, 2nd Session; Part 2. Washington, 1880.

8. U.S. Congress, Senate Report 693, 46th Congress, 2nd Session; Part 2. Washington, DC, 1880, 288.

9. U.S. Congress, Senate Report 693, 46th Congress, 2nd Session; Part 2. Washington, DC, 1880, 289

10. U.S. Congress, Senate Report 693, 46th Congress, 2nd Session; Part 2. Washington, DC, 1880, 288–295.

11. U.S. Congress, Senate Report 693, 46th Congress, 2nd Session; Part 2. Washington, DC, 1880, 293.

12. U.S. Congress, Senate Report 693, 46th Congress, 2nd Session; Part 2. Washington, DC, 1880, 291.

13. U.S. Congress, Senate Report 693, 46th Congress, 2nd Session; Part 2. Washington, DC, 1880, 295.

14. U.S. Congress, Senate Report 693, 46th Congress, 2nd Session; Part 2. Washington, DC, 1880, 291.

15. U.S. Congress, Senate Report 693, 46th Congress, 2nd Session; Part 2. Washington, DC, 1880, 292.

16. U.S. Congress, Senate Report 693, 46th Congress, 2nd Session; Part 2. Washington, DC, 1880, 294.

17. *William Reynolds v. Board of Education of the City of Topeka, of the State of Kansas. In the Supreme Court of the State of Kansas, 1890.*

18. *William Reynolds v. Board of Education of the City of Topeka, of the State of Kansas. In the Supreme Court of the State of Kansas, 1890.*

19. Brief for the Plaintiff, *William Reynolds v. Board of Education of Topeka,* January Term 1903, vol. 66, 627–637.

20. *William Reynolds v. Board of Education of the City of Topeka, of the State of Kansas. In the Supreme Court of the State of Kansas, 1890,* 3–4.

21. The court cases were *Reynolds v. Board of Education, Topeka,* 1903; *Cartwright v. Board of Education, Coffeyville,* 1906; *Rowles v. Board of Education, Wichita,* 1907; *Williams v. Board of Education, Parsons,* 1908; *Woolridge v. Board of Education, Galena,* 1916; *Thurman-Watts v. Board of Education, Topeka,* 1924; *Wright v. Board of Education, Topeka,* 1929; *Graham v. Board of Education, Topeka,* 1941; *Webb v. School District No. 90, South Park Johnson County, Kansas,* 1949.

22. Author interview with El. Dorothy Scott, October 1992.

23. "Ku Klux Sentiment Entering Public Schools." *Topeka Plaindealer,* September 28, 1928.

24. January Term, 1930. Kansas State Supreme Court, vol. 129, 853.

25. 72 Kansas 629.

26. *Topeka Plaindealer,* Friday, January 26, 1940.

27. The attorneys for the *Reynolds* case asked for a writ of mandamus to compel the school board to admit the plaintiff to Lohman Hills Elementary School. The writ as denied in an opinion filed on April 11, 1903. The opinion is written in response to four parts, each section addressing the unconstitutionality of Kansas segregation laws. The first question states that the law establishing separate schools on the basis of race was not within the legislative authority of the Kansas legislature. Citing the two previous Kansas school cases which were established in cities of the second class that had no clear legislative authority to do so, the plaintiff tried to argue that a statute that created segregated schools in cities of the first class was not uniform. Though "[t]he question is not free from difficulty," the opinion of the court will set a precedent for the next forty seven years in Kansas (Kansas State Supreme Court, p. 673). The amendment that stipulated that boards

of education could establish separate schools based on race in cities of the first class was not invalidated by having been written to amend a former statute. The plaintiff also tried to argue that the act of 1879 could not stand because its title was not sufficient. The court found that the act contained only one subject.

Lunch counter sit-in at John A. Brown's department store, August 27, 1958, Oklahoma City. The fact that the activists are being served drinks illustrates how the boundaries of racial segregation were permeable when directly challenged (courtesy of the Oklahoma State Historical Society).

3

"Invisibility Blues"

Black Women and the Public Sphere in Guthrie, Oklahoma, 1890–1910

This chapter discusses early civil rights struggles, demonstrating the importance of the historical situation and intersection of cultural goals in the development of institutionalized means to achieve social change. In the preceding chapter the competing ideologies of racial inclusion and exclusion were examined in the border state of Kansas. This belief system underpinned an uneven system of racial segregation limited primarily to its public schools. We now turn to a different border state, Oklahoma, which developed its own system of segregation on a different trajectory than Kansas. Like Kansas, Oklahoma's geographical location bordering northern, southern, and western states shaped its ideologies of race. Its cultural values of liberty and freedom were also tempered by northern abolitionism and free soil mentalities, southern racial exclusion, and Western frontier beliefs about rugged individualism.

Kansas's lack of a unitary hegemonic racial ideology (Harding 1984, 386) shifted the racial discourse from overt legislative attempts to reserve citizenship for "whites"—as was the case in the South—to a more covert manipulation of the color line through restrictive real estate covenants and municipal restrictions in public facilities such as restaurants and theaters. As cities like Topeka grew, their expanding system of public schools became the primary institution where racial politics were played out, eventually resonating nationally with the 1954 *Brown* case. Supported largely by property taxes, public schools became neighborhood-defining institutions, gradually turning into symbols of social class, status, and racial exclusion. The Master Narrative obscures this nuanced negotiation of the color line and the importance of regional variance in challenges to the color line.

Oklahoma's more restricted color line reveals how individual action adapted to specific social situations. These types of nuanced civil rights struggles are overlooked by the Master Narrative. Though Oklahoma shared *de jure* segregation with its southern neighbors, its civil rights protests are often ignored. In Oklahoma, racial prejudice was fueled by its much larger Native American and African American populations. The forced relocation of thousands of Native Americans to Oklahoma lands began in the 1830s, and after the famous "land run" in 1889, thousands of African Americans also began to pour into the territory. Oklahoma offered the opportunity for black Americans to "create towns and colonies where black people would be free to exercise their political rights without interference" (Taylor 1998, 144). Edwin P. McCabe, originally a leader of Kansas's Exoduster movement (discussed in Chapter Two), directed his efforts toward Oklahoma as a place where "the negro can rest from mob law, here he can be secure from every ill of the southern policies'" (145). It was even rumored that McCabe, a Republican, hoped to be appointed the first governor of Oklahoma Territory, something Oklahoma's Democrats used to "brand all Republicans dangerous and unworthy of white support" (145).[1]

Race, Gender, and Women's Historical Agency

After statehood in 1907, the Democrats successfully took political control of Oklahoma and immediately implemented a comprehensive system of *de jure* segregation. Though Oklahoma's system of segregation was shaped and codified by cultural values of racial hierarchy, it was also influenced by the competing cultural values of collective responsibility and frontier individualism, as outlined in the previous chapter. In addition, Oklahoma's racial and ethnic dynamics of the frontier were also influenced by heightened anxieties about being marginalized by the East, economically and culturally. The Master Narrative undermines appreciating the ways in which marginalized and disenfranchised groups, like African Americans and women, were able to circumvent racism and sexism through forming their own institutions.[2]

Examining women's historical agency provides an alternative to the masculine bias of the Master Narrative. Women, just as African Americans in Kansas after the Civil War, were excluded from the public sphere and created their own segregated institutions in which they gradually were able to "redefine not only women's roles but also the state in relationship to its citizens" (Haarsager 1997, 3). Also, as suggested about black Kansans in the last chapter, women's historical agency was "sometimes strongest when policies for women were the least liberal" (Haarsager 1997, 364). Disenfranchised African Americans were able to express their ideas in terms of the American work ethic and formed institutions to seek access to training and education in order to uplift their race from slavery. So, too, were women able to create their own organizations in which to "express their ideas (and make them acceptable) by attaching them to the values of the home" by extending their "traditional female roles as caretakers, teachers, and moral guardians" (Haarsager 1997, 23-24).

The Master Narrative focuses on charismatic leadership and the resources provided by the institutional structures of black churches and activist organizations—for the most part arenas of male activism. As in the South, African Americans developed their own community institutions that were eventually used to channel insurgency. But this exclusion from the public sphere also opened up opportunities for women to enter politics through nonpolitical women's literary clubs and benevolence associations. As citizenship during this time was a male prerogative, women from both sides of the color line were similarly confined to the domestic sphere. While Kansas had less restrictive segregation, thus allowing black men to more openly publicly challenge it, Oklahoma's unyielding color line succeeded in limiting the efforts of black men while at the same providing opportunities for women to operate within the boundaries of their domestic roles. Using the Border Campaign, we bring into focus the ways in which black women led the forces of resistance in claiming legitimacy for their actions on the basis of their assertion of respectability and dignity as wives, mothers, daughters, and sisters.

Women's involvement in social reform came about because of their memberships in various voluntary associations during the Progressive Era (1890–1920) (Rynbrandt 1997, 203). The Progressive Era is most often remembered for governmental reforms in the name of efficiency, direct political participation, and governmental regulation of business, particularly at the federal level (Chafe 1980). This period is especially important for the ways in which middle- and upper-class women began to participate in civil society by transcending the ideology of separate spheres for men and women (Kerber 1988). "Women were assigned the task of defending their homes and families in the private sector but were increasingly unable to do so without becoming involved in public political reform in the more modern, industrial society" (Rynbrandt 1997, 203). Acting as a "bridge for women between the private home and the public world" (203), women's clubs would play a significant role in facilitating broader participation of women in the public sphere.

On one level, women's clubs fostered conformity by embracing the ideology of the late nineteenth century cult of domesticity celebrating women's "innate" moral superiority. In a frontier town such as Guthrie, Oklahoma, with a transient population, women's literary societies and charity organizations were a means of acculturation for newcomers. Women's clubs were important sources of friendship and moral support as women on the frontier were often lonely and socially isolated. As Haarsager (1997, 5) observes, "[w]omen used clubs for identity formation, both as women and as part of a group of bounded by class, by culture.... Women isolated in nascent towns without services or amenities especially needed this association.... Clubs created a female space outside the home and church where none had existed before."

The importance of this "female space" is reflected by the rapid development of women's clubs. The General Federation of Women's Clubs (GFWC) was founded in 1890. Though excluded from joining the GFWC, African American women soon formed their own clubs, including the National Association of Colored Women (NACW) in 1896 (Giddings 1985, 93). The NACW became the institutional means by which African American women would be able to redefine women's moral role to include "moral uplift" of their race. The charge to use women's moral authority to undertake racial uplift was expressed in the following way by Anna Julia Cooper: "Only the Black Woman can say 'when and where I enter, in the quiet, undisputed dignity of my womanhood, without violence and without suing or special patronage, then there the *whole Negro race enters with me*'" (1892, 31; emphasis in original).

Though white women in the West were invisible in this period (Rynbrandt 1997, 200), Wallace (1990, 5)argues that black women faced the dilemma of "*high visibility* together with their almost total lack of *voice.*" Not only are black women objectified by sexism and racism, but they are presumed to lack agency in shaping activism. This contradiction is due in part to African American women being embedded in a "double and sometimes triple context—as blacks and as women to white Americans, as women to black men, and as individuals of particular class backgrounds to and for themselves" (Lengermann and Neibrugge-Brantley 1998, 160). For example, Cooper's description from the 1890s of the "multiple effects of race, gender, and class was offered in the form of a simple narrative set in a place no African American, then or now, would fail to recognize: the racially segregated, Jim Crow car of a railroad train.... And when farther on in the same section our train stops at a dilapidated station ... and when looking a little more closely, I see two dingy little rooms with 'For Ladies' swinging over one and 'For Colored People' over the other while wondering under which I come" (Lemert 1997, 179).

Race, Gender, Class, and Activism in Oklahoma

The Master Narrative characterizes the color line in masculine, almost militaristic language, representing racial practices using terms filled with control and domination. However, the particular way in which segregation was codified in Oklahoma also shaped understandings of racial etiquette in terms of gender and class. By being sensitive to the local situation, Oklahoma's particular social, cultural, and political conditions provides a setting in which to consider the constraints of gender in terms of the frontier and hegemonic Southern culture understandings of race. African American women lived, as Lengermann and Niebrugge-Brantley remind us, "in a double and sometimes triple context ... to and for themselves." Given that segregation curtailed black women's movements because of race, along with the contested meanings of gender on the frontier, they were further confined by the "cult of domesticity" consigning women to the private or domestic sphere as a woman's "proper place." "Further, black women had to address the ever-present, rarely publicly spoken charge of sexual immorality" making the ideal of genteel womanhood even more difficult for them to claim (160).

One way in which black women could get around these constraints was through community involvement, working to "uplift" their race and foster a sense of self-efficacy. "Self-preservation demands that [Black women] go among the lowly ... to whom they are bound by ties of race and sex ... to reclaim them" (160). These ideas helped foster the growth of women's clubs and benevolence organizations nationally and on both sides of the color line. In Oklahoma, women's benevolence organizations grew out the activism of the Women's Christian Temperance Union (WCTU) involved in the break up of the "whiskey towns" between Oklahoma Territory, where liquor was legal, and Indian Territory, where it was not (Gumprecht 1996, 146). Before statehood, whiskey towns did a very lucrative business selling illegal liquor to Indians. Contemporary accounts described these towns as "where saloons lined the streets, bootleggers came to stock up, gambling was widespread, and brothels did a brisk trade in upstairs rooms" (146). After the Oklahoma Land Run of 1889 and before statehood in 1907, the traffic in illegal liquor diminished due in part to efforts by the WCTU (151).

The temperance movement illustrates how women worked together to bring about social change when they lacked political and civil rights. But women were not without historical agency. For example, when public protests and petitions failed to close a saloon, the ladies of one temperance society in Lincoln County ostracized the wives whose husbands were involved in selling liquor. "We just did not call on ... [the wives] ... or invite them to visit us. Soon the woman was so lonesome that she persuaded her husband to move away from there."[3] Efforts by these women and others of the WCTU resulted in Oklahoma endorsing prohibition in every county in Oklahoma Territory when it became a state in 1907 (167).

The land rush in 1889 also brought in a flood of white European settlers who worked to establish an ideology of racial superiority reinforced by white dominant institutions. In the territorial capital of Guthrie, this shift toward white dominance is reflected in the gradual *de jure* segregation of public schools. In December 1890, due to the rural nature of the population, the territorial legislature passed Bill No. 2, making it a county-level decision to determine every three years whether schools would be segregated or integrated. As in Kansas, many towns, including Guthrie, practiced an informal system of integration. But one year later, in 1891, Logan County, which included the city of Guthrie, voted to segregate schools. By May 1893, voters passed a school bond to build and equip four permanent buildings, one of which was designated for black students.

The school census in Guthrie that May was 1,326 white and 876 African American children. This meant that each of the three white schools had an average of 442 pupils, while the black school had to accommodate approximately twice that many. But an overcrowded school was just one of the many problems now facing African Americans in Guthrie: over the next fifteen years they would see their rights and liberties slowly erode and almost taken away as Oklahoma and the rest of the country became increasingly segregated (Taylor 1998, 216–218). In the Republican stronghold of Logan County, where African Americans had experienced some success in being elected to public office, black candidates increasingly encountered more difficulty being elected, especially after statehood, which ushered in several decades of dominance by the Democratic Party.

As the Oklahoma Constitutional Convention convened in 1906, the convention's president, William H. Murray, articulated the new dominance of the Democratic Party by urging the new state of Oklahoma to adopt a provision prohibiting racially mixed marriages and provide for not only separate schools, but also all public institutions in the state, including railroad cars and phone booths.[4] Ensuring that its segregation laws be obeyed uniformly, Oklahoma even enacted civil and criminal penalties for school administrators who mixed the races in its public schools. Worried that President Theodore Roosevelt "would refuse statehood if segregation were written into the constitution, the Democrats waited until the first legislature convened" (Reese 2003, 330).

In codifying segregation, Oklahoma's interpretation of Southern culture and ideology about the mixing of races in public accommodations went to an extreme. Its ideology about how to regulate the movements of women went even further. Writing about the frontier in the 1890s, Frederick Jackson Turner wrote, "Frontiers were as devoid of women as the Great Plains was devoid of trees." This statement reflects the overall invisibility of women of any color from the narrative of the West (Taylor and Moore 2003).

As previously noted, women built strong support networks within the confines of the domestic sphere shaped in varying degrees by kinship, religion, and political and class sympathies. This subculture of female friends and relatives was ruptured and difficult to reconstruct in places like Oklahoma, where women found themselves isolated by distance or privation. As historian Susan Armitage notes "'frontier individualism was forced upon these women: they had to be more self-reliant and less communal than they had been before'" (Haarsager 1997, 9).

After settling in frontier towns like Guthrie, Oklahoma, women sought out other women in voluntary associations to not only improve themselves but also to refine their raw communities.

The Public Library Movement and Racial Segregation

During the Progressive Era, public libraries became important places where women could venture and not violate moral codes about propriety. The expansion of public libraries in the South remained slow due to its rural nature and general lack of public funding. Southern white citizens, including white Oklahomans, viewed libraries as a luxury, and only the biggest cities had the money to support them (Robbins 2000, 38–39). Because of segregation, African Americans had little access to public libraries.

Community approaches to providing library resources to African Americans varied by city. Using grants from Andrew Carnegie and the Carnegie Corporation, eleven segregated public libraries were built in the South between 1905 and 1925, constituting "an access point for black intellectualism, a confirmation of black African Americans as literate" (Malone 1996, 1, 23). But these libraries were the exception, not the rule. Access to library services for most African Americans was limited to what was available on the campuses of their segregated schools where public libraries would sometimes provide limited access to its services. In 1904, the African American Library of Galveston, Texas, established a board of directors, which quickly built an addition at Central High School to provide quarters for a public library (Gleason 1941). Other cities established branch libraries for their black citizens. In 1903, the North Carolina legislature passed an act for establishment of an independent branch library for "the colored people of Charlotte." When Louisville, Kentucky, opened its public library in 1905, it planned for two of its ten additional branches to be designated specifically for blacks.

In Oklahoma, ten Carnegie libraries were built before statehood in 1907, and fifteen more were built between 1908 and 1916 (Finchum and Finchum 2001), African Americans were not allowed access. One obstacle African Americans faced in obtaining their own grant from

Carnegie's library program was that it only provided start-up funds to pay for a building; local governments needed to impose a special tax to pay for the operating costs (Van Slyck 1995). As noted earlier, it was not impossible for African Americans to receive a grant, but Carnegie's policy closely linked support for public libraries with local governments. Given that racial segregation excluded their participation in local government as well as access to most public facilities, it is not surprising that so few black Carnegie libraries were built.

In Guthrie's Carnegie library grant application, the city maintained that the new library was "... for the thousands of common people, black and white, old and young, rich and poor, who inhabit the flourishing capital city of our young territory." It was quietly understood that the black community would not be welcome to utilize the new public facility. Though Guthrie's library upkeep would eventually be supported with public funds (Finchum and Finchum 2001, 464), it also meant that African Americans were paying for public facilities they could not use.

Though most public libraries were closed to African Americans, they became a new public space for both black and white women to venture. In the broader discussion of the progressive movement's importance to women's gradual involvement in politics, public libraries are an often overlooked mechanism by which women of both races were able to operationally transform their domestic ideals into public issues (Malone 1996, 30–32; Stiefmiller 2001). For white women, public libraries offered an option outside of private homes to hold women's club meetings. These rooms were often styled after Victorian family parlors, making them both familiar and gendered in the sense that they created a zone or safe space of non-interference for women to meet (Malone 1996, 40). For African American women, public libraries became a very important social domain in which to articulate how reading and its relationship to education was an important way in which the limited resources of black women could be spent wisely in order to uplift their race. Championing the cause of public libraries was also a way in which black women could use their high visibility to find a voice that whites would begin to listen to.

We turn now to the story of how one African American woman, Judith Carter Horton, who was able to use literacy to fight racial prejudice as well as create a public space for African Americans in an increasingly segregated society.

Judith Carter Horton and the Founding of Guthrie's Excelsior Library

Horton was born in Wright City, Missouri, in 1866. Determined from an early age to secure an education, she overcame her father's objections (her mother died soon after she was born)—that attending school was a "foolish and unnecessary activity"—and left home at age 13 to do domestic work in order to earn an education (Horton 1914, 5). The family she worked for moved to St. Louis in 1882, and Horton took advantage of the city's expanded educational opportunities in order to prepare for college. Against all odds, she managed to save enough money to set out for Oberlin College in 1884, first attending Oberlin Academy and eventually earning a teaching degree in 1891. Though less famous than other African American Oberlin alumni—Mary Church Terrell and Julia Adams Cooper, both graduating in 1884 (Lengermann and Niebrugge-Brantley 1998, 156)—Horton's Oberlin experience shaped her activism for the next several decades. Horton later recalled, as she neared graduation, that she promised herself "in spite of the fact that you are now a 'Nobody,' without culture, social standing or money, you must some day accomplish what no Negro women (sic) has ever attempted" (Horton 1914, 17).

After teaching for a year in Columbus, Kansas, Horton eventually found herself living in Guthrie, marrying a teacher named Daniel Gibbs Horton, in 1894, with whom she had six children, only three living to adulthood. Horton managed to travel to Washington, DC, in July 1896, to be present at the merging of the National Federation of Afro-American Women and the National League of Colored Women to become the National Association of Colored Women (Stiefmiller 2001, 9). Just as Oberlin prepared her intellectually for being aware of racial and social injustice, the NACW provided an important organizational structure from which to carry out her social activism. The NACW's stand against racial segregation and lynching would later bring nationally renowned figures like Mary Church Terrell and Ida B. Wells to Oklahoma, helping to facilitate racial justice in Guthrie (Strong 1957, 54).

Like her Progressive Era sisters from both sides of the color line, the timing of Horton's activism revolved around the demands of her domestic life. For the next ten years, between 1896 and 1906, Horton was involved in raising her children. In early 1906, Horton was finally able to organize the first African American women's club in Oklahoma: the Excelsior Club of Guthrie (42). Though broadly concerned with moral uplift, this club would provide an important social outlet for African Americans, as well as an organizational platform from which to focus on issues related to race.

As the Guthrie Carnegie Library was being built and finally opened in February 1903, the black community followed its progress through the *Oklahoma Guide,* the weekly African American newspaper. The *Oklahoma Guide* also provided details about the role of the city in funding its maintenance, in particular the city council's decision to pass a mill levy. Though African Americans were also paying for the "free library," no one challenged this fact until Daniel Horton tried to get a library card in 1907.

Horton was turned away because "no provision had been made for Negroes" (Stiefmiller 2001, 14). Horton recalls that her husband came home and told her "the time had come for me to carry out my pledge to something unusual." Though "prospects for such an undertaking looked very dim . . . I . . . began to work out a plan for its execution" (Horton 1914, 17).

Horton was guided by her conviction "to hasten the education and uplift our people by the establishment of reading rooms, and libraries in every community. When we become a reading people, we will be a thinking people" (27). Horton drafted a plan for a library and "approached a group of local businessmen who acknowledged both the need and feasibility of her plan" (Stiefmiller 2001, 15). Next, she sought support from the Excelsior Club. But when she asked the club to sponsor her project, only six of its twenty-one members supported her plan. Despite the jeers from members of her own race, Horton undertook a letter-writing campaign and solicited help from community leaders from both sides of the color line. She secured a building, and with the help of "white Club Women of this city have promised to aid us [to] the extent the purchase can [be] made. Now, what are the colored citizens of City and State going to do?" (16–17). Now called the Excelsior Library, the library campaign was further aided by a benefit appearance of Mary Church Terrell, the civil rights activist and nationally known leader in the black women's club movement.

Using the Carnegie Library as a model, Horton petitioned the city council to gain tax support for the maintenance of a black library. This final, but crucial, step was hindered by the sudden appearance of a petition signed by twenty-three Guthrie citizens objecting to the proposed location of the Excelsior Library (18). The library appropriation was removed and added to other municipal appropriations. The mayor, however, vetoed this move, reminding the councilmen that failing to fund the segregated library would mean that it would be difficult to continue to legally justify reserving the existing Carnegie library for only whites—since Guthrie "having levied annually a tax upon all the property of the citizens for the support and maintenance of a Library from the privileges of which a certain class of our citizens are denied."[5] Though African Americans were legally denied access to public facilities, they enjoyed equal representation as taxpayers. The black citizens of Guthrie had used their status as taxpayers to demand their right to access public facilities they had helped finance. As in the funding of Kansas's public schools, Guthrie's black citizens realized that paying taxes gave them the basis from which to launch campaigns questioning exclusion from public accommodations. The Guthrie City Council eventually approved the levy and the Excelsior Library was dedicated on September 24, 1908 (Horton 1914, 23).

As a symbol of education and its promise of moral uplift, the Excelsior Library also served as a community center for Guthrie's black citizens.

Horton understood that having access to a library provided the opportunity for African Americans to develop intellectually, "no matter what race Thinkers belong they are considered 'Good Citizens'" (24).

Judith Carter Horton eventually expanded her efforts to improve the plight of other marginalized groups, including helping to found the State Training School for African American boys at Boley and the African American Orphans' School at Taft (Stiefmiller 2001, 20). In all her efforts directed toward racial uplift, Horton worked through coalitions on both sides of the color line. As discussed in the next chapter, similar types of coalitions would play an important role fifty years later in the civil rights movement.

Conclusion: Race, Class, Gender, and the Civil Rights Movement

Unlike the Master Narrative, the Border Campaign emphasizes the local situation as an important way to study "internal processes of social movements" and the historical agency of "decisive shapers of reform" (19–20). The Border Campaign also finds problematic the "view of activists only as harbingers of change—colorful, politically impotent, socially isolated idealists, and malcontents who play only fleeting roles in the drama of American political history" (29–30). When Guthrie opened the first Carnegie Library in Oklahoma to be tax-supported (Finchum and Finchum 2001, 464), African Americans used their legal status as tax payers to challenge their lack of access to the new public library. This challenge was also gendered because as a cultural institution, libraries were one of the few public spaces women could enter. Given the circumscribed actions of women, the public library was also a particularly significant space in which African American women could enact and claim the same legitimacy as white women.

The attenuation of gender to social class and racial practices brings ideologies of race, ethnicity, and gender to the center. In codifying segregation after statehood in 1907, Oklahoma's interpretation of Southern racial practices created an extreme system of segregation. Its frontier ideology of managing respectability in the absence of strong governmental controls worked to further objectify women and cultivate their moral superiority. The growing civic participation of middle- and upper-class women in Progressive Era Oklahoma demonstrates how women's volunteer activity and grassroots organizations were stimulated by the politics of segregation following statehood in 1907. Women from both sides of the color line sought to improve the living conditions and enhance the well-being of African Americans in light of the harsh and unyielding segregation practices peculiar to Oklahoma. When public libraries became designated "for whites only," black and white women in Guthrie, Oklahoma, worked together to organize an alternative public library system. This led to their benevolence work being transformed into a full-fledged politicized movement of "gendered radicalism."

In the early civil rights movement, women's actions were not the kind that were readily visible or easy to define. Their behind-the-scenes roles—including fund-raising for school boycotts—combined qualities of mediating leadership and grassroots volunteerism. In his study of Greenwood, Mississippi, Payne (1995) discovered that African American women worked tirelessly in that community to aid voter registration efforts. Their actions were channeled outside formal leadership roles and their efforts were important in keeping the momentum of the movement going.

The Master Narrative emphasizes male leadership as politically oriented and tends to marginalize the contributions of women despite recent studies by McAdam (1992) and Robnett (1996) focusing on women's participation in civil rights activism. West and Blumberg (1990, 8–9) argue that politically centered interpretations of social protest are inherently patriarchal and tend to ignore significant contributions by women, especially when they are politically oriented in the public sphere outside women's circumscribed domestic social domain.

The political and public leadership bias of the Master Narrative is captured by Morris (1984, 277) who argues that "in my view the civil rights movement was essentially a political phenomenon in that blacks were engaging in struggles for power against whites" while "the political nature of the civil rights confrontations ... [was] their defining characteristic." West and Blumberg (1990, 8) argue for social movements to take a more "women-centered" approach in order to be responsive to how women experience events differently than men, particularly in matters related to race. They contend an emphasis on political leadership makes "political women 'invisible,' men reinforce the dualistic worldview of themselves as political and women as apolitical.... Inclusion of women changes the assumptions and categories that men have set up."

Payne (1990) characterizes African American women's involvement as "overparticipating" during Freedom Summer (1964) in Greenwood, Mississippi. He attributes this overparticipation of women as an extension of their family roles. Though many of the women in this Southern community filled traditional roles by housing and feeding civil rights workers, they were also deeply involved in other aspects of the campaign. Women "canvassed more than men, showed up more frequently at mass meetings and demonstrations, and more frequently attempted to register to vote" (Payne 1990, 156). Payne concludes that the "sense of personal efficacy" women received from their civil rights work was more of an inducement for overparticipation than "their religious beliefs" (165). He suggests that the "organizational life" of the community of Greenwood was more "dependent on women" and their own networks of communication rather than the institution of the local African American church, something the Master Narrative focuses on.

Blumberg (1990) argues that economics played an important part in the civil rights activism of northern white women. During the 1950s and 1960s, the high participation of white mothers was related to the fact that "white mothers of young children were not engaged in full-time paid work." By studying the linkage between mothers who were naturally involved in youth groups and "church-related volunteerism," Blumberg (166) discovered that these unpaid, voluntary activities coincidentally drew them into civil rights activism.

Payne's study (1990) of Greenwood, Mississippi, also suggests that the same held true for the other side of the color line. African American women were less likely to suffer from economic reprisals since their salary, if they worked for a wage at all, "was likely to be perceived as less important to the family than the husband's. If anyone was going to be fired, better it be the woman. In short, it was simply safer, more cost-effective, for women to participate" (158).

The Border Campaign helps to contextualize civil rights struggles as localized responses to the continual strains of racial control and dominance. It also provides insights to the study of social movements by closer examination of the historical agency of women from both sides of the color line. In the next chapter we explore how fifty years later in Kansas another challenge to the color line launched by African American taxpayers helped finance a new school their children would not be allowed to attend. These events, occurring in the late 1940s so close to the time of the *Brown* case, have also become obscured by the Master Narrative.

Notes

1. Oklahoma's complicated history of race relations includes three important landmark Supreme Court cases: *Hollins v. Oklahoma* (1935), which outlawed all-white juries; *Sipuel v. Oklahoma State Regents for Higher Education* (1948); and *McLaurin v. Oklahoma State Regents for Higher Education* (1950), which desegregated higher education.

2. While teaching at the University of Oklahoma, writer Michelle Wallace (1990) observed that, "I've become fascinated by the unwillingness of 'American history' to include Oklahoma in its big picture. It's like one of those nuclear dump sites, some place nobody wants to know something about" (99). Wallace argues this is because Oklahoma did not "whiten up until the 1920s."

3. Indian Pioneer Project, 69:102.

4. The only state to enact this specific of a statute.

5. Guthrie City Council Minutes, microfilm: Guthrie City Record Series, Roll 42, August 4, 1908, Oklahoma Territorial Museum (OHS), 470.

Teacher Corinthian Nutter and the Walker Walk-outs, 1949 (courtesy of the Johnson County Museum, Kansas).

4

"Going Where We Could Not"

Race, Gender, Class, and Religion in Merriam, Kansas, 1948–1949

The previous chapter discussed how African American women in Guthrie, Oklahoma, used their marginalized status to obliquely protest racial injustice. As a gendered civil rights struggle, their actions demonstrate how black elites from this era avoided public displays of protest in order to maintain the status quo (Frazier 1957; Wilson 1961). As in Guthrie, this civility could be strained to the point where the blacks were compelled to take action. However, their course of action was limited by the doubly circumspect role society assigned to them as women of color. So, they avoided public outbursts, opting instead for behind-the-scenes bargaining. They channeled their activism through nonpolitical women's clubs and literary societies. These struggles by means of caution and activism are rarely mentioned by the Master Narrative.[1]

The American notion of citizenship was expanded early in the twentieth century by granting women voting rights in 1920[2] and citizenship to Native Americans in 1924.[3] This progressively more inclusive political climate forced black elites to work harder to reconcile the contradictions of maintaining their status created by segregation while at the same contending with the daily humiliations of racism. By the middle of the twentieth century, this growing racial consciousness would develop into a more militant activism, one that would eventually directly challenge the racist foundations of American society.

71

The Master Narrative does not provide an adequate benchmark to measure the actions and tactics utilized in places like Topeka, Kansas, or Guthrie, Oklahoma, given the prevailing cultural values about racial segregation. Drawing on nonpolitical types of leadership and activism, these civil rights struggles have also been forgotten because a heterogeneous type of action was employed. In Guthrie, this meant channeling women's activism through clubs and benevolent organizations. Briefly defined, nonpolitical leadership and activism are conceptualized as not being closely associated with formal organizations, which are implied by the Master Narrative. As in the previous chapter, the actions of the nonpolitical leaders and activists discussed in this chapter use behind-the-scenes negotiations rather than public displays. However, this chapter shows how caution is being replaced by more radical activism as civil rights struggles become more intense. But even by the late 1940s, the looser coupling of Kansas's segregation laws still tended to diffuse targets of racial injustice, making it difficult to organize public tactics. As in previous decades, there is more of a tendency to engage in smaller protests than mass mobilizations.

Border Campaign: Time, Place, and Rhythm of Action

Historically more firmly entrenched as a system of stratification in the South, racial segregation in the Master Narrative is conceptualized as monolithic and static. On the other hand, the Border Campaign considers the color line in terms of its components: time (historical situation), place (geography), and rhythm of action (timing and intensity). We have already considered how Kansas and Oklahoma fostered social practices and institutions that mixed time and place on the borders between North and South, and East and West. Next, as discussed in this chapter, we consider how the magnitude of the color line is also influenced in terms of the rhythm of actions (timing and intensity) that challenge it.

Moving beyond Border Campaign as referencing a specific historical time and context to a unit of analysis of social movements, "Border" calls attention to the mixture of cultural values and racial ideologies. After Stinchcombe (1965, 142), Border Campaign conceptualizes segregation and segregationist practices as sets of "social relations deliberately created, with the explicit intention of continuously accomplishing some specific goals or purposes." Rather than an unchanging system of relations, the Border Campaign's fluid conceptualization of segregation operationalizes it as a social institution dominated by people who possess the symbolic power to define the situation. In this way, segregation operates in terms of a negotiated order (Goffman 1983). While the Master Narrative emphasizes white dominance, the Border Campaign recognizes that the people who have the symbolic power to control the interaction can come from both sides of the color line. This conceptualization eliminates the categorization of segregation as simply a dominant white hegemony, but rather illuminates its subtle complexity and the underappreciated agency of African Americans, who in some cases (such as black elites), use it to their own advantage. Regardless of how stable it might appear to be, segregation is comprised of social practices that are constantly recreating it. In Border Campaign, the negotiated context of segregation refers to a limited repertoire of actions, attitudes, and practices.

By emphasizing nonpolitical leadership and activism, Border Campaign emphasizes how racial boundaries are not necessary political, and as such, it draws attention to the blurred boundaries between contrasting cultural practices concerning segregation. Border Campaign also illustrates the types of struggles and actions on the margins of segregationist and integrationist impulses, between antecedent and mass mobilization phases of the civil rights movement, between local and national initiatives, and between individual or small group actions and mass mobilizations.

Finally, considering the rhythm of action will draw attention to how its tempo increases and decreases given the historical context and local situation. In this chapter, we come to the historical situation when civil rights struggles reach the level of a collective campaign. After Marwell and Oliver (1984, 12), *campaign* "refers to discrete units of collective or social action directed toward a specific goal embedded within a broader social movement." A "collective campaign" then is "an aggregate of collective events or activities that appear to be oriented toward some relatively specific goal or good, and that occur within some proximity in space and time." In this way, Border Campaign approaches understanding social movements as long-term aggregates of collective campaigns. This conceptualization also aids in understanding the disparate actions of early civil rights struggles. It is a way to study or "break out" these early efforts to challenge segregation apart from the broader civil rights movement. The concept of a campaign, insofar as it appeals to the unfocused aggregate rather than formal structure, is useful in studying early civil rights struggles.

By the late 1940s, the rumblings along the color line were heading towards a crescendo. In this period, civil rights struggles were less disparate and were beginning to take on the form of a collective campaign. An important distinction between a collective campaign and a social movement is that social movements are generally related to higher-level (i.e., more abstract) goals than are collective campaigns. In the historical period discussed in this chapter, challenges to segregation were still discrete and limited. Whereas the civil rights movement challenged everything related to segregation, including its ideological foundations, the campaigns discussed here involve a much more limited repertoire of social actions focusing on goals that are confined to a specific time and place.

Career Activist

In order to appreciate the significant rhythm of action, the Border Campaign illuminates micro-level individual social action. As outlined in the last chapter, the Master Narrative obscures the historical agency of women by its masculine conceptual logic of political action. The discussion in this chapter, therefore, focuses on how the Border Campaign avoids the Master Narrative's tendency to collapse agency into structure. First, the Border Campaign draws on Weber's (1978, 24–25) logic of value-rational social action to avoid assuming activism can be explained in terms of a social movement's objective, material goals. Weber defines value-rational social action as being "determined by a conscious belief in the value for its own sake of some ethical, aesthetic, religious, or other form of behavior, independently of its prospects of success." The actors (or participants) in early civil rights struggles are typified by individuals who reflect most particularly the values of value-rational social action.

Therefore, these individuals are called "career activists" because they do not fit into the neat categories of political leadership or organizational affiliation used by the Master Narrative. Existing models in the literature suggest that activism is carried by organizations, leaders, and communication networks "ready" to provide resources to a campaign. The concept "career activist" is a way to explain how civil rights struggles and campaigns are sustained by individual interventions rather than the resources of an organization or its political leadership.

Career activists also aid in distinguishing individual action when it occasionally intersects with political leadership and formal organizations. The Master Narrative subsumes the agency of single activists under leadership and organizations. By considering activism in terms of a career, Border Campaign avoids fixed notions of action—individual or collective. After Swidler (1986), this method recognizes that people draw from "cultural tool kits" to generate action from which they formulate "strategies of action." This approach suggests a way to study the causal logic between culture and action by emphasizing the means (tools or dispositions toward segregation used by career activists to formulate "strategies of action") rather than focusing on the ends (as the Master Narrative does) toward which that action is directed. Career activists bring culturally inscribed dispositions about segregation into Border Campaigns, thus linking micro practices of segregation to the broader social order. Finally, using the conceptualization of segregation as a negotiated order in which career activists interact provides insight into how early civil rights struggles evolved, as well as a general understanding of the multiplicity of actions involved in social movements.

More broadly, the narrative in this chapter demonstrates how Border Campaign links analysis of subjective meaning (agency and value-rational social action) with structural forms (nonpolitical leadership and nonorganizational elements of collective action and activism). Since analysis of social reality involves a process of abstraction, which is achieved through a selection process from a "category of facts" (Hekman 1983, 30), the Border Campaign guides collection and categorization of data without surrendering "inconvenient" facts (Weber).

The actions challenging the color line in South Park, Kansas, in the late 1940s occurred in a small, unincorporated section of northeast Johnson County. At this time, South Park was predominantly African American, but the town that grew up around it was called Merriam, which was also an unincorporated community that was predominantly white. The plaintiffs involved in the school desegregation case were from South Park, and the white woman who helped them, Esther Brown, lived in Merriam. Sometimes "South Park" and "Merriam" are used interchangeably since the two areas are so close to each other. In the next section of this chapter we return to Kansas in order to discuss how Esther Brown, as a career activist, drew on resources related to her race, class, gender, and religion. These factors all contributed to her being drawn into school desegregation struggles in the late 1940s. Esther Brown illustrates how someone without political leadership, organizational affiliation, and no personal stake in issues related to the color line can become involved in activism.

De Facto School Segregation in South Park

De facto, or illegal, school segregation that existed in second-class cities—populations less than fifteen thousand—developed out of racially isolated settlement patterns.[4] "Cities of the second class ... were divided into wards. Each ward had its own elementary school, and since blacks were concentrated in one or two areas of the city, de facto segregation was the result" and these "separate facilities ... were grossly inferior" (Woods 1983, 187–188). Since South Park was primarily (but not completely) African American and Merriam was primarily (but not completely) white, the school district creatively made up two wards.

Geographically, South Park is located just across the Kansas River, south of Kansas City, Kansas, directly west of downtown Kansas City, Missouri, and approximately twenty miles east of Topeka. It was named for a company of five real estate developers from Kansas City who formed the South Park Improvement and Investment Company and planned the village called South Park in 1887. The whites who originally settled in South

Park were of German immigrant descent and migrated from Kansas City, Missouri, into Johnson County. By 1900, there were 250 residents in South Park, many of whom worked at Crowe Spring Works, a buggy and carriage springs manufacturer (Bednar 1959; Van Delinder 1994).

In the 1880s, the rural county school district of Johnson County labeled South Park as "School District Number 90," and in 1888, a one-room school was built "for the colored and white children who lived in the area." A survey of the county schools records that there were four black families living in South Park whose children attended school with the white children (Allen 1959, 37–38). Consistent with outlying areas around Topeka discussed in Chapter Two, rural county school districts "each having a school house with all elementary grades taught in one room … were generally … [racially] … mixed" (Woods 1983, 188). Like Topeka, as the population of both races increased, segregation was gradually implemented. Olathe, a nearby village in the same county, also began to segregate public schools, "following an influx into the community of several hundred Negroes from 1879 to 1881.… [T]he school board decided it would be better if blacks had their own school with their own teachers" (Woods 1983, 188).

South Park began to segregate when a new school was constructed in 1912, which would be used by the white children, and the African American children were to remain in the original building.[5] The first administrator and only teacher in what was now known as the "colored school" was Mr. Thomas Henderson, an African American. In 1917, there were a total of sixty-five pupils between the two schools (Allen 1959, 39).

Across the river to the north of Kansas City, Kansas, the African American community was much larger and more established than in South Park. In 1880, around the time South Park began to be inhabited, "one out of every five … [residents] in Kansas City, Kansas, was a Negro" (Woods 1983, 186). Kansas City, Kansas, had the only segregated high school—Sumner High School—originally built in 1905 and rebuilt in 1937.[6] African Americans living in South Park who wanted to go on to high school were sent to Sumner, twenty miles away.[7] White students from South Park attended high school at Shawnee Mission North, just a few blocks away.

By 1929, the African American school in South Park had fallen into disrepair. The basement had problems with standing water, eventually rusting out the furnace. That same year, South Park African American parents complained to the school board about the conditions at the school. The school board approved the expenditure for minor improvements to the school building. Blackboards were put up, a sump pump was installed in the basement for water removal, and the furnace was overhauled (Allen 1959, 45). However, problems with the physical structure persisted for another twenty years. Norma Fields, a former pupil, remembered the school's furnace problems when she attended classes there in the 1940s: "We had a furnace that was in the basement and when it rained a lot of water would get in and we couldn't have no school. The janitor—the janitor couldn't get down there to make a fire. So there were times like we've had it poured rain we'd be out of school maybe one or two days."[8]

Fields remembers the Walker School as

> a small school. We had this one great big room that was divided by those folding doors that really made two rooms. We had one teacher with four grades. We had two teachers—there would be one that taught grades one through four and the other—the fifth through the eighth.... My mother even went to that school. So you know it was old. When she was a little girl.... [We] didn't have a kindergarten. You started when you were six—and you started the first grade.[9]

When asked about the differences between the segregated Walker School and the white South Park School, Fields replied, "Oh, well see, the South Park School it had a teacher for each classroom and they also had kindergarten and they had a nice cafeteria where ... [food] could be cooked there to prepare the lunches and all ... which we didn't have.... [P]art of the time we went home for lunch."[10]

The disparity between these schools became the focus of attention when the Johnson County School Board decided to build a new elementary school in South Park in 1947. School enrollment had increased steadily during the 1940s as the overall population expanded. John Anderson, who served as Johnson County Attorney from 1946 to 1953, remembered that during his time in office "this county was growing ... at the rate of 5,000 to 10,000 people a year."[11]

The rapid population growth in Johnson County also meant school overcrowding in Merriam and South Park. Between 1942 and 1945, the combined enrollment in South Park's African American and white schools increased from 232 to 287. This prompted the school board to split these children into two buildings and begin planning a new grade school on the site of the old South Park Grade School in 1946.

The proposed $90,000 bond issue to finance a new grade school for white students precipitated a request by South Park residents Alfonso Webb and William Swann to upgrade the facilities for African American children. They were concerned that with the new school being built, the dilapidated Walker School would not be updated. Alfonso Webb timed his request for an upgrade to the Walker School so that it could be included as part of the bond issue: "At the time we called this school board to the Walker School the last bond floated for the common school of South Park had not been voted upon so we had plenty of time to get consideration."[12]

A week later, Alfonso Webb received a telephone call from school architect, B. A. Larson, offering to make improvements to the Walker School if

Webb would not publicly oppose the bond issue. Webb refused. "I was not a private citizen. We had already retained an attorney."[13] Within a week of Webb's and Swann's meeting with the local school board they had already obtained legal counsel.

Alfonso Webb's wife, Mary Webb, recalls that October 1947 meeting with Johnson County School Director Virgil Wisecup, school board member Vernon Hoyt, and school architect Larson:

> Since they were going to build the new school up there—well, first of all, ... well, [we will] just try [for] some improvements on the [Walker] school, now. Two rooms for eight grades. Two teachers. They just had a partition through the rooms, you know, divided into grades. And, all the facilities were outside. And, coal and wood for the stove. But, anyway, after the day they were talking about this new school building, they were going to build it, this school up here. Well, then ... [we] asked about improvements, you know, for South—for this one down here. And what they was handing down, wasn't going to bring it up in no kind of way, you know. There wasn't going to be any inside facilities and wasn't going to be any new school books. And all that kind of stuff.[14]

Swann and Webb were told by the school board that if they wanted to upgrade the segregated school they would have to raise the money themselves, through their churches.[15] Alfonso Webb owned a house in South Park and was self-employed as a concrete contractor. His wife remembers that "[h]e did a lot of the laying of the sewer lines through here in Johnson County. All over. And he did a lot of the patios, porches, the sidewalks, and things like that."[16] Webb also paid a considerable amount in property taxes to the county, some of which went to finance the new school his children would not be allowed to attend.[17] Near the end of 1947, the school board offered to make improvements to the Walker School. They agreed to install a stop sign and put up a mailbox.[18]

In January 1948, William Swann's wife, Helen, went to work for a young couple with small children, Esther and Paul Brown. Esther's husband recalls "in January 1948, we decided to forego basic needs in order to hire a part-time black maid, Mrs. William Swann, who lived with her husband and six children in South Park, a nearby integrated area located in Merriam."[19] Unbeknownst to Esther and her husband, Mrs. Swann was already active in a school segregation struggle. Once Esther heard that African American children were being excluded from attending a new school being built in her community and were being forced to attend the dilapidated, segregated Walker School, Esther made up her mind to help.

Esther later reported in the NAACP's *The Crisis* magazine (Williams and Fultz 1949, 140-141) that the condition of the Walker School was deplorable. It was "a two room frame building with outside toilet facilities, little to no heating, and a basement that was filled with water."[20] A few weeks after employing Mrs. Swann, Esther Brown attended a school board meeting with six African Americans and four white supporters. They tried to encourage the school board to make needed improvements (Katz and Tucker 1995, 238). Mary Webb remembers that Brown was "the person that really came to our aid. . . . She could open doors and get in where we could not."[21] The school board agreed to install new light bulbs and transfer old desks from the white school to the Walker School (238). The tone of the public meeting was civil, if not cordial, according to Brown's husband, Paul.[22]

However, the next day, Esther received a telephone call from Larson, the school board architect.[23] Larson reportedly told the Browns not to get involved, remarking that "'the people in South Park were getting along very well in handling . . . [the problem] . . . and they aren't complaining." Larson reminded Brown of what had happened to a white druggist in nearby Shawnee who had spoken up for the black community: the druggist soon found himself without customers and was forced to leave town because no one would sell him or his family food, clothing, gas, or other necessities (238).

The next evening Esther was invited to speak at a "small meeting" with the white community about the conditions she had discovered at the Walker School. Against the wishes of her husband, she decided to attend the meeting, reluctantly accompanied by her husband.[24] The meeting turned out to be a crowd of three hundred hostile, white Merriam residents. Brown was accused of trying to foster integration, even though she had only spoken in favor of equalizing the schools. She stated that she only wanted a decent school for African American children. For the next several days, she and her husband were subjected to a series of abusive telephone calls. Threats were also made to burn down their house.[25]

As a woman and a Jew, Brown had violated not only gender norms but also the civility of the color line. She spoke out against racial prejudice not only in regard to blacks but also implicated other Jews. In trying to organize a local chapter of the NAACP to sustain civil rights activism, she would also violate African American norms of self-sufficiency. The Master Narrative emphasizes formal organizations as important resources and a precondition for collective action. In South Park, an important formal African American organization was created when collective action was already under way.

The Kansas City, Kansas, NAACP chapter helped South Park African Americans organize a local branch after Brown contacted them asking for assistance in the South Park school segregation problem (Katz and Tucker 1995).[26] The Kansas City, Kansas, NAACP branch president, Reverend E. A.

Freeman, and the state NAACP president, Dr. Porter Davis, were present when the South Park NAACP had its first meeting in early 1948.[27] Alfonso Webb was elected as the first president of South Park's NAACP. At this meeting, it was resolved that the organization would take further action on the school situation in South Park.[28] In February 1948:

> With encouragement from the Kansas City, Kansas, NAACP, South Park hired William Towers, a local black lawyer and Republican [state] legislator from Wyandotte County, to represent them. Towers met with the board and demanded remedial action to make Walker School comparable to South Park's new school. The board told the black parents to make their requests at another meeting—without an attorney.... [Esther] Brown volunteered to represent the black community in lieu of Towers. (239)

Towers's demand for equalization of the Walker School was consistent with local NAACP branches' push to "ensure the 'equal' part of 'separate-but-equal' ... worried that desegregation would destroy black institutions, including schools" (Patterson 2001, 7–9). For example, in 1937, Towers was influential in passing a special law in the Kansas State Legislature allowing Kansas City, Kansas, to build a new segregated high school (Kurland and Carpe 1975, 804).

Webb, the Swanns, and Esther Brown attended a meeting of the school board on April 9, 1948. Daring the school board to equalize the black school, Webb and Swann requested that their children be admitted to the new South Park elementary school (Katz and Tucker 1995, 239–240). The school board refused to consider this request and responded by tightening the zoning by gerrymandering South Park into two school districts, one of which included only whites and the other only African Americans. However, whites and African Americans were not concentrated in any one area. The lines of the two districts zigzagged up and down streets and alleys:[29]

> At a special meeting held on May 15, 1948, adopt a resolution fixing the boundary of the attendance areas of the two schools. The metes and bounds of these attendance areas does not divide the district East and West or North and South, but meanders up streets and alleys, and by reason thereof all of the Negro students are placed in the Walker School attendance area. Under this allocation the white children walk past the Walker School. There may be white families in the Walker area and Negro families in the South Park area.... Such designation does attain the result of segregating the Negro children in the Walker School whether such result was intentional on the part of the school officials or not.... There is no statute, nor does the law

of this state sanction the segregation of Negro pupils in a common school district.

The South Park NAACP—supported by the Kansas City, Kansas, NAACP—directed attorney William Towers to initiate a lawsuit against the school board, demanding that they admit African American children into the new South Park elementary school beginning with the fall 1948 term.[30] This shift from equalization to request integration might have been a strategic attempt by Towers to extract improvements for the Walker School. Towers's actions also reminded the school board that school segregation was illegal in cities of the second class. Probably knowing that they were legally on shaky ground by segregating, black demands for integration produced results: on July 27, the attorney for the school board, Carey Jones, wrote Towers informing him that the board was willing to spend the necessary money to improve the Walker School building in time for the fall 1948 school term.[31] Towers then apparently stopped pushing the request for integration, and when no further action was taken by Towers, Esther Brown wrote the national NAACP in New York and asked for their help in motivating Towers to take action.[32] The New York branch responded by recommending the services of Topeka civil rights attorney, Elisha Scott (who was involved in school desegregation cases discussed in Chapter Two).[33] Brown pressured the South Park NAACP to fire Towers and hire Scott, which it did on August 11, 1948, over the objections of the Kansas City, Kansas, NAACP (Katz and Tucker 1995, 240).

Brown's action was prompted by a July 27, 1948, letter Towers had received from Jones. This letter stated that the school board was willing "to settle this matter on a reasonable basis for all parties concerned."[34] Brown was worried that Towers would want to settle with the school board and that "the local NAACP no longer were interested in a compromise deal" (240).[35]

Walker Walk Outs

Elisha Scott pursued the request for integration, and the African American residents of South Park made plans for an alternative school for their children in the fall. Rather than attend the unsatisfactory Walker School, thirty-nine of the forty-one African American students attended school in the homes of their parents.[36] They came to be known as the "Walker Walk Outs." Former "Walker Walk Out," Norma Fields remembers, "[W]e had school.... [T]here was a couple of people that opened their homes and we had school in their homes. And then finally [we] had school in church.... [W]ell, these two teachers ... taught us while we were trying to be integrated.[37]

The two teachers teaching the "Walker Walk Outs," Corinthian Nutter and Hazel McCray Weddington, indicated that the African Americans, not the teachers, were indignant about the school's physical condition.[38] Nutter recalled:

> I was the only certified teacher at both of the schools [the Walker School and the Walker Walk Out School]. There was never more than two of us. Before the opening of the school year, in September 1948, the Walker school case was already on file. The NAACP aided parents in providing classrooms and teachers for pupils during the trial, which was predicted to last about two or three months. It lasted the entire school year. Hazel Weddington ... taught grades one through four in the home of Mr. and Mrs. Ernest Gay, while my classes, five through eight were taught in the home of Mr. and Mrs. Berry. After two or three months, our classes moved to a small church in the community where we taught the remainder of the year. Two substitute teachers, Miss Randall and her sister, were hired by the Board of Education to teach at Walker School during the trial. It was predicted that those teachers taught one child each, because most parents refused to send their children to Walker School.[39]

Nutter was not paid for teaching the Walker Walk Outs, and it was a hardship for her and her husband. She recalls that the parents paid her in goods and services rather than cash. She says she survived due to her husband's income and because she had a garden.[40] Nutter was caught between a personal obligation to help children and the strategic shift by the NAACP Legal Defense Fund to push for school integration. Her activism came at a high personal price and a type of struggle unnoticed by the Master Narrative.

Some South Park African Americans were opposed to challenging school segregation. According to an editorial in the *Kansas City Plaindealer* on July 22, 1949, the South Park community was divided on the issue of whether or not to give up the Walker School. The editorial claimed the only reason for wanting to keep the school open was to selfishly preserve jobs for African American teachers. Mary Webb recalled, "We had our own people that were giving us negative feelings. Because it wasn't going nowhere."[41]

Morale was low among the South Park African Americans, especially when the Kansas Supreme Court denied a plaintiff petition requesting a temporary injunction to end segregation in South Park School on December 16, 1948. "As the case continued into the New Year, a determined effort by Brown, Webb, and other black leaders was necessary to keep the people united and the boycott school in session. This became especially difficult when the school board bribed the parents with free school lunches and threatened not to graduate their children" (Katz and Tucker 1995, 242).

After South Park was denied an injunction to end school segregation, some African Americans who had initially supported the case also began to be discouraged. Alfonso Webb, with the help of Esther Brown, sent a telegram to Franklin Williams at the NAACP Legal Defense Fund office, stating that the residents of South Park ". . .were losing confidence" (242). This appeal to the national office was followed by a personal letter from Brown to Williams, stating her doubts about Elisha Scott's handling of the case.[42] Brown requested the personal intervention from the Legal Defense Fund, but its funds were too limited to pay the expenses for an attorney to come from New York to Kansas.[43] Eventually, the national NAACP Legal Defense Fund did assist in the preparation of the brief in the spring of 1949, but the plaintiffs had to wait until early summer before they heard the decision of the Kansas State Supreme Court.

The Kansas State Supreme Court finally ruled in favor of the plaintiffs in *Webb v. School District No. 90 in Johnson County* on June 11, 1949. Although Alfonso and Mary Webb were the first named plaintiffs for their minor children Harvey Lewis Webb and Alfonso Eugene Webb, Jr., there were three other plaintiffs listed on the brief.[44] Beginning with the 1949–1950 school year, "the colored pupils and all pupils in District No. 90 must be permitted to attend the 'South Park District School.'"[45] The unlawful separation of the races begun in 1912 ended, and once again African American and white children were attending the same grade school in South Park.

Despite the ruling, on September 7, 1949, the school board announced it intended to keep the Walker School open, now staffed by three teachers instead of two. However, no African American child attended the Walker School the next day. Finally, on September 9, 1949, all school-age African American children enrolled in the South Park School, and on September 12 they began attending classes. Both of these actions occurred without any incidents. Also in the fall of 1949, seven African American students enrolled in Shawnee Mission North High School, instead of riding the bus to segregated Sumner High School in Kansas City, Kansas.

Race, Gender, Class, and Religion: Jews and Civil Rights Struggles

Brown's civil rights activism is related to her marginalized status as a woman and a Jew. Born in 1917 as Esther Swirk, she was the daughter of Russian Jewish immigrants. Her father, Ben Swirk, was a watchmaker and earned his living at a small jewelry store in downtown Kansas City,

Missouri. Her mother, Jennie Schneiderman, died of ovarian cancer when Esther was twelve. Esther was raised by two men: her father and uncle, who were both active in labor and socialist organizations. Esther's daughter Susan recalls:

> After my grandmother's death my mother became involved in my grandfather's socialist activities. Even though she was only twelve years old, she would attend socialist meetings with my grandfather. He didn't want to leave her at home alone. My grandfather belonged to many socialist organizations including the Workmen's Circle, the International Workers Order, the Human Rights Club, and the Jewish Progress and Cultural Society. Esther attended these political meetings with her father and her uncle, Isaac Price. My mother later told me that attending these socialist meetings made a lasting impression on her. She joined the Young Pioneers, a left-wing children's group, and read leftist writings like the *New Masses,* which my grandfather always had lying around the house.[46]

Esther's first act of protest occurred when she was still in high school. She joined a picket line of striking workers at a cosmetics manufacturer. After graduating from the Paseo High School, in 1934, she moved to Chicago. She supported herself by working as a sales clerk at Marshall Fields department store. Although she had hoped to attend a four-year college, she never was able to afford it.[47]

During the summers of 1936 and 1937, Esther attended a leftist labor-affiliated training school called Commonwealth College, in Mena, Arkansas.[48] While in Arkansas, she also worked as an organizer for the Southern Tenant Farmers Union. According to her husband, Paul, her activities also included recruiting new members for the Communist Party.[49] The valuable experience she gained in canvassing door to door for the Southern Tenant Farmers Union would later be used to organize resistance in South Park.

Esther returned to Kansas City in 1939, and her experience in union organizing helped her obtain a job as an interviewer with the Works Projects Administration (WPA) in Kansas City, Missouri. She was dismissed from this job in 1941 after the FBI did a routine background check. Her husband later wrote that

> she had supposedly misrepresented herself on her job application including her age, education, prior places of residence and work experience. She denied having attended Commonwealth College, although she had told fellow office workers that she was a Communist. On June 28, 1940, she signed an affidavit denying being a communist or a member of the communist party. While she was employed by the WPA, she was outspoken about her Russian heritage and critical about the United States

giving military aid to Britain. She always thought that she had been fired for her communist activities rather than for lying to the federal government about her education, job experience, and political affiliation.[50]

Two years after being fired from her job, she married her childhood friend Paul Brown. At the time of their marriage, Paul did not know about her prior communist activities, which would later lead to him being discharged from the Air Force reserve in 1951.[51] When Esther married Paul, he was a captain in the Intelligence Division of the U.S. Army Air Corps, stationed in Miami, Florida. After she moved with him to Miami, Florida, Esther had to adjust to living in the South. Paul recalled, "one day Esther came home upset after riding the Miami city bus. Apparently she had not been aware that there was a whites only section in the front of the bus, and had unknowingly seated herself in the back, near the Negro passengers."[52]

After his discharge from the service in early 1947, Paul and Esther moved with their two small children into the small community of Merriam, Kansas, and Paul went to work in his father's auto parts store. As Esther's involvement grew in the South Park school desegregation case, Paul recalled in interview that his father gave him a message from Joseph Cohen, an influential Jewish politician, that "Esther was making waves throughout the state. He appealed to my father for his help in getting Esther to withdraw from her leadership role." Esther's activism was also drawing unwanted attention to Kansas City's Jewish community.

When Paul refused to tell his wife to stop, his father said he "would no longer tolerate Esther's 'radical activities' ... and insisted that I influence her to stop immediately." Brown refused, and his father fired him.[53] He turned to his father-in-law for help: "[W]e had returned to the area [Kansas City] in late 1945, after almost five years in the Air Force, and bought the two-bedroom house ... [in Merriam] with the help of a down payment from my father, plus a GI loan."[54]

Throughout the South Park litigation, Esther worked tirelessly in support of racial justice. She even went door to door, asking for help from anyone who would listen to her. Paul Brown remembers: "After depleting our own limited funds, raising money became almost an obsession with Esther. She organized bake sales, and appealed for donations at churches. She approached personal friends, mostly in the Jewish community, who responded generously.... Because it would have been simpler to pursue her interest without depending upon others for costly legal advice and procedures, Esther frequently voiced regret that she was not a lawyer."[55]

By the time the South Park case was resolved, the Browns were no longer living in Merriam.[56] They had bought a larger house in a suburb further south. But this move away from Merriam did not end Esther's civil rights activism. When she tried to push the Wichita NAACP to commence a lawsuit to challenge school segregation, Wichita's African American teachers defeated the attempt.[57] She also became involved in Topeka's school desegregation. Jack Greenberg, the NAACP Legal Defense Fund attorney who worked on the *Brown* case recalled her as "being someone who could get things done."[58] Topeka plaintiff and NAACP Local Branch Membership Secretary Lucinda Todd stated later that Esther Brown provided invaluable assistance to the plaintiffs (Kluger 1975, 390).

In the later 1950s, Esther's activism led her to affiliate with women's religious organizations. For example, she became more involved in the Sisterhood of the (Reform) Temple B'nai Jehudah and the Reform Jewish Commission on Social Action. Adler (1972, 253) attributes Brown's new religious involvement to her activism rather than to any strong commitment to the principles of Reform Judaism: "To suppose that an example of active Reform Jewish leadership was the influence would be pleasant, but idle in the light of a prior record of inaction by religious spokesmen in general ... and of Esther Brown's background.... A Reform Jewish Commission on Social Action, created in 1948 ... confined itself mainly to issuing generalized pronouncements."

In 1956, the B'nai Jehudah Temple Sisterhood presented a luncheon program called a "Bouquet of Neighbors." The "Bouquet of Neighbors" was a panel of five women

> of different races and religions who talked not about generalities, but about how they themselves, as individuals, had met with prejudice. There was no sermonizing; no call for specific action. Each woman panelist (a Jew, a Catholic, a Negro, a Chinese American, and a white Anglo-Saxon Protestant) spoke ... about how she felt about prejudice and what she was doing about it. Esther Brown, as moderator, fielded probing, soul-searching audience questions. (257)

The panel discussion was planned as a one-time thing, but it "gave rise to a national volunteer movement" (257). The name was changed to "Panel of American Women," and Esther Brown became its national coordinator. She continued to act as moderator and answered mail and telephone requests from other women in neighboring cities to set up similar panels. Dottie Harder, Topeka coordinator of the Panel of American Women, was impressed by Brown's commitment to social justice. "She wanted to demonstrate that if people were face to face with people of different colors and creeds, they would see for themselves that there was nothing to fear. She firmly believed that racism was based on fear and ignorance.... Esther Brown was tireless. She was convinced that the Panel was the only way to fight racism since it brought people face to face with each other."[59] Brown's daughter Susan recalled that during this time their home had "two telephone lines, and people were constantly coming and going. It was exciting. I thought everyone lived like that."[60]

As Brown extended her activism beyond the small communities of Merriam and South Park, she also began to be drawn into the organizational life of her temple. If, as Adler (253) argues, her activism was not driven by a strong sense of religiosity, then a probable conclusion is that her temple was a space that gave her a renewed sense of community once the South Park case was resolved. As the civil rights movement progressed, many Jewish women were drawn into civil rights activism since it gave them "an opportunity to create existential meaning in their lives through moral action." As women, this involvement "also provided adventure, 'authentic' experience (in which theory and practice were linked), a sense of community, and escape from boring jobs, difficult families, and the prospect of marriage and life in suburbia" (Schultz 2001, 24). Given Esther's strong sense of commitment to social justice as well as her adventurous spirit, her career as an activist was driven by complicated and often conflicting reasons.

Conclusion: Career Activism and Social Movements

Formal organizational affiliation and leadership fails to explain the unique leadership role that career activists like Esther Brown play in social movements. By operating primarily outside the context of established economic and political organizations, white women could make crucial contributions to the civil rights movement in ways that did not displace African American leadership. As an isolated housewife in suburban Johnson County, Kansas, in the late 1940s, Esther Brown's life was changed dramatically when Mrs. Helen Swann, an African American woman, came to work for the Brown family.

As a white woman of Russian Jewish heritage, Esther was somewhat marginalized from the mainstream in terms of her gender, religion, and ethnicity. Her history of communist activism, compounded by the lack of a college degree, held up her ambitions for a professional career. Once married, her responsibilities as a housewife and mother of small children gradually provided her with an opportunity to pursue a new vocation: social activism. "White women did perceive their struggle against racial injustice as being connected to their roles as mothers (Blumberg 1990, 168; Crawford, Rouse, and Woods 1990; McAdam 1982; and Payne 1995). As a Jew, her sense of social justice was fostered by her father and uncle who facilitated her involvement in socialist and communist labor organizations, such as the Southern Tenants Farmers Union. These previous examples of activism helped her develop a strong sense of public justice that went beyond her maternal role.

Esther Brown's activism in South Park and later in Topeka, Kansas, indicates that reliance on organizational labeling to indicate the "type" of leadership in early civil rights struggles can be misleading. Career activists often can take on leadership roles without being formally affiliated with any one organization; sometimes this leadership role serves as a communication link between two organizations. McAdam, Tarrow, and Tilly (2001, 142) refer to this type of person who connects different organizations as a "broker." However, this term tends to reify leadership as politically oriented, obscuring how someone, like Esther, could at various times take on a leadership role by acting as an intermediary between the white school board and African American community. When the school board refused to hear their demands, Esther planned and implemented a boycott of the school. The national office of the NAACP even came to describe Esther as a "one woman show" and the presumed leader of the school desegregation efforts, even though she was acting as an intermediary for the African American community rather than a formal leader.

After the school board was forced to allow the African American children to attend the new school, Esther went on to assist in school desegregation in Wichita and Topeka, Kansas. Once schools were desegregated nationally after 1954, Esther became involved in other social justice protests, including combating anti-Semitism. It is more useful to assume responses to segregation are likely to have been some mixture of accommodation and protest, not in one extreme, mutually exclusive category or other. The point is to avoid a dichotomous characterization of leadership and thereby lose the more nuanced movements of agency.

The individual activism suggested by Esther Brown's actions in Merriam, Kansas, in 1948 and twenty miles away in Topeka, Kansas, in 1950, were not confined to any one particular case. The relationship is not strictly causal but rather suggests the continuity of an individual's activism or agency carrying them over into different forms of protest and leadership. It also brings to the forefront those types of leadership actions that have been previously ignored by the Master Narrative because of their seemingly indirect nature.

Oftentimes career activists' paths will cross—like Elisha Scott, the person Esther Brown contacted to handle the school desegregation lawsuit in Merriam, Kansas. Scott is the father of Charles and John Scott, who later argued the initial *Brown* case in Federal District Court in the early 1950s (see Chapter Five). Scott's career activism can be easily dismissed as idiosyncratic since over his long career he would argue both for and against racial segregation. However, the importance of desegregation as the broad desire for black Americans diminishes when focus is shifted away from objective goals to more intermediary ones or, in this case, toward more immediate values and beliefs. Just as understanding how Esther Brown's outsider status enabled her to pursue social justice in a variety of ways consistent with her own biography, so too does Scott's membership in the black bourgeoisie help us understand how his loyalty to his own elite status group led him to both challenge and defend racial segregation.

Scott symbolizes some of the ironies of pre-*Brown* struggles by black Topeka. For several decades prior to *Brown,* Scott argued civil rights cases on behalf of African Americans and local Indian tribes. He diligently pursued school desegregation in places where it was illegal—Coffeyville, Weir City, and South Park—and which were not first-class cities (with a population more than fifteen thousand) and therefore did not have the legal mandate to segregate (see Chapter Two). However, he did not challenge segregation where it was legal, as in Topeka, Kansas, during the *Graham* case.

Scott's involvement in school cases came about because of his law practice and organizational affiliation with the Topeka NAACP. When Topeka's school segregation was challenged in 1941 by the *Graham* case, Scott represented the interests of the African American teachers, some of whom were his relatives, who sought to retain their jobs by keeping segregation intact. Scott argued in support of segregation since it was legal in Topeka. During the *Graham* case, he even helped to establish a rival NAACP chapter and was elected president. Though Scott's actions appear to be inconsistent with civil rights issues, his actions *are* consistent when considered in terms of his own biography. He pushed for integration only in cases where segregation was illegal and was not a threat to black institutions, particularly schools.

Scott's activism displays a type of agency that was constrained by race as well as organizational and professional roles. As an African American, he was committed to values consistent with desegregation, but at the same time he was constrained by the interests of his status group membership that benefited from segregation. As one of the few black lawyers in Topeka, he enjoyed a certain security in handling cases and clients that white attorneys did not want. Desegregation would open the floodgates for others (white and black) to enter into the professional class that in the black community included doctors, dentists, barbers, beauticians, morticians, and teachers. In one interview with a middle-aged black man from Topeka, who had grown up during segregation, the man bitterly recalled how his dream of attending law school was dashed when he was told "there was not enough business" in the black community to support more lawyers. He became a social worker instead due to a higher demand for that profession in the black community.

This chapter suggests that the individuals described in these cases did not suddenly decide to become activists. But in examining the broader societal context, their actions were also not easily explained as simply an outgrowth of ongoing sporadic desegregation efforts. The characteristics of the struggles described in these communities were due, in part, to the forms that activism took in relationship to changing contemporaneous local social conditions and opportunities. These cases also provide a better understanding of the importance of culture, as well as the structural context (political and economic) in explaining how individual troubles contribute to how some people become involved in collective action. These cases also illustrate the sometimes overlooked contribution of agency, generally, in social movement theory (McAdam and Paulsen 1993; McAdam, Tarrow, and Tilly 2001).

This chapter has provided specific examples of how personal troubles can carry individuals into activism. It shows that even the formation of organizations may result from activism rather than be a necessary precondition for it. The joint action represented by Helen Swann, Alfonso Webb, Esther Brown, and other participants eventually merged into longer strips of action able to successfully challenge the color line in Merriam, Kansas; all this occurred before a local chapter of the NAACP was organized or a "local movement center" existed. Esther Brown's social justice orientation eventually brought her to religious involvement with her Temple Sisterhood rather than the other way around. Ultimately, she became a formal leader of the Panel of American Women. This, too, developed out of her self-initiated and sustained career of activism.

The South Park campaign calls attention to the possibility of significant participation in other social movements by individuals who were not a part of an established organization or leadership. *Career activist* conceptualizes a tendency observed in early civil rights struggles for persistent, committed individuals to make decisive contributions to collective action. It reflects the capacity of some individuals to be self-starting, self-directing, and self-sustaining in their activism, rather than either the formal leaders or the mobilized followers of an organization. Career activists tend to inject themselves into collective action through their own value-rational agency. The career of their activism tends to extend beyond any particular campaign. Although, conceptually, their actions are characterized as nonorganizational, career activists may cooperate with organizations during a campaign. However, the tendency is for career activists to attempt to utilize organizations (even to the point of attempting to transform them), rather than be controlled by them. Career activism continues outside of and beyond the affiliation with an organization and tends to be directed by personal value-rational agency.

This emphasis contrasts with the Master Narrative's representation that formal and political leaders and organizations are central to civil rights episodes. The contrast is made not to dismiss the Master Narrative's conclusions, but to indicate the need to also conceptualize and explain nonorganizational actions. In the episodes studied here, the individuals often acted in consequential ways apart from organizations. Career activist Esther Brown sometimes appeared to be working inside the local NAACP when she used that organization's resources and membership networks to raise funds, obtain legal advice, and secure the services of civil rights attorneys. Typically, however, Esther Brown was out ahead of established organizations.

Career activists often engage in *individual activism*—an intermediary between a formal leader and an individual acting alone helps to explain the sometimes ambiguous forms of leadership that emerge in social movements. This concept helps to get beyond the Master Narrative understandings of leadership, as well as beyond the confines of a specific protest movement.

In conclusion, early civil rights struggles in Kansas are characterized by the inconsistency of state segregation laws. Rather, it is primarily through internal value-rational commitments rather than external motivational factors or goals that mobilize nonpolitical leaders and individual activists. The Border Campaign attempts to capture the irregularities and inconsistencies of diffuse protest actions ignored by the Master Narrative. It also provides a framework by which to compare the rhythm of this type of action with more coherent and regularized types of protest. Leadership and organization are not always static social structures but can be fluid under some circumstances (Gusfield, 1981).

Depending on the circumstances, different persons may have taken on the role of leaders or informal leaders in one respect or other. In general, the civil rights episodes discussed in this chapter differ from the later mass mobilization era since they are concerned with different issues, attacked with contrasting tactics, and were from different community locations. The protest was sometimes carried forward and sustained by informal leaders and individual activists, whose important, but sometimes discontinuous trails of activism can be uncovered only by examining the local context of early civil rights episodes. However, their joint actions are often obscured when civil rights activism is examined as a large structural framework. The significance of value-rational agency is related to its effect rather than its substance. By focusing on the interplay between individuals who act as a formal leader and an individual acting alone helps to explain the complicated relationship between agency and collective action. The framework used here to discuss cases of individual agency might also be helpful to expand our previous understandings of agency beyond the confines of any specific protest movement toward a better appreciation of the contribution of agency to social movements.

Notes

1. Writing about the Progressive Era in Greensboro, North Carolina, William Chafe (1981) argues that black leaders used similar tactics to address grievances, see pp. 21–22.

2. The Nineteenth Amendment was proposed on June 4, 1919, and ratified on August 18, 1920. Women had voting rights in Wyoming (1869) and Utah (1870), although the U.S. Congress disenfranchised Utah women in 1887. Other Western territories and states

granted women the vote in the late nineteenth and early twentieth centuries, but women were not allowed to vote in federal elections until 1920.

3. Also called the Snyder Act, the 1924 Indian Citizenship Act (43 U.S. Stats. At Large, Ch. 233, p. 253) (1924) granted citizenship to Indians born in the United States. Some Indians had previously obtained U.S. citizenship through marriage—or through military service, allotments, treaties, or special laws. But most were not citizens, and they were barred from naturalization.

4. Other second-class cities that had illegal school segregation were Ft. Scott and Olathe. (*History of Kansas,* II, 1073, 1453). Hiawatha and Emporia had integrated grade schools, but the teachers were all white (*Topeka Colored Citize*n, November 8, 1879).

5. At 9420 West 50th Street Terrace.

6. Kansas Laws 1879, c. 81, sec. 1. Kansas Laws of 1905, ch. 414, sec. 1. *General Statutes of Kansas,* Topeka, Kansas, Kansas laws of 1937, Chapter 309.

7. Author interview with Corinthian Nutter, Merriam, Kansas, November 30, 1994.

8. Oral History interview with Norma Fields, August 23, 1994, Merriam, Kansas. Johnson County Museum, Shawnee, Kansas. Interviewed by Susan Klarlund.

9. Ibid.

10. Ibid.

11. Interview with author, February 23, 1995. Overland Park, Kansas. Anderson, as the county attorney, would later be named as a defendant in the Merriam desegregation case (in 1949). Anderson also later became governor of Kansas.

12. Testimony of Alfonso Webb, Transcript of Commissioner's Investigation, September 22-23, 1948, *Webb v. School District No. 90,* case file 37,427, p. 35. Records of the Kansas State Supreme Court, Library and Archives Division, Kansas State Historical Society.

13. Testimony of Alfonso Webb, Transcript of Commissioner's Investigation, September 22-23, 1948, *Webb v. School District No. 90,* case file 37,427, p. 35. Records of the Kansas State Supreme Court, Library and Archives Division, Kansas State Historical Society.

14. Oral History interview with Mary Webb, August 1994, Merriam, Kansas. Johnson County Museum, Shawnee, Kansas. Interviewed by Daryl Williams.

15. Testimony of Alfonso Webb and William Swann, Transcript of Commissioner's Investigation, September 22-23, 1948, *Webb v. School District No. 90,* case file 37,427. Records of the Kansas State Supreme Court, Library and Archives Division, Kansas State Historical Society.

16. Oral History interview with Mary Webb, August 1994. Merriam, Kansas. Johnson County Museum, Shawnee, Kansas.

17. Testimony of Alfonso Webb and Helen Swann, Transcript of Commissioner's Investigation, September 22-23, 1948, *Webb v. School District No. 90,* case file 37,427. Records of the Kansas State Supreme Court, Library and Archives Division, Kansas State Historical Society.

18. Testimony of Alfonso Webb and Helen Swann, Transcript of Commissioner's Investigation, September 22-23, 1948, *Webb v. School District No. 90,* case file 37,427. Records of the Kansas State Supreme Court, Library and Archives Division, Kansas State Historical Society.

19. Author interview with Paul Brown, November 22, 1994, Leawood, Kansas.

20. Appalling as the conditions in the Walker School were, it was indicative of the general living conditions of the South Park African American enclave. According to Mary Webb's oral history interview, South Park African Americans did not have running water, indoor plumbing, sidewalks, or paved streets. Webb recalled, "The only water at that time that we had was—unless a person had a well on their property . . . [was] down there on Antioch, there used to be a public well there. And that's where we would get our water. You'd have to haul it down there to the house. That's how I got all of my water to do my laundry and everything." Oral History Interview, August 1994. op.cit. Sewage, water, and gas lines

were not installed in African American homes in South Park until it was annexed by the city of Merriam in 1967. See "South Park Overview" by LeAnn Schmitt, Johnson County Museum, May 1994. See also Norma Fields, Oral History Interview, August 23, 1994, who remarked about the improvements made in South Park after 1967 as being "a great big change ... like I said, paved streets from rock and dirt road, sewers, and has water inside and gas, we used to have coal furnaces or coal and wood stoves ... well you might say just electricity we didn't have in the beginning."

21. Oral History interview with Mary Webb, August 1994.

22. Paul Brown memorandum dated June 10, 1994. Johnson County Museum, Shawnee, Kansas. File: "Remembering South Park."

23. When Paul Brown recalled these events for me, he would not identify the caller, but only called him a "spokesman for the school board." He and his wife were upset by the phone call, but it only made Esther more determined to be involved in the challenge to school segregation. Author interview with Paul Brown, November 22, 1994, Leawood, Kansas.

24. Author interview with Paul Brown, November 22, 1994.

25. Author interview with Paul Brown, November 22, 1994.

26. Susan Brown Tucker is Esther Brown's daughter. Interview with author, October 1992, New York City, NY.

27. Mildred B. Sharp to *Glouster Current,* January 9, 1948, Merriam, Kansas, 1945-1955, Kansas NAACP Branch Office files (microfilm 1392), Library and Archives Division, Kansas State Historical Society.

28. Edna Hill to *Glouster Current,* January 14, 1948, Merriam, Kansas, 1945-1955, Kansas NAACP Branch Office files (microfilm 1392), Library and Archives Division, Kansas State Historical Society.

29. Supreme Court of Kansas, January term, 1949, Vol. 167, pp. 399-400.

30. Testimony of Alfonso Webb and Helen Swann, Transcript of Commissioner's Investigation, September 22-23, 1948, *Webb v. School District No. 90,* case file 37,427. Records of the Kansas State Supreme Court, Library and Archives Division, Kansas State Historical Society. Towers filed a writ of mandamus before the Kansas Supreme Court on May 25, 1948.

31. Correspondence from W. C. Jones to William H. Towers, July 17, 1948, printed in *Webb v. School District No. 90.* Case Files: *Webb v. School District No. 90. Brief for the Plaintiff.* Kansas State Historical Society, Topeka, Kansas.

32. Author interview with Susan Brown Tucker, New York City, NY. October 6, 1992.

33. Author interview with Susan Brown Tucker, New York City, NY. October 6, 1992.

34. W. C. Jones to William H. Towers, July 27, 1948, *Webb v. School District No. 90.* Case File, Kansas State Historical Society, Topeka, Kansas.

35. After Elisha Scott was hired on August 11, 1948, Towers filed a motion for a hearing in Johnson County before the beginning of the school term on September 9, 1948. This followed up on previous action taken by Towers, who had filed a similar motion on July 2. See Paul Brown memorandum, June 10, 1994, Johnson County Museum, Shawnee, Kansas.

36. Kansas City *Call,* September 20, 1948.

37. Interview with Norma Fields, August 23, 1994.

38. According to Corinthian Nutter, Hazel McCray Weddington had at one time been employed at the Walker School but had not taught there for several years. Her teaching certification had expired. Author interview with Corinthian Nutter, November 22, 1994.

39. Author interview with Corinthian Nutter. Mrs. Nutter also has numerous newspaper clippings and photographs in her personal possession. She was generous enough to let me photocopy them for my dissertation.

40. Author interview with Corinthian Nutter, November 22, 1994. Mrs. Nutter was shy about being recorded about the hardships she and her husband endured during the

Walker School desegregation cases. The information about her income was recorded in my field notes immediately after the interview. Nutter also showed me a letter dated March 22, 1949, from Franklin Williams, attorney, NAACP Legal Defense Fund, summarizing the significance of Corinthian Nutter's personal sacrifice for the court case: "This letter comes as a word of appreciation from this office for the unselfish role you are playing towards the successful prosecution of the school case in South Park, Kansas. We realize that your continuing to teach these children in return for such a small compensation must be quite a personal sacrifice. We are hopeful of obtaining a successful conclusion of this suit within the next month or so. Needless to say, your energies have resulted in contributing to the maintenance of morale among the Negro parents and students of Merriam." Private papers of Corinthian Nutter.

41. Mary Webb oral history interview, August 1994. Johnson County Museum, Shawnee, Kansas.

42. Author interview with Susan Brown Tucker, October 1992.

43. This is not surprising since the number of attorneys on staff of the Legal Defense Fund was very small, four or five full-time lawyers. Author interview with Constance Baker Motley. New York City. October 6, 1992. The NAACP recommended the services of Carl Johnson, an attorney affiliated with the Kansas City, Missouri, branch, Kansas City *Plaindealer,* December 31, 1948.

44. The other plaintiffs were "Shirley Ann Turner and Norbert Edward Turner, minors, by their parents and next friends, Thelma Turner and Ernest Burrell Turner, Jr.; Delores Gay; and Patricia Black, a minor, by her parent and next friend, Thomas Black." Supreme Court of Kansas, January Term, 1949, Vol. 167, p. 395.

45. See Reports of Cases Argued and Determined in the Supreme Court of the State of Kansas. Vol. 167. No. 37,427, *Webb v. School District.* p. 404.

46. Susan Brown Tucker, interview with author, New York City, October 6, 1992. Esther Brown died of breast cancer on May 24, 1970.

47. Author interview with Susan Brown Tucker, October 6, 1992, New York City, NY.

48. Esther's daughter, Susan Brown Tucker, referred to this school as being a communist organization. Interview with author, October 6, 1992.

49. Author interview with Paul Brown, November 22, 1994.

50. Paul Brown memorandum dated June 10, 1994. Johnson County Museum, Shawnee, Kansas. File: "Remembering South Park." According to Susan Brown Tucker, Esther never attended the University of Chicago or Northwestern, although she often told interviewers she had attended these institutions. Interview with author, October 6, 1992, New York City, NY.

51. Author interview with Paul Brown, November 22, 1994.

52. Author interview with Paul Brown, November 22, 1994.

53. Paul Brown memorandum dated June 10, 1994, Johnson County Museum, Shawnee, Kansas. File: "Remembering South Park," p. 4.

54. Author interview with Paul Brown, Leawood, Kansas. November 22, 1994.

55. See Paul Brown memorandum, June 10, 1994, Johnson County Museum, Shawnee, Kansas. Also see Katz and Tucker (1995, 241–242).

56. In December 1955, the now integrated South Park District 90 became annexed to School District 110, Overland Park, Kansas.

57. Susan Brown Tucker interview with author, October 6, 1992, New York City, NY.

58. Interview with author October 7, 1992. Jack Greenberg was reserved during my interview, but when I asked him about Esther Brown, his first reaction was physical. He immediately straightened up in his chair and his expression brightened as he exclaimed, "Of course I do! She was someone who could get things done!"

59. Interview with author, Topeka, Kansas, February 12, 1993. Dottie Harder coordinated the Topeka panel for several years and served as moderator and on the panel as "a white Anglo-Saxon Protestant." Mrs. Harder lent me her personal papers while I was writing my dissertation. Also, according to her husband Paul, Esther was involved in actions that led to the abolishment of fraternities and sororities from Missouri high schools. She thought such organizations were discriminatory. This reasoning was based on her own experience in high school when she was excluded from membership in a high school sorority because of her Jewish heritage.

60. Interview with author, October 6, 1992, New York City, NY.

Miss Hunt's first-grade class at the State Street School, Topeka, Kansas, January 1955. Racial integration was implemented in Topeka a few months following the 1954 *Brown* decision (courtesy of J. E. Schrock/Kansas State Historical Society).

5

Behind the *Brown* Case, 1944–1954

Topeka, Kansas is famous for being the setting of the 1954 *Brown v. Board of Education* school desegregation case, but the Master Narrative overlooks Topeka as an important locale. Topeka is overshadowed by its southern companion cases, specifically *Briggs v. Elliott* (South Carolina) and *Davis v. County School Board of Prince Edward County* (Virginia) (Kluger 1975, 466–471, 475–48; Smith 1965, 31–69). This neglect is due in part to the subdued nature of the activism in Topeka that was organized around its distinctive color line practices, as discussed in Chapter Two. One other reason for this neglect is that the Master Narrative emphasizes desegregation as a goal, shunting antecedent challenges to segregation that were more directed toward finding a common ground. By placing more weight on the types of episodes that came to fruition *after* 1954, the Master Narrative has failed to fully consider the relevance of how local-level issues were historically situated prior to the national push to desegregation.

The Border Campaign ideal type's logic of action as multidimensional helps to maintain conceptual uniformity when confronted with cases of data heterogeneity and nonlinear causality. The Master Narrative emphasizes homogeneity of data and a linear causality of action that is directed toward specific goals. Given the historical importance of the *Brown* case, this tendency toward finding exceptional individuals who focus their efforts through key organizations represents the conventional understanding of social movements in general and the civil rights movement in particular.

The Border Campaign offers an alternative approach by examining movement objectives situated in terms of the historical influences on the local context. Chapters Two and Three discussed the relevance of how this gap between cultural goals and institutional means in uncovering collective action that furthered the autonomy of African Americans from state control by reinforcing their control over their own public institutions. For example, it is easy to overlook the implication of African American women claiming the same access to the public sphere that white women had in turn-of-the-century Guthrie, Oklahoma (Chapter Three). Given their gender and race, middle-class African American women realized that public libraries were respectable spaces for them to gather. The opening of a segregated library might be interpreted as a step back when measured by the Master Narrative's linear model. In contrast, the Border Campaign's allowance for the nuance of the local situation opens up a multidimensional understanding of collective action mediated by cultural meanings and understandings of racial etiquette. Using their middle-class status, African American women were to claim the same rights of access to the public sphere as white women. This did not result in racial equality, but the underlying logic of using their civil status as taxpayers to legitimize their claims in order to gain access to closed public institutions is a tactic that would be used fifty years later in Topeka, Kansas, as well as in many other locations in the modern civil rights movement.

As discussed in Chapter Two, changes in the organization of Kansas's schools in the 1920s pressured school boards to enforce segregated education as cities like Topeka expanded. The introduction of junior highs and their more specialized curriculum drew attention to the growing division between segregated and nonsegregated schools. Actions directed toward access to education arose from parents who did not want to see their children attend poorly funded schools. In Chapter Four, Esther Brown acted as an intermediary, linking the African Americans living in South Park, Kansas, to important formal institutions (the NAACP) and individuals (attorney Elisha Scott). By placing less emphasis on exceptional or charismatic individuals as rational agents of change and more stress on how individual activists are guided by value-rationality as career activists, the line of inquiry shifts away from conflating action as either agency or structure.

The preceding chapters all provided different examples of how the gap between cultural goals and institutional means is characterized in different eras and how this gap affects the possibility of changing race relations in nineteenth- to mid-twentieth-century Kansas as well as turn-of-the-century Oklahoma. By the mid-twentieth century, the possibility for a dramatic change in race relations was closely becoming a reality. This chapter begins to examine how localized claims to full citizenship were beginning to resonate at the national level. The expanded notion of unlimited access to society had its antecedents in Guthrie residents petitioning for access to the public library and South Park residents wanting to attend their neighborhood school. Again, in these cases, their limited claims against segregation were legitimated by status as local taxpayers.

By the mid-twentieth century, the entire institution of segregation would begin to be targeted. Though there had been gradual modifications to segregation, the Master Narrative's linearity ignores these slow but positive shifts in practice and ideology toward full racial inclusion. Examining the local situation behind the *Brown* case using the Border Campaign provides a way to better understand the how history, biography, and social structure intersect. As a significant historical event, the *Brown* case provides an example of how the Border Campaign offers a broad and systematic approach to studying social movements by emphasizing the importance of individual action without sacrificing the relevance of its relationship to social structure.

Rising Expectations and Social Unrest

The 1940s brought dramatic changes to American society, particularly in how it reconfigured the color line. Advocates of more egalitarian race relations became bolder in pointing out the contradiction between maintaining a system of segregation at home, while at the same time assuming the role as leader of the "free world." This rising militancy, especially among African Americans, has been attributed to their participation in the armed forces during World War II—a war for freedom and democracy (Patterson 2001). When blacks returned home, many decided to fight the war on a second front by directly challenging the inequalities of Jim Crow, or segregation.

America's new world dominance after World War II encouraged those in segregated settings to develop their own "revolution of rising expectation" toward the cultural value of equality suggested within integrated settings. Though the mass mobilization era of the civil rights movement would not fully mature for another ten years, this embryonic period of civil rights activism provides a useful way to study the impact of culture on social structure in terms of activism.

It is within this revolutionary context that we can understand the unusual importance of the Border Campaign for generating civil rights activism. We can draw a parallel here between Crane Brinton's analysis of the Puritan, American, French, and Russian revolutions and the early appearance of the civil rights movement within border states more than in the Deep South. Brinton wrote: "First, these were all societies on the whole on the upgrade economically before the revolution came, and the revolutionary movements seem to originate in the discontents of not unprosperous people who feel restraint, cramp, annoyance, rather than downright crushing oppression" (1952, 318; see also Tocqueville 1955, 177; Davies 1962b, 5, 17; Sztompka, 1993, 309-318). We can generalize Brinton's argument so as to include not only economic oppression but also racial oppression. It was in the border states rather than the Deep South that we find "restraint, cramp, annoyance, rather than downright crushing oppression."

Direct action perspectives emphasize formal organizations and leadership as being crucial to the development of mass mobilizations such as the Montgomery Bus Boycott in 1955 (Killian 1984; Killian and Smith 1960; Morris 1984; McAdam 1982; Oberschall 1989). The type of civil rights activism encountered in Topeka, Kansas, prior to the *Brown* case involved intermediate stages, aimed at transitional goals. The social changes eventually wrought out of this activism were neither immediate nor resulting from a specific action or cause. Participants in Topeka did not necessarily take the shortest route to their desired objective. They also undertook numerous actions that on first scrutiny appear to be unrelated. This is due to the fact that the some of these actions were peaceful negotiations requesting inclusion of African Americans in all public facilities: movie theaters, swimming pools, and schools.

As at the turn of the century, the black middle class led the vanguard in challenging segregation. But the tactics would shift from eradicating illegal segregation—in a sense sustaining the legality of segregation—to directly challenging it. Also, as discussed later in this chapter, as the *Brown* case unfolded in Topeka, the black clergy would prove as likely to be agents of caution as agents of change, which the Master Narrative predicts. Initial alteration would be more slowly carried forward by lawyers, in particular two sons of attorney Elisha Scott (see Chapter Two)—Charles and John—who were training for a legal career at Topeka's Washburn University Law School. These two brothers, along with another attorney named Charles Bledsoe, would slowly put together a legal case and later play a prominent role in preparing the initial brief for the *Brown* case.

The eventual desegregation of Topeka's schools developed out of civil rights actions that began by challenging segregation in public accommodations during the 1940s. These challenges were initiated by individuals addressing singular grievances and were joined by others who were affiliated with various types of organizations, including the civil rights–oriented NAACP, as well as community-based ones such as the American Veterans Committee (AVC) and Parents Teachers Association (PTA). Challenges to segregated schools were orchestrated through the NAACP but included an ad hoc Citizens Committee, as well as individual efforts from attorneys Charles and John Scott, and Charles Bledsoe.[1] School desegregation efforts were furthered by challenges undertaken by white elites opposed to the school superintendent Kenneth McFarland along with a campaign to remove unsympathetic school board members. Other efforts to eliminate school segregation were directed through the white PTA, and were opposed by the black PTA and African American teachers. Diverse actions, separately controlled, loosely combined into what became the 1954 *Brown* case.

Challenges to Segregated Public Accommodations, 1944–1948

Topeka's color line practices limiting the movements of African Americans resulted in a challenge to public accommodations in 1944 (Kluger 1975, 375). The local NAACP protested the proposed repeal of a municipal licensure requirement that "prohibited state universities, colleges, public schools, inns, hotels, or vehicles of public transportation" from discriminating on the "basis of race, color, or previous condition of servitude."[2] In the words of the president of Topeka's local chapter of the NAACP, R. J. Reynolds, by repealing this law, "Topeka will be showing the rest of the cities in Kansas how to find a loophole in the law to deny Negroes of their rights."

Reynolds's action stalled the tightening of the color line for three more years, but this ambivalence toward segregation soon shifted toward exclusion when an African American patron named Phillip Burton sued a local movie theater after he was denied admission because of his race. The theater managers were found guilty of violating the local municipal ordinance prohibiting discrimination on the basis of race, color, or previous condition of servitude. They were both fined ten dollars.[3] This successful challenge to segregation resulted in a backlash against integration when a few weeks later the Topeka City Commission repealed its permissive licensing requirement for local theaters on October 1, 1947.[4]

Three days later, Ava and Arthur Lee Stovall were refused admission to the same Dickinson Theater that Burton had sued a month earlier.[5] Though once again the local NAACP protested as it had done in 1944 to prevent reinforcement of the color line, this time its efforts were unsuccessful: the legal grounds to sue local businesses over limited access to public facilities had been removed.[6] Movie theaters, as well as any other public facility in Topeka operating under a municipal license, could segregate as they wished (Kluger 1975, 391). This setback caused the NAACP to shift attention from public accommodations to public schools; another phase of civil rights activism was initiated in 1948.

As recently returned World War II veterans, the Scott brothers were active in a biracial veteran's organization—the local American Veterans Committee—seeking to redress race issues. The AVC was founded in 1946 by returning World War II veterans as an alternative to the American

Legion, which was segregated (391). Its efforts challenging segregation coincided with those of the local NAACP. Though the AVC also targeted segregated institutions, its actions were limited to peaceful, public demonstrations.[7]

The Scott brothers had experienced the indignities of segregation in the military and were determined to create a better world once they returned home. Though these initial challenges were similar to the earlier school desegregation cases—initiated by individuals addressing singular grievances—they gradually broadened to include numerous plaintiffs when they decided to target school segregation. And, though the local chapter of the NAACP was involved in organizing these challenges, it was the ad hoc Citizens Committee that became the public face of these challenges. Challenges to racial injustice were no longer isolated individual requests for privileged access to whites-only institutions. The rising expectations of postwar America facilitated the growing racial consciousness of Black Americans and the growing awareness that segregation was no longer an option: autonomy and self-sufficiency would be yielded for full legal equality.

These challenges were carried forward from both sides of the color line. Another group of veterans, who joined the Scott brothers in forming the American Veterans Committee (AVC), were newly hired staff members employed at the renowned Menninger Foundation, many of whom were Jewish and not from Kansas. They had a reputation for "leftist" activities, which included campaigning for Henry Wallace's Progressive Party in 1948. "The AVC nucleus included a number of Jewish staff members at the Menninger Foundation, who were seen as menacing 'pinkos' from the East Coast.... [The AVC] helped the Scotts raise money to cover the costs of their action to de–Jim Crow the public pool in Gage Park and other legal measures."[8]

Years later, Marita Burnett Davis, daughter of Topeka's NAACP president McKinley Burnett, argued that school desegregation in Topeka was secretly funded by some Jewish physicians who worked at the nearby nationally renowned Menninger Clinic.[9]

"Separate Schools Are Here to Stay": Challenges to Elementary School Segregation in Topeka, 1948–1950

The local NAACP split during the *Graham* case, a successful lawsuit against segregated junior high schools in 1940 and discussed in Chapter Two. On one side were the African American teachers and administrators who sought to protect their jobs along with hostile white community leaders who sought to preserve the racial status quo.[10] On the other side were those people who were sympathetic to desegregation and the injustice it sought to redress. It was this faction, oriented toward civil rights and desegregation, which had gained control as the official, local NAACP chapter after 1941 and remained in power throughout the desegregation era.

In 1948, the NAACP petitioned the Board of Education in 1948 to equalize the financing for the segregated schools. When the school board failed to respond favorably, it decided to appear before the local school board and request that the board compose a plan for integration. However, the NAACP formed an ad hoc Citizens Committee to undertake this task instead of using the formal auspices of the local NAACP (Kluger 1975, 393). This committee knew that, since 1942, the board's segregation policy was to keep the status quo in Topeka's schools. Superintendent Dr. Kenneth McFarland later recalled: "We were operating the schools under essentially the same structure that we took them over in 1942. . . . We have no objective evidence that there is any substantial desire for a change among the people that the board represents. . . . [T]here is nothing in the record historically, that it's the place of the public school system to dictate the social customs of the people who support the public school system."[11]

McFarland's administration of Topeka's public schools reflected the realignment of the school board to continue the *tightening* of public segregation begun during Topeka's urban expansion and population growth in the 1920s and 1930s. According to Topekan Samuel Jackson, McFarland held "back the tide" (404). However, the local NAACP hoped to exploit the fact that the school board was divided on the issue of continuing segregation. Jackson continues, "[t]he school board might have gone along with desegregation . . . if McFarland had not resisted." Charles Scott's law partner Charles Bledsoe wrote Robert Carter of the NAACP in New York that "one of our good friends of the white race has polled every member of the Board of Education; two of them were bitterly against integration, and four of them would welcome a lawsuit, in order to take the load off their shoulders. . . . We interpret this as meaning that the Board will not wage an all-out defense; but this is opinion only."[12]

A strong leader, McFarland was adamant that school segregation was consistent with Kansas law (segregation was legal in the primary grades) and the school board gradually hardened its stance toward segregation. As a result of this realignment, McFarland consolidated and dissolved the power of its committees into his office; he could then override the elected authority of the elected school board (380).

McFarland's "iron hand" policy included hiring Harrison Caldwell as director of Negro school education to administer and closely supervise the segregated schools.[13] Caldwell played on the existing fears of African American teachers by reminding them that they would all lose their jobs if the schools were integrated.[14] Caldwell conducted yearly performance reviews of the teachers that included assessing their teaching in the classroom by how positive or negative they were toward the administration and its policies (381).[15] Mamie Williams, a teacher at Buchanan School and later principal at Washington School, recalled that the teachers did not protest this practice for fear of losing their jobs: "Since nobody had tenure then, and most of the teachers were unmarried women dependent on their salaries for their livelihood, you went along" (381).[16]

Divisions in the African American community over integration were also reflected in school organizations, such as the Negro Parent Teachers Association (PTA). According to Speer (1968, 27) and Adler (1972, 253, fn103), the African American teachers, in turn, put pressure on Topeka's Negro PTA to oppose challenges to segregation by influencing the parents of the children they taught. This resulted in African Americans acting in support of a white supremacist segregationist policy in order to preserve community and economic stability. McKinley Burnett stated that "the Negro PTA ... [had] sent a letter to the Board of Education expressing their official support of the *Board* position. Public ... [segregated] school teachers hesitated even to comment on the case as it was being prepared for court" (Speer 1968, 27; emphasis in original).

The local NAACP tried to overcome the teachers' reluctance and win their support for school integration. NAACP President McKinley Burnett later recalled: "At one point we called a meeting of the team. First, we had a man from the National Office (NAACP), a lawyer, who was going to speak to us.... We invited the teachers to come. They didn't come, not a one."[17]

A concurrent second challenge to Topeka's Board of Education was an effort by white elites to remove Superintendent McFarland. The white elites' challenge and the African Americans' challenge were separate but complementary actions against McFarland and his policies, thereby indirectly challenging segregation.

McFarland's leadership of Topeka's schools was seen as autocratic, and by the late 1940s his opponents had articulated several grievances against him besides supporting segregation.[18] Frank Wilson, principal of Sumner Elementary School, indicated that during McFarland's era one was either a "company man" and went along with his policies, or one sought employment elsewhere.[19]

McFarland's management style and dictatorial manner in which he overrode the school board culminated in a direct challenge by white elites to both school board members and McFarland. While the *Brown* brief was being prepared for court in April of 1951, half of the school board responsible for hiring McFarland in 1942 was up for reelection (Wilson 1994, 25).[20] On April 3, 1951, those school board members were voted out of office.[21] A few days after the election, on April 5, 1951, Superintendent McFarland turned in his resignation effective August 1951.[22]

The election of new school board members and the resignation of Superintendent McFarland changed the commitment the Board of Education had with segregation. In September 1953, two and a half months before the state of Kansas was to reappear before the United States Supreme Court in defense of its permissive segregation statute, the Board of Education of Topeka, Kansas, voted to abolish segregation in its elementary schools.[23]

The *Brown* "Story"

The "story" of the *Brown* case begins in September of 1950, when Oliver Brown took his young daughter Linda by the hand and walked the four blocks from their house to Sumner Elementary School to enroll her for the coming term. When Brown and his daughter arrived at the school, school principal Frank Wilson remembers he courteously refused to enroll Linda as a pupil.[24] Although the Browns lived near the school, and Linda was the correct age to attend elementary school, she was not eligible to attend Sumner because of her race. Instead, Oliver Brown was directed to return his daughter to the Monroe School, almost twenty blocks away. It was the school designated for African Americans living in that particular neighborhood. Oliver Brown sought to redress the injustice of segregated schools in Topeka and the rest of the nation by managing to convince twelve other parents to join him in a lawsuit, eventually enlisting the aid of the national NAACP (Berman 1966).

The above story of the white school's refusal to admit Oliver Brown's daughter Linda, and the subsequent crediting of Brown as the initiator of the lawsuit, is often found in accounts about the origins of the case (Kluger 1975, 409). Kluger's suggestion that Oliver Brown was not key to the origins of the case is often overlooked. In his biography of Thurgood Marshall, journalist Carl Rowan (1993, 182–183) characterized Oliver Brown as the "[a]ngry minister Brown" who "went to his friend and former classmate at Topeka High School, Charles Scott, who was the local attorney for the NAACP, and they agreed to file suit against the Topeka school board."

Though much has been written about the national significance of *Brown* (Patterson 2001), this research discusses how events in Kansas directly leading to Oliver Brown's actions were part of this broader effort to challenge segregation on behalf of all African Americans in Topeka. Though courageous, the actions of Oliver Brown most likely were motivated by concern for his daughter's welfare during her long daily trips to and from a segregated grade school. They were also embedded in and completely understandable only in terms of a local collective campaign against segregation in Topeka.

One overlooked aspect of the *Brown* story and subsequent legal case is the role of the plaintiffs. The Master Narrative emphasizes formal organization and leadership in assessing collective action, while the Border Campaign type emphasizes the actions initiated and sustained by career activists. Since the *Brown* plaintiffs' actions were only partially explained by their membership in the NAACP, it was useful to consider career activist tendencies (already suggested for the Border Campaign type by their importance in Guthrie and South Park) in assessing their participation in the Topeka campaign. Recruitment and participation in collective action varies according to factors related to incentives, rewards, and personal commitment (Turner and Killian 1987, 262). Further, participation in collective action is described by Turner and Killian (325) as falling on a continuum somewhere between minimal ("segmental involvement") and complete ("total absorption").

McAdam and Paulsen (1993, 645) also argue that it is important to recognize that "social ties may constrain as well as encourage activism." Popular accounts about the *Brown* case, as discussed above, assume that Oliver Brown, the lead plaintiff, "acted" as a result of his personal convictions and sense of injustice. However, this overlooks his overlapping and sometimes conflicting social roles as a husband, father, part-time minister, and Sante Fe Railroad employee. His studying for the ministry should have fueled his sense of militancy since the Master Narrative frames the emergence of radical protest as being largely due to the role of the black clergy. This "sense of injustice" attributed to Oliver Brown overshadows the participation of twelve other parents who were also named plaintiffs in the case. It also overshadows his job security as a union employee at the Sante Fe Railroad.

The involvement of the several other plaintiffs in Topeka indicates that Oliver Brown was not acting alone; many other African Americans in Topeka shared his point of view about the injustice of the segregated school policy (Henderson 2003).Also, being sympathetic and aware of an injustice is not enough to prompt action because "most of the attitudinally predisposed and even the overt sympathizers take no active part in a movement" (Turner and Killian 1987, 325). To explain this discrepancy between sympathy and action, Turner and Killian argue that "other variables must be combined with compatibility between individual attitude and movement value orientations to provide a fuller explanation for movement adherence and activism" (325–326).

Former NAACP Legal Defense Fund attorney Jack Greenberg, who worked on the Kansas brief, attributes the credit given to Oliver Brown in "starting" the case as a byproduct of the way in which cases with multiple plaintiffs are listed alphabetically by the courts. Greenberg (1994, 127) argues that Oliver Brown "was neither more or less involved than any other ... because Brown was first in alphabetical order, they captioned the case *Oliver Brown, et al. v. Board of Education of Topeka, Shawnee County, Kansas.*"[25]

The original brief filed in federal district court in 1951 does not list Oliver Brown as the first of thirteen plaintiffs: he was preceded alphabetically by Mrs. Darlene Brown, though later ones obviously put his name first.[26] A careful examination of the court documents and the surviving papers of attorney Charles Scott indicated two other possible explanations for Oliver Brown to be listed first. First, Oliver Brown was the only male plaintiff. Second, his daughter, Linda, lived the furthest from a segregated school while living closest to a white school.

The original complaint listed Leola, not Oliver, as the adult plaintiff representing their daughter Linda.[27] Indeed, all the other plaintiffs petitioning on behalf of their minor children were also female.[28] The reason why Leola Brown was replaced by her husband, Oliver Brown, as lead plaintiff occurred when she became pregnant in the fall of 1949. Leola Brown recalls: "He being the man there for our family, because I wasn't there ... he stepped forward."[29]

The written record offers little explanation for the other mothers, not the fathers, being listed as plaintiffs. Oral history interviews of the surviving plaintiffs yielded the following information. Leola Brown recalled that the women were involved before the men because "all the women were volunteering. I don't know if any of the rest of the men were there.... They ... [might have been] there with their wives. [But] the wives were the ones who took ... [the men] in."[30]

However, Leola Brown recalls that her husband was active in the NAACP: "He was at all the meetings because he was that type. He believed in trying to get what was fair for all his people.... [T]he NAACP was very much alive and in evidence here in Topeka at that time and most black people here belonged to it."[31]

The question of Oliver Brown's involvement is not settled by his positive orientation toward the NAACP. Did he become involved only because his wife could not? Or did he become involved for some other reason than organizational affiliation or career activism? Evidence indicates that the decisive factor was his lifelong friendship with Charles Scott. His wife recalled that it was through his friendship with Charles Scott that Oliver Brown *finally* overcame his reluctance to be a plaintiff: "Charles Scott really prevailed upon him to do it because he was a friend of Charles Scott.... I don't think ... [Oliver Brown] ... really volunteered at first but he prevailed upon him. So he finally said yes."[32]

Charles Scott also recalls that Oliver Brown was initially reluctant to be a plaintiff: "Not all of the parents took part in the suit with great enthusiasm. That was certainly true of Oliver Brown.... Mr. Brown was anything but eager to act as plaintiff. In fact, he agreed only after we persuaded him that nothing bad would happen to him."[33] The activism of

Charles Scott, while not as dramatic as Esther Brown's in South Park, was essential in the process of recruiting several of the *Brown* plaintiffs.

One of the other plaintiffs had attended integrated schools outside of Topeka, and was another possible factor encouraging participation. Plaintiff Vivian Scales was born in Winfield, Kansas, and had attended an integrated school. When she moved to Topeka, she was introduced to segregated education. Mrs. Scales recalled, "I went to white school first, because we lived in Winfield and there was no black school there. [When we moved to Topeka] we . . . had to get adjusted to it [school segregation], it was different, just like everything else. Of course we were a little more advanced than some of the kids in our grade, but it was all right, because we always got good grades. We did notice some different things, but the kids that were already there, they didn't know the difference."[34]

Besides the difference in curriculum, Mrs. Scales remembers being subjected to traveling a long distance to school. "We had to be bused to school. The bus passed three white schools. . . . When you stop to think about it, that was crazy. We lived two blocks from a school, and they bused us."[35] Having these experiences in mind, Mrs. Scales stated that when it came time for her daughter to attend school, she was "determined to hang in there, so our children and grandchildren wouldn't have to go through what we went through. . . . I had to take . . . [Ruth Ann] . . . to [a segregated] school, and Parkdale was right there [nearby]."[36] A longtime member of the Topeka NAACP, Mrs. Scales was an early supporter of the challenge to school segregation. But her daughter, Ruth Ann, only had to travel seven blocks to school and not face the same hardship that Linda Brown did in having to travel twenty-one blocks.

Thus, neither organizational affiliation nor career activism on the part of the plaintiffs themselves could adequately explain the participation of the *Brown* plaintiffs. Their diverse backgrounds and situations, along with evidence of hesitation by some of the participants, support the hypothesis that participation as a plaintiff was based largely on friendship networks and personal relationships. What united these thirteen plaintiffs to jointly petition the school board? One likely explanation was Charles Scott's activism. Operating through friendship networks and personal relationships, Scott coordinated the petition process for the *Brown* case through his civil rights law practice and local NAACP contacts: "And so we—when I say we I'm referring to the committee that we had at that time—we solicited and gained the consent from these parents to use their names as well as the children in the test lawsuit."[37]

The lead plaintiff, Oliver Brown, ambivalent about having a place in the collective action challenging segregated schools, was drawn into the case primarily due to his friendship with Charles Scott and not due to his personal convictions or value orientations. Therefore, his participation cannot be understood in terms of career activism. This led to the conclusion that the primary basis for participation by the *Brown* plaintiffs was through personal relationships, which situated their activism on a continuum between organizational affiliation and career activism. This finding demonstrates the need for a broader conceptualization of activism than considering only continuum endpoints such as organizational membership or career activist. The intensive social interaction that was occurring within these friendship networks was not organizational, but rather merely *associated* with organizations. Career activism and organizational affiliation by the plaintiffs were not decisive factors explaining participation as plaintiffs in this instance. However, the local NAACP provided an overall organization context in which Charles Scott's career activism operated through networks of friendship to recruit these plaintiffs into their crucial roles in the Topeka campaign.

The Master Narrative's emphasis on the crucial role of the black clergy in carrying forward protest has caused Oliver Brown to be characterized as an "angry minister" (Rowan 1983, 183). However, oral history interviews and careful examination of the historical record uncovers a slightly different causal relationship. The clergy in Topeka were divided about how to challenge segregation, according to Reverend E. B. Hicks: "As the Case moved on to the courts, mine was low profile. I learned a long time ago to operate on a low profile. There would be less [sic] problems."[38]

At the time of the *Brown* case, Oliver Brown was attending seminary part time in the evening where Hicks taught. Hicks recalled that his involvement in the case came about even though "I wasn't intending to be but I was." Hicks had been called out of town a few days on business, and when he returned, he discovered his name in the paper protesting against the Topeka Board of Education. Hicks related a typical telephone conversation with a male parishioner soon after the ad appeared in the newspaper: "This was an ad about the Board of Education saying that this special committee was attacking the Board of Education for its stand. 'Do you know Rev. Oliver Brown?' 'Yes. I know him quite well. In fact, he is one of my students.' He [the parishioner] said, 'Well, what are you going to do?' I said, 'I'm not going to do anything.'" Hicks also recalled "I only remember three ministers who were really involved in it," and none of them were Oliver Brown.[39]

The role of the black clergy in civil rights protest is more complicated than characterized by the Master Narrative. During segregation, the black clergy was influential on both sides of the color line, in terms of carrying forward complaints of their parishioners to the white power structure. But they also could be agents of caution, like Rev. Hicks, who though sympathetic to injustice, preferred to remain anonymous and work quietly behind the scenes. Hicks's recollection that Oliver Brown's involvement in the case was not closely related to being a clergy member contradicts what is emphasized by the Master Narrative. Rather, using the Border Campaign, Brown's involvement is more multidimensional in suggesting he was drawn into activism due to the overlap of his private roles as husband and father, his public roles of concerned citizen and future minister, along with his close personal relationship with attorney Charles Scott.

Conclusion: Local Initiatives in Social Movements

The civil rights actions that resulted in school desegregation in Topeka were undertaken within various types of organizations, including the civil rights–oriented NAACP, as well as community-based ones such as the American Veterans Committee (AVC) and the PTA. This contrasts with the Master Narrative's weight toward action located in the black churches (Morris 1984). Though African American churches, long-standing mainstays of their communities, mobilized crucial resources in the Southern mass-mobilization campaigns, in Topeka they served more as part of an informal network for the *Brown* plaintiffs. Though Oliver Brown was a part-time member of the clergy, he was not a recognized community leader; his primary status for being selected was his union job at the Santa Fe Railroad.

The social action was more heterogeneous, reflecting the combined efforts of formal and informal leaders as well as civil rights organizations such as the local chapter of the NAACP. There was not a concentrated location of collective action within the black church, even though the lead plaintiff, Oliver Brown, was studying for the clergy and worked part-time in St. John's A.M.E. church. Participants in civil rights activism were primarily drawn from numerous community organizations and individuals working outside of established organizations. The eventual desegregation of Topeka's schools developed out of these early types of civil rights actions that began by challenging segregation in public accommodations during the 1940s. School desegregation was furthered by challenges undertaken by white elites opposed to Superintendent McFarland's administration, including removal of unsympathetic school board members at the next election. Some of these efforts to eliminate school segregation were directed toward the white PTA, and were responded to by the black PTA and teachers. Diverse actions, separately controlled, loosely combined into what became the 1954 *Brown* case.

Scholarship on the origins of the civil rights movement includes how national organizations brought change into local communities (Lawson 1991). Others examine the communities themselves (Chafe, 1980; Colburn, 1985; Norell 1985). Interactive studies connecting local and national issues with social and political factors include McAdam (1982), Morris

(1984). McAdam (1982) and Tarrow (1994) emphasize the structural pre-requisites to civil rights protest, such as the advantageous internal political opportunity structure that developed in the early twentieth century brought about by the mass migration of blacks to the northern cities and the emerging political power of the Northern black vote. In particular, McAdam emphasizes rising national political opportunities for African Americans to exercise power dating back to the New Deal politics of the 1930s. McAdam argues that these political opportunities permitted the groundwork for the new national political insurgency that was to follow in the 1950s and 1960s. An important external political opportunity structure is related to America's role in Cold War politics emphasizing freedom and democracy; this pressured Americans to reevaluate their own racial practices within their own borders.

Local contexts are an important way to study the "internal processes of social movements" and "decisive shapers of reform" (Carson 1986, 19–20). It is also problematic that these studies disregard the individual activist "only as harbingers of change—colorful, politically impotent, socially isolated idealists and malcontents who play only fleeting roles in the drama of American political history" (29–30). McAdam, Tarrow, and Tilly (2001) have begun to address the importance of the different ways in which individuals facilitate activism by suggesting a "relational" approach sensitive to "webs of interaction" (22–23). But their method is so broadly defined that it does not help us understand why specific people are drawn into activism (Polletta 2002, 582) For example, members of Topeka's black middle class involved in desegregation were not "socially isolated idealists" but rather realists who sought a constructive way to bring about social change. They moved between existing organizations, like the NAACP, and also formed ad hoc community groups to carry forward their reforms, as they did just before the Brown case. As the culture of segregation changed in the 1940s, so did the actors and tactics who wanted to dismantle it.

The Master Narrative overlooks civil rights struggles in Kansas due to their different type of historically situated activism. Instead of focusing primarily on charismatic leadership or the political resources provided by the institutional structures of black churches and activist organizations, I ask: What were the indigenous patterns of accommodation and paternalism that had to be broken before change could occur? Which forces paved the way for protest? Who led the forces of resistance? How did the resistance use the same ideals of American freedom and liberty to justify the exclusion of a whole class of citizens on the basis of race?

The types of civil rights actions utilized to end segregation in Topeka were shaped by the ambiguity of color line practices in Kansas and were organized around local level issues. As the city limits of Topeka expanded to incorporate rural communities, the city created new fault lines along the color line because its practices were renegotiated as part of the confrontations between real estate developers, city government officials, the board of education, and parents of school-age children. The civil rights actions used to help eliminate segregation were shaped by Kansas's mixture of segregationist and integrationist cultural patterns. The state's permissive segregation statute prohibited publicly funded school segregation except for elementary schools in its "first-class" cities with a population of more than fifteen thousand.[40] The expansion of Topeka's city limits through annexation in the first part of the twentieth century resulted in some African Americans being moved from integrated rural county schools to segregated city grade schools. This shift in the boundaries of the city also shifted color line practices in the newly annexed areas.

Those African Americans who were caught between pressures to preserve segregation within Topeka's city limits brought the resulting challenges to the color line to maintain the informal tradition of integration to which they were accustomed outside of the city limits. The period between 1944, following the 1940 *Graham* case (which desegregated the junior high schools), and the 1954 *Brown* decision (which desegregated the elementary schools) can be characterized as a curious mix of accommodation and exclusion. Throughout the early civil rights era, there were whites and blacks who were responsible for initiating challenges and those who resisted. Both blacks and whites perceived existing race relations as unjust and were willing to participate in programs to fight segregation. They were opposed by those who sought to preserve segregation, from both sides of the color line, who, for different reasons, sought to keep racial integration at a minimum.

In the next chapter, we return to Oklahoma, where challenges to segregation after the 1954 *Brown* decision begin to take on characteristics of Southern direct action campaigns. We also examine the agency of a black woman named Clara Luper, who used her status as a teacher in segregated schools to launch a series of challenges to segregation by recruiting young people to stand up for their rights at Oklahoma City's lunch counters.

Notes

1. As discussed in Chapter Two, during the *Graham* case, the Topeka NAACP split into two rival factions. Civil rights attorney Elisha Scott, who did not support desegregation of the junior high schools in Topeka in 1941, led one faction, which represented the interests of African American teachers, including a relative of Scott's who taught in the segregated schools. As indicated above, some African American teachers did lose their positions after desegregation of the junior high schools. After *Graham,* Scott's group gave way to the faction in favor of desegregation, one of which included Scott's' two sons, Charles and John.

2. General Statute 21-2424, 1935.

3. General Statute 21-2424, 1935. *Kansas City Call,* September 26, 1947, and November 24, 1947.

4. *Kansas City Call,* October 17, 1947.

5. *Kansas City Call,* October 17, 1947.

6. *Kansas City Call,* October 10, 1947.

7. Charles S. Scott Papers, Kansas Collection.

8. Ibid.

9. Interview with author. See oral history transcript of Marita Burnett Davis, August 1994.

10. "Meetings of the Topeka NAACP were generally not attended by more than a dozen members" (Speer 1968, 22). "The NAACP meetings that Burnett chaired rarely drew more than a dozen or so people and usually degenerated into gripe sessions" (Kluger 1975, 393). The Citizens Committee did not present itself as an NAACP delegation, since "mention of the NAACP, it was presumed, would have earned the back of the school board's hand" (393). There were four segregated elementary schools in Topeka: Buchanan, McKinley, Monroe, and Washington.

11. *Brown v. Board of Education,* 98 F Supp. 797 (1951); transcript of record in lower court, 234.

12. Correspondence from Charles Bledsoe to Robert Carter, Topeka NAACP Branch Files. Kansas State Historical Society, Topeka, Kansas.

13. Caldwell had worked under McFarland in Coffeyville, Kansas (Kluger 1975, 381). For a personal account of Caldwell, see Merrill Ross's oral history transcript, *Brown v. Board* Oral History Project. Ross was a coach and teacher under Caldwell during the 1940s.

14. Caldwell was described by the Citizen's Committee as "stumbling block to our progress and had … reduced the morale of the colored teachers 'to an all time low'" (Kluger 1975, 393).

15. Author interview with Stan Stalter, July 17, 1994, Topeka, Kansas.

16. During the *Graham* case, Mamie Williams taught sixth and seventh grade at the Buchanan School. See brief for the defendants, *Graham v. Board of Education of Topeka* (19). During the time of the *Brown* case, Miss Williams was principal at Washington School.

17. McKinley Burnett interview with Hugh Speer, April 1967 (Speer 1968, 27).

18. Author interview with former Randolph School principal Stan Stalter, July 17, 1994, Topeka, Kansas. Mr. Stalter recalled that faculty at Washburn University who had children in Topeka's public schools were particularly opposed to Superintendent McFarland's policies. Stalter felt that the "movement" to remove McFarland began in the schools around Washburn University.

19. Author interview, October 1994. Frank Wilson was principal of Sumner Elementary when Oliver Brown tried to enroll his daughter, Linda, in 1950.

20. Author interview with Stan Stalter, July 17, 1994, Topeka, Kansas.

21. Two years later, on April 7, 1953, the remaining half of the members of the board of education was voted out of office. All who had been on the board when the *Brown* lawsuit was filed were off the board by August 1953. The *Brown* case went to the U.S. Supreme Court on December 7, 1952. Memorandum on *Brown* compiled by the University of Kansas Law Library Reference Desk, August 1995. Copy in the private collection of the author.

22. Topeka *Capital,* April 4, 1951, and April 5, 1951.

23. There was only one negative vote, by Oberhelman, who stated that "he was no [sic] opposed to the policy, but felt that an orderly program should be worked out before the resolution was passed." Segregation Policy, Topeka Board of Education. Charles S. Scott papers, Kansas Collection, University of Kansas.

24. Author interview August 1994.

25. See also Kluger (1975, 407): It is one of the idiosyncrasies of U.S. constitutional law that cases of profound consequence are often named for plaintiffs whose involvement in the original suit is either remote or merely fortuitous.

26. Former Kansas assistant attorney general Paul Wilson noticed this also in his analysis of the *Brown* case. See Wilson (1994, 21-22).

27. Charles S. Scott Collection, Kansas Collection, Spencer Research Library, University of Kansas, Lawrence, Kansas. See Box 1.

28. Mrs. Richard Lawton (daughters Victoria Jean and Carol Kay), Mrs. Lucinda Todd (daughter Nancy Jane), Mrs. Andrew Henderson (daughter Vicki Ann and son Donald Andrew), Mrs. Vivian Scales (daughter Ruth Ann), Mrs. Lena Carper (daughter Katherine Louise), Mrs. Shirley Hodison (son Charles), Mrs. Marguerite Emmerson (sons Claude Arthur and George Robert), Mrs. Sadie Emmanuel (son James Meldon), Mrs. Iona Richardson (son Ronald Douglas), Mrs. Alma Lewis (sons Theron and Arthur, daughters Martha Jean and Frances), Mrs. Darlene Brown (daughter Saudria Dorstella), Mrs. Shirla Fleming (sons Duane Dean and Silas Hardrick). *Brown v. Board of Education,* 98 F Supp. 797 (1951).

29. Leola Brown Montgomery oral history interview transcript. November 1991, Topeka, Kansas. *Brown v. Board* Oral History Project, Kansas State Historical Society.

30. Leola Brown Montgomery oral history interview transcript. November 1991, Topeka, Kansas. *Brown v. Board* Oral History Project, Kansas State Historical Society.

31. Leola Brown Montgomery oral history interview transcript. November 1991, Topeka, Kansas. *Brown v. Board* Oral History Project, Kansas State Historical Society.

32. Leola Brown Montgomery oral history interview transcript. November 1991, Topeka, Kansas. *Brown v. Board* Oral History Project, Kansas State Historical Society.

33. Charles S. Scott papers, Box 1, Kansas Collection, University of Kansas Libraries. (RH: MS: 494, 1).

34. Author interview with Mrs. Vivian Scales, October 30, 1991.

35. Author interview with Mrs. Vivian Scales, October 30, 1991.

36. Author interview with Mrs. Vivian Scales, October 30, 1991.

37. Transcript of an interview with Charles S. Scott by Dr. James C. Duram and Mr. Robert Bunting on June 25, 1970. Dwight D. Eisenhower Library, Abilene, Kansas.

38. Author interview with Reverend E. B. Hicks Topeka, Kansas. p. 24.

39. Author interview with Reverend E. B. Hicks, Topeka, Kansas. January 1992.

40. Wilson, p. 39.

6

"Standing Up in the Heartland"

The Oklahoma City Lunch Counter Sit-Ins, 1957–1964

As discussed in previous chapters, the Master Narrative provides a static description of social action, obscuring the complicated relationships between agency, culture, social structure, and situations in social movements. The Border Campaign provides an alternate, more dynamic typology by incorporating spatial, temporal, and cultural dimensions to structural axes of inquiry. This approach better captures the disparate actions of individuals by considering how their actions coalesce into collective action without collapsing or eliding them into agency or structure. Emphasizing the relationship between agency and structure illumines how they are mediated by ideas embedded in cultural systems and thus influence people's actions.

The border state protests discussed in previous chapters have provided some important examples of how using the 1954 *Brown* case as a watershed, the Master Narrative emphasizes mass mobilizations and direct action protests. Just as the 1955–1956 Montgomery bus boycott is the Master Narrative's defining moment for characterizing mass mobilizations, so too are the 1960 Greensboro, North Carolina, sit-ins for typifying direct action protests. Just as the *Brown* decision subsumes previous desegregation challenges as discussed in Chapters 2, 3, 4, and 5, so too this approach overlooks an important tactic challenging racial segregation: economic boycotts.[1]

This chapter examines some overlooked economic boycotts testing racial segregation occurring in border states, during the intervening years between two Master Narrative watershed moments: the aforementioned 1954 *Brown* school desegregation case and the 1960 Greensboro, North Carolina, sit-ins. The Greensboro sit-ins led by four male college students resonate as the iconic moment of youthful dissent against the racial status quo. The Master Narrative's tendency to elide antecedent events is illustrated by its failure to acknowledge the significance of earlier sit-ins in Wichita, Kansas, on July 19, 1958, and in Oklahoma City, Oklahoma, on August 17, 1958.[2]

These border state sit-ins anticipated the student sit-in movement by almost two years. The July 1958 sit-ins in Wichita were organized after two years of discussion preceded by various attempts of African Americans to desegregate Wichita's movie theaters and restaurants (Eick 2001, 3). Within weeks, sit-ins occurred in other nearby Kansas towns and spread across the border into Oklahoma, where sit-ins were staged not only in Oklahoma City but also in Enid, Tulsa, and Stillwater (43). That these boycotts are not considered significant by the Master Narrative is partially due to their lack of a contagion effect in spreading like a wildfire across the South (Morris 1981, 751).[3] Further, since the Oklahoma City sit-ins were organized and led by a woman, Clara Luper, they also fail to meet the Master Narrative emphasis on the necessity of direct action being masculine led, which was the case with the Greensboro sit-ins. By considering these earlier sit-ins within the context of their local situation, the seemingly disparate actions of individuals are less incongruent.

The Border Campaign approach is more fluid and multidimensional in considering agency and structure as distinct domains mediated by ideas embedded in cultural systems (Archer 1996). In the Border Campaign, we link agency with structure, characterized by value-rational action using the concept of career activist. Because early civil rights protest cannot simply be characterized in terms of objective goals, career activism helps bring into focus some significant instances of human agency. It also avoids the masculine bias of the Master Narrative in failing to recognize the leadership contributions of women, acting as intermediaries who link people to protest situations and institutions by allowing them to interact with other individuals, to influence, or even to become formal leaders, and, finally to connect structurally with organizations and social institutions. Career activists are linked to social structure through the combined qualities of social and collective action. Again, the qualities of career activist social action are derived from Weber's typology of value-rational action, or a type of action that can only be understood in the context of an individual's own life and values, rather than from the goals of any organization or institution to which they might belong.

The Border Campaign focuses on the "interplay" between agency and structure, avoiding the fallacy of the "central conflation" by not conceptualizing agency and structure as being tightly constitutive (Archer 1996). In this way, agency or the properties of interaction are kept analytically separate from the properties of structure. Assuming that neither agency nor structure is totally coherent or conflictual, this approach emphasizes where they intersect, their interplay, in terms of beginning to distinguish "the orderly or conflictual relations pertaining between groups of actors (the degree of social interaction) from the orderly or contradictory relations prevailing between parts of the social structure (the degree of system integration)" (xvi). In this way, there is a distinction made between the logical consistency or ideas of a cultural system and the causal consensus or influence of ideas on people (socio-cultural interaction).

By focusing on the interplay between agency and structure, without conflating them to the top, bottom, or middle, we can begin to unravel which systemic relations impinge upon agency (socio-cultural interaction) as well as which social relations affect how agents might respond to and react back on the cultural system. Analysis of agency leading to collective action can begin by "examining the effects of holding ideas with particular logical relations (of contradiction or complementary to others)—not with the (socio-cultural) reasons for these being held" (xxii).

The Master Narrative stops with static abstractions conceptualization of collective action. Instead of looking for importance in terms of local movement center dynamics focusing on the role of black clergy to coordinate mass mobilizations by linking churches with existing protest organizations (Morris 1981, 753–754), the Border Campaign analysis considers protest action in terms of the cultural significance of the situation. The Master Narrative does not provide an adequate benchmark to measure the actions and tactics utilized in Kansas, Oklahoma, and even Louisiana. As in Topeka, Kansas, and Guthrie, Oklahoma, these types of civil rights protest have been forgotten because they employed a heterogeneous type of collection action.

For example, the 1953 bus boycott in Baton Rouge, Louisiana, was preceded by negotiations between local black community leaders and the city council. As in Merriam, Kansas, the Oklahoma City dissent is led by a woman, Clara Luper, but even though Luper is African American, she does not fit the Master Narrative masculine model of black leadership clustered among the clergy. Luper's coordination of the Oklahoma City sit-ins flouts prevailing gendered understandings of leadership on sides of the color line. As events that do not precisely fit within the Master Narrative, events in Oklahoma City are worthy of consideration using the Border Campaign framework since these boycotts are examples of how important it is to first consider the local situation before making generic conclusions about their significance.

Economic Boycotts and the Rise of Consumer Society

The rising expectations of middle-class blacks to fully participate in American society were increasingly obstructed by racial segregation in public transportation, stores, and restaurants (Frazier 1957; Ayers 1993). The search for economic solutions to racial inequality made targeting public facilities such as mass transportation and restaurants obvious ones long before the 1950s (Weems 1998). "The battle over the racial ordering of modern transportation" began with the growth of railroads and streetcars between 1880 and the early 1900s (Hale 1998, 128). "Because many whites found it difficult to imagine African Americans as anything other than poor and uneducated, finely dressed blacks riding in first-class [railroad] cars attracted their particular ire" (129). The white denial of black prosperity was shattered as "middle-class blacks entered the semi-public spaces of railroads ... plac[ing] their better attire and manners in direct juxtaposition with whites' own class signifiers" (128–129). Fears of racial purity emerged "in an increasingly anonymous world where class and race status depended on appearances, racial disorder endangered the very meaning of white identity" (129).

Attempts by state legislatures to limit access to public accommodations according to racial boundaries met with resistance across the South. For example, streetcar boycotts appeared in every Southern state that enacted Jim Crow laws between 1891 and 1906 (Barnes 1983; Meier and Rudwick 1969; Roback 1986). In 1907, the year Oklahoma became a state, segregated streetcars were legal in Virginia, Texas, Louisiana, Mississippi, and Tennessee. Attempts to enact uniform statewide legislation were met with resistance in Florida and Alabama and, as in Topeka, Kansas, municipal trespassing laws were used to enforce segregation.

From 1900 to 1902, blacks protested streetcar segregation fifty years before the 1955–1956 Montgomery Bus Boycott (Meier and Rudwick 1969, 758). Though the Master Narrative characterizes this boycott as an effective tactic (Morris 1984, 48), it fails to take into account the historical context in shaping subsequent actions. Unlike the Baton Rouge and Montgomery bus boycotts in the 1950s, which sought to change the racial order from vertical to horizontal, the early twentieth-century streetcar boycotts were a "conservative protest" in that they were "seeking to preserve the status quo—to prevent a change from an older and well established pattern" (Meier and Rudwick 1969, 770). The boycotts were organized by black business elites and clergy as a "multifaceted response to oppression that protested and yet avoided confrontation with the discriminating whites" (773). All these boycotts eventually failed, though, in part because black leaders started riding the segregated cars, and in part because of the lack of black-owned streetcar companies to be able to compete with the larger, better-capitalized, white-owned mass transportation companies (765).

Efforts to use economic tactics to protest racial segregation continued in the 1930s by the picketing of stores and restaurants that refused to employ blacks. These protests were coordinated by "don't buy where you can't work" organizations in Chicago, New York, and Washington, DC (Bunche 1940). Other protests include black rent strikes organized in Norfolk, Virginia, in 1932 (Meier and Rudwick 1976, 336). Some of the earliest sit-ins were organized in 1942 by CORE in Chicago and in 1944 by the Howard University NAACP chapter in Washington, DC (Bunche 1965; Farmer 1965). These earlier sit-ins are neglected by the Master Narrative's tendency to date the beginning of the civil rights movement to the late 1950s and early 1960s.

This neglect of the historical precursors to the civil rights movement is due in part to the historiography of the civil rights movement. Graves (1981) notes that historians of the early civil rights movement such as John Hope Franklin (1974, 476) and Richard Dalifume (1968, 90–116) are "misleading because … [they] … fail … to mention the importance of the sit-ins." Franklin writes of Greensboro as "the beginning" of the sit-in movement and Dalifume "stresses the March on Washington (MOWM) of the 1940s … [but] … does not mention an equally important phenomenon—the sit-ins" (Graves 1981, 293–94; cfn, 46–47).

The economic boycott came of age with the 1953 bus boycott in Baton Rouge, Louisiana. This event was preceded by negotiations between local black community leaders and the city council, which agreed to change the contours of the color line by passing an ordinance in March 1953 to allow blacks to be seated on a first-come, first-served basis (Morris 19984, 16–18). The bus drivers, all of whom were white, promptly went on strike, and the ordinance was quickly rescinded; permitting blacks to be seated next to whites was declared "illegal because it conflicted with Louisiana's segregation laws" (18).

Though the city buses were technically already integrated in that blacks and whites shared a common space, this was not a violation of existing state segregation law in that blacks either sat separately in the back or had to stand when their section of the bus was full. But this type of integration was vertical, not horizontal, in that the inferior status of blacks was sustained. Once the spatial boundaries of this limited integration was challenged by blacks petitioning to be seated in the front or even to sit beside whites, the careful equilibrium of limited racial interaction was upset. Horizontal integration pointed toward the taboo of racial equality.

When the black community of Baton Rouge boycotted the buses for ten days in June 1953, the economic impact of the lost revenue forced the city to negotiate with the protesters. Though the Baton Rouge boycott ended with a compromise, it symbolically sustained segregation by reserving the front two seats for whites and the long rear seat for blacks (24). But Reverend Jemison saw ending the boycott as an opportunity to begin legally challenging all bus segregation through the courts (24). Rather than interpreting the subsequent Montgomery Bus Boycott a year later as an abrupt, watershed event, using the Border Campaign typology it is brought into focus as the redeployment of an economic boycott tactic that accompanied the enactment of segregation laws fifty years previously. Depending on the prevailing cultural norms about racial equality, the boycott is both a conservative and avant-garde protest tactic. As a way to object to racial segregation through avoidance rather than confrontation, it also encourages "group unity" while "aggressively upsetting the white-controlled economy" (Meier and Rudwick 1969, 773). In the early twentieth century the streetcar boycotts occurred during a period of adjustment as black Americans' access to public facilities was being carefully controlled, a movement which was sustained by the courts.[4] Fifty years later these boundaries were being sharply contested as the legality of segregation was being dismantled.

Gender, Leadership, and Innovative Organizational Tactics

The meaning of the local situation of the Baton Rouge Boycott is also shunted aside by the Master Narrative's focus on the mass mobilization and leadership of black clergy, particularly Reverend T. J. Jemison, in an effective use of black churches to forge "institutional link(s) to the masses" (Morris 1984, 21). This tactical innovation is later institutionalized in the organizational structure of the Southern Christian Leadership Council (SCLC), founded in 1957, using churches for mobilizing mass protests (Garrow 1989, 272). The emergence of the SCLC directly challenges the more staid legal tactics of the older, more established NAACP that the Master Narrative posits as against abrupt change (Morris 1984, 124). But what is largely ignored during this period after *Brown* is the changing nature of the cultural meaning and acceptance of integration from partial (vertical) to complete (horizontal). The Master Narrative's conceptualization of integration is static and one-dimensional. The Border Campaign provides a more nuanced understanding of the dynamics of integration by taking into account its cultural meanings. As seen by the bus boycott in Baton Rouge and the vertical integration of its buses, the boundaries of segregation are not evenly drawn in places like Louisiana, a former slave state.

After the Montgomery Bus Boycott, the charismatic Rev. Martin Luther King, Jr., asserted a new image of black masculinity that resonated with accepted cultural ideas about white gender arrangements: men lead and women follow (Robnett). Though the NAACP was largely male led at the national level, its decentralized organizational structure did allow some room for diverse leadership, and women often assumed leadership positions at the grass-roots level.[5] Women often served as chapter officers—Lucinda Todd in Topeka, Kansas, and Daisy Bates in Little Rock, Arkansas, for example—while others like Rosa Parks in Montgomery, Alabama, and Clara Luper in Oklahoma City, Oklahoma, also served as advisors to NAACP youth councils.

These women all share important leadership characteristics in challenging racial segregation, though Parks is most commonly associated with the Montgomery Bus Boycott and Bates for organizing the integration of Central High School in Little Rock, Arkansas, in 1959. Though Morris (1984, 124) notes "[a] disproportionate number of ... [Youth Council] ... advisors were women," the masculine logic of the Master Narrative renders their leadership contributions indistinct by emphasizing community organizing as a means of power rather than focusing on organizing relationships to build community (Stall and Stoecker 1998, 729). Though Parks and Bates are more familiar, Luper of Oklahoma City and Vera Pigee are even less known since their actions are further obscured by the Master Narrative's tendency to collapse agency, culture, social structure, and situations. These women contributed extraordinarily to the civil rights movement, while at the same time they had to continuously negotiate cultural meanings attributed to gender as individuals in interactions within specific situations.

By maintaining the categorical unity of civil rights leaders as male, the Master Narrative not only represents the civil rights movement as largely confined geographically to the South and bound by a single defining issue—race—but also typifies it "as a movement of African American men" (Ferree and Roth 1998, 627). This aspect of the Master Narrative considered here—its underlying masculine logic—means that even when considering the internal dynamics of social movements as gendered, it emphasizes successful outcomes by its "militaristic language" that concentrates on goals and targets (Taylor 1998, 675). By singling out successful strategies and tactics, the Master Narrative places movement participants in "finite categories," obscuring important gendered dynamics and tensions within movements (675). In contrast, the Border Campaign emphasizes the interplay between groups of actors (the degree of social interaction) from the orderly or contradictory relations prevailing between parts of the social structure (the degree of system integration). It complicates gender participation in social movements by incorporating the dynamics of value-rational agency along with means and rationality. In this way, gender can be considered without dichotomizing it as either a freedom or a limitation.

As discussed in Chapter One, the label "campaign" is a dynamic one that makes discrete events bounded by a specific place and time, rather than abstract goals, the focal point (Marwell and Oliver 1984, 12). While, as discussed in Chapter Four, value-rational agency conceptualizes activism within the context of an individual's biography.

Esther Brown, a white woman, illustrates how women can be drawn into activism through the transformation from their role as mothers (of their children) into "activist mothering" (of many children) (Irons 1998, 695). In examining how women's participation varied by race, Irons (694) argues gender is but one of many "structures of constraint" that "shape[s] ... social movement experiences." The actions of Luper's activism were tempered not only by racism—she was a black woman— and sexism, but she also had to contend with a similar sexist ideology from members of her own race. Like Brown, Luper's multidimensional activism only becomes known when viewed through the lens of value-rational agency, which gives equal weight to situational meanings and action. As Einwohner, Hollander, and Olson (2000, 680) point out, "gender can be used by social movement participants who wish to construct their image in a certain light, frame an issue in a particular way, or claim legitimacy as actors in a certain arena."

Conceptualizing gender as a "cultural resource" (Williams 1995) that actors in a social movement arena can use to further their goals" (Einwohner et al. 2000, 81) provides a way to discuss how these meanings are employed both by movement participants as well as their opponents. As Einwoher et al. argue, "movements are also gendered to the extent that opponents and other third parties evaluate them in terms of gender" (688). But movement insiders can also use dominant cultural meanings of gender to hamper women's leadership roles in organizations (as happened in SCLC and later in SNCC). By emphasizing the dominant role of the male black clergy in organizing collective protests through their churches, the Master Narrative obscures how "culturally specific ideas about gender shape interactions" within organizations (Einwhoner et al. 2000, 689). This is particularly relevant when examining the role of the NAACP youth councils in organizing sit-ins. There were rumblings along the color line between 1956 (the end of the Montgomery Bus Boycott) and February 1, 1960, when four black youths initiated a sit-in at Woolworth's in downtown Greensboro, North Carolina. Though many of these earlier sit-ins were led by women, it is this watershed male-led student sit-in movement in Greensboro, North Carolina, that resonates with the Master Narrative (Graves 1981; see also Chafé 1980).

Luper's long-term struggle to desegregate Oklahoma City public facilities provides an example of the dynamic interplay between agency and structure mediated by ideas embedded in a particular cultural system of racial segregation. In this case we are examining influences of the local situation in Oklahoma City, Oklahoma—another type of border circumstances. As discussed in Chapter 3, Oklahoma had its own unique system of racial practices patterned after the hegemony of Southern white supremacy tempered by frontier rugged individualism. Even though Oklahoma's Jim Crow is characterized as the most hegemonic of the border states, on closer scrutiny its color line, like Kansas's, was more permeable than first realized. Like Topeka, there were no formal segregation laws in Oklahoma City. Instead, trespass laws were used to enforce segregation and by the 1950s these now *de facto* racial practices were entrenched through social interaction. However, the boundaries of the vertical racial segregation (Graves 1981) in Oklahoma City were redrawn horizontally as African Americans sought to sit down and be served.

Racial Segregation in 1950s Oklahoma City

By the middle of the twentieth century, the segregationist practices in the community of Oklahoma City visibly resembled many Southern cities: blacks were thoroughly segregated in housing, employment, and education (Saxe 1969, 3). But there were cracks forming along the color line in a similar manner found in other border states: segregation was sustained more by social convention than by ideology. Like other border states, Oklahoma's economy never rested on the foundations of slave labor, and so its principles of racial inferiority were not simply a codification of preexisting social norms. At the time of statehood in 1907, there was a national trend toward codification and uniform enforcement of segregation laws (Meier and Rudwick 1969, 758). Though Oklahoma's constitution "rivaled any of the southern states" for its strict separation of the races (Saxe 1969, 16), it was written during a time of a tightening, nationally, of racial boundaries.

The Oklahoma Constitution even defined as "colored . . . all persons of African descent who possess *any* quantum of Negro blood" (18; italics not in original). There were civil and criminal penalties for school administrators who mixed the races in its public schools, a miscegenation law forbidding mixed race marriages, and statues stipulating separate railroad cars (17–18). Oklahoma even determined that the races use separate phone booths (18).

Given these unambiguous segregation statues mirroring those found throughout the southern region, one would assume challenges to segregation would be met with similar hostility. However, as the major thrust of this chapter demonstrates, civility and not incivility would characterize challenges to segregation in Oklahoma City. In his book on the civil rights movement in Greensboro, North Carolina, historian William Chafé (1983) defines civility as "the cornerstone of North Carolina's progressive mystique, signifying courtesy, concern about an associate's family, children, and health, as well as a personal grace that smoothes conflict with strangers and obscures conflict with foes." Civility was what white progressivism was all about—a way of dealing with people and problems that made good manners more important than substantial action. Significantly, civility encompassed all of the other themes of the progressive mystique.

Graves (1981, 162) argues that a border state civility is reflected in how the Oklahoma City sit-ins "dramatized" the "undemocratic nature" of racial segregation. The direct-action campaigns were preceded by negotiations "before resorting to sit-ins." Oklahoma's "progressive mystique," what Chafé (1983) typifies as "abhorrence of personal conflict, courtesy toward new ideas, and a generosity toward those less fortunate than oneself" is illustrated by the way in which the white press would expose uncivil behavior toward African Americans. Oklahoma City's morning and evening newspapers, the *Daily Oklahoman* and *Oklahoma City Times* were both owned by the Oklahoma Publishing Company, also had controlling interests in the city's major television and radio stations and owned an important trucking company and several other specialized publications, including the monthly *Farmer-Stockman,* which had a significant readership (Saxe 1969, 38–39).

Though politically conservative and never an outspoken advocate of racial equality, the *Daily Oklahoman* did indirectly champion racial equality by "speak[ing] out against the Klan when it was most active in the 1920s and 1930s (38–39). A survey of editorials in these newspapers revealed that between 1921 and 1930 there were more than eight hundred news items about the Klan's activities in Oklahoma. These virulent attacks gradually led to the political demise of many politicians who openly associated with the Klan. Just as in Topeka during the *Brown* case, white elites were able to bring about reforms by using the "undemocratic nature" of racial issues to point toward other undemocratic activities and organizations. Forty years later, the Oklahoma City sit-ins facilitated the coalescence of elites in challenging the city's one-party dominance and its maintenance of control through the ward-style political system (Saxe).

As discussed earlier in this chapter, rising expectations during and after World War II influenced how blacks began to redefine their role in American society. In Oklahoma City, U.S. defense installations created a steady demand for labor between 1940 and 1954 (69). Like other states in the region, Oklahoma experienced a steady urbanization of its black population during this time period, though its total black population remained stable: 19,709 in 1940 and 22,665 in 1950.[6] Because the inflow of migrants into Oklahoma City was matched by an outflow to northern and western states, the black residential areas were not unduly congested (66–67). The ability to find adequate housing was also aided somewhat by the Supreme Court's formal removal of restrictive covenants in 1948[7] and the intervention of white homeowners—primarily Jewish—who publicized racist practices of local property developers in the local newspaper.

Though the Oklahoma City School Board had officially desegregated all public schools by 1955, this action did not provide equal access to public accommodations (16–19, 49, 162). This restriction on individual freedom despite school desegregation was noticed particularly by the city's NAACP youth council and its adult advisor, Clara Luper (Reese 2003). Luper taught history at Dunjee High School in Spencer and was active in the Fifth Street Baptist Church. Her initial efforts to challenge segregation began when she reorganized the Oklahoma City NAACP Youth Council in January 1957, and by May of that same year she organized a letter-writing campaign to area churches requesting them to begin a dialogue about integration. The white churches ignored her request. On the other side of the color line, African American churches declined to be "officially" involved in desegregation challenges but, nevertheless, offered to quietly provide indirect support. Luper recalls that they let her use their church facilities for meetings, took up collections to finance her cause, and made announcements about her activities from their pulpits to interested parishioners (Luper 1979, 3–4).

After "wait[ing] for fifteen months between deciding to desegregate and actually protesting," Luper and the NAACP Youth Council finally took action on August 19, 1958 (4). The participants ranged in age from seven to fifteen years old. The initial target was Katz Drug Store in downtown Oklahoma City. Luper's eight-year-old daughter, Marilyn, suggested "they just sit somewhere until they were served" (DeFrange 1998, 8). In the weeks to come, Luper's efforts were focused on coordinating sit-ins at other lunch counters in the downtown area (1979, 14). She organized rides downtown for demonstrators, recruited participants, and was herself arrested twenty-six times (DeFrange 1998, 8): "I knew I was right because somewhere I read in the 14th Amendment, that I was a citizen and I had rights, and I had the right to eat."

Luper later recalled that as early as 1957 she was laying the groundwork to directly confront segregation by organizing sit-ins, even seeking the help of national leader Reverend James Lawson to train her group on how to properly conduct sit-ins (Morris 1984, 125). However, Luper's initiative did not receive much encouragement from the national NAACP organization, as Lawson later recalled, "[t]he NAACP opposed [sit-ins]. The parent body, the branch body, chastised the school teacher [Luper] who was responsible for it, chastised them, told them to desist" (Morris 1984, 125).

Even though the sit-ins resulted in Katz Drug Store desegregating its thirty-eight outlets in Missouri, Oklahoma, Kansas, and Iowa over the next few weeks, the sit-in movement met with mixed results and would stop and start up again for the next several years. Finally, on June 2, 1964, the Oklahoma City city council finally passed a public accommodation ordinance prohibiting segregation in public restaurants (Luper 1979, 284). Luper's tireless efforts to challenge segregation did not cease with the successful resolution of the sit-in protests. She worked toward the recognition of a Fair Housing Ordinance, better working conditions for sanitation workers—including assisting them in organizing a strike in August 1969—and the establishment of the Freedom Center in 1968.

Luper's informal leadership practices and individual activism are evidenced through her continual, singular attempts to meet with local business leaders as well as recruiting the help of sympathetic whites. For example, in 1961 a group of white women conducted their own sit-in at John A. Brown's, a local department store in downtown Oklahoma City, largely through the behind-the-scenes efforts of Luper (46). Like their African American counterparts involved in early civil rights activism in turn-of-the-century Guthrie, Oklahoma (Chapter 4), white women engaged in less visible or "low-risk activism" (Irons 1998, 692). This type of activism involved such activities as letter writing campaigns and making telephone calls rather than direct confrontations. Though they acknowledged the injustice of racial segregation, their activism was carried out within their circumscribed roles as wives, mothers, and community volunteers. They were less publicly associated with the sit-ins and preferred less visible roles. "The sit-in movement involved more than the people . . . [white and black] . . . who went downtown" (DeFrange 1998).

Working indirectly through the NAACP Youth Council, Luper managed to change the structure of Oklahoma City's race relations. Even though her efforts took more than ten years to be fully realized, Luper's persistence and dedication to desegregation was a higher priority than any one organization. Though she sometimes worked within the confines of formal organizations such as the NAACP, she just as readily worked outside those institutional boundaries to effect change.

Conclusion: Master Narrative and Border Campaign Analyses of Social Movements

The Master Narrative's analysis of the sit-in movement after February 1, 1960, emphasizes the importance of organizationally affiliated leadership. The importance attributed to formal organization stems from the success of the Student Nonviolent Coordinating Committee (SNCC)—founded in April 1960, in Raleigh, North Carolina—and the ongoing influence of the Congress of Racial Equality (CORE) in recruiting participants to undertake nonviolent protests against segregated lunch counters. College students, who were undoubtedly crucial as participants, are also assumed to have provided the "necessary" leadership for these sit-ins. Oberschall's (1989, 39) "diffusion of protest" model explaining the emergence of the 1960s sit-ins assumes congruence between leadership and organization. At some point, Oberschall (39) thinks it is "necessary" that the protest group "surrender" to a "leadership group that invests them in organization." When the sit-ins occurred in Oklahoma City in 1958, the SNCC did not yet exist. The primary organizational vehicle was the NAACP Youth Council, which consisted of a subgroup that was attached to the local NAACP branch comprised of high school students (Walters 1996). Ronald Walters, a student who participated in early sit-ins in nearby Wichita, Kansas, around the same time (in 1959) points out that the sit-ins were planned without leadership or organizational support. Walters (21) recalled, "Our confidence was devoid of both the deep religious basis of the Southern Movement and the presence of a charismatic leader. Our effort also lacked external support."

The Oklahoma City sit-ins, while not as dramatic as the more numerous ones that occurred later across the South from 1960 to 1963, are significant because they were organized and sustained without the assistance of any formal organization and leader. Luper's efforts were assisted indirectly by black churches and concerned citizens, those institutions and persons "who were uncomfortable with any public display."

Oberschall (1989, 39) conceptualizes organization "as a continuum from absence of organization, through loose structure, all the way to tight structure." He disagrees with Morris (1984) over categorizing organizational characteristics into either "a loose structure" or "tight structure." Another conceptualization of organization is suggested by Robert White (1964) in his study of how CORE organized sit-ins in Tallahassee, Florida. White argues that CORE was not only the "primary organization vehicle" in the local movement, but it brought with it twenty-two years of experience in nonviolent tactics (77).

Formal organizations—indigenous, local, or national—were less important in the early challenges to segregation prior to the mass mobilization era. Individuals who were loosely or not at all affiliated with an organization made significant contributions to the campaigns in several instances. As similar to what happened in Oklahoma City, the students enlisted the advice of civil rights attorneys (Luper 1979, 33), but acted outside the bounds of any formal organizational capacity or the direction of formal leadership. The participants and their families all lived and worked in the community.

On the other hand, college students involved in the more famous Greensboro sit-ins were likely to be temporary residents and not have economic and social ties to the community (Oberschall 1989). In the post-1960 sit-ins, the sojourner status of college students has been one explanation for their willingness to participate in direct action (Oberschall 1989). This analysis is not adequate for the Oklahoma City and, later, Wichita sit-ins, although the sit-ins seem similar due to their relative absence of organizational control. Though the sit-ins were not particularly violent in these Midwestern cities, they did involve bold challenges to the color line using civil disobedience tactics. As these sit-ins and the school segregation actions undertaken in Merriam and Topeka demonstrate, antisegregation protest is more diversified than has been described in the literature, which concentrates on mass movements in the South. One purpose of studying obscure campaigns such as those in Merriam and Topeka is to move toward a more heterogeneous sociological framework to better understand these early desegregation efforts.

Comparing the Master Narrative and Border Campaign helps focus on how the disparate actions of individuals coalesce into collective action. Clara Luper illustrates the activism of someone who had to contend with a lack of credibility from not only critics outside the civil rights movement but also from within the accepted leadership channels of the NAACP's organizational structure. Luper's coordination of the sit-ins flouts gendered understandings of leadership in both the black and white communities; she also marshals very young children into activism.

This approach suggests that the women described in these cases did not suddenly *decide* to become activists. Their actions were also not simply an outgrowth of sporadic desegregation efforts conducted by African Americans dating back several years. The characteristics of the antisegregation protest described in these communities were due in part to the forms that activism took in relationship to changing contemporaneous local social conditions and opportunities. The Merriam, Kansas, case was overshadowed by events in nearby Topeka, while the local activism in Topeka has been overshadowed by the 1954 court case decided by the U.S. Supreme Court now called *Brown v. Board of Education of Topeka*. This landmark decision is often associated with the civil rights activism that followed in the 1950s and 1960s. The sit-ins in Oklahoma City in 1958–1959 were overshadowed by the events of February 1, 1960, in Greensbor, North Carolina, and the formation of the Student Nonviolent Coordination Committee in April that same year. When Barbara Posey entered Katz Drugstore in downtown Oklahoma City in August 1958, the SNCC did not yet exist. However, individual activists such as Clara Luper (1979) in Oklahoma City, through loose affiliations with the NAACP Youth Council, organized successful sit-ins in this community.

Leadership in the Master Narrative obscures the actions of those who participated in protest but could not be characterized as leaders in the traditional sense, even though they were important to successful protest outcomes. For example, the Oklahoma sit-ins emerged without a formal organizational structure to sustain enough interest to promote mass participation. These sit-ins were undertaken without the benefit of earlier successful demonstrations, providing positive opportunities for later ones, as was the case with Baton Rouge "helping" Montgomery (Morris 1984). The student sit-in movement of the early 1960s, which did succeed in creating a formal organization—the SNCC—has obscured these early sit-ins.

The early civil rights episodes discussed in this chapter differ from the later mass mobilization era since they concerned different issues, attacked with contrasting tactics, and were from different community locations. The protest was sometimes carried forward and sustained by informal leaders and individual activists, primarily women, whose important, but sometimes discontinuous trails of activism can be uncovered only by examining the local context of early civil rights episodes. Their actions are obscured when civil rights activism is examined as a large structural framework. The significance of individual activism and informal leadership is related to its effect, rather than its substance. However, people like Clara Luper and Esther Brown were crucial links in sustaining activism that cannot be completely captured by categories of gender status and formal leadership alone.

Notes

1. Such as the June 1953 Baton Rouge, Louisiana, Bus Boycott, which preceded both *Brown* (1954) and the Montgomery Boycott (Meier and Rudwick 1976, 365–66).

2. For a complete discussion of the Wichita, Kansas, sit-ins, see Gretchen C. Eick, *Dissent in Wichita: The Civil Rights Movement in the Midwest, 1954–1972* (Urbana: University of Illinois Press, 2001). This book offers some interesting data on the Wichita sit-ins. Like Oklahoma, students were an important resource during the sit-ins.

3. Morris (1984) argues that the Greensboro sit-ins are more significant because they set off "sit-ins across the South at an incredible pace" (751).

4. *Plessy v. Ferguson* (1890).

5. This alternative avenue to leadership was largely closed to women in SCLC, which was dominated by male clergy whose authority was additionally reinforced by biblical scripture (i.e., Ella Baker's later defection to SNCC).

6. U.S. Census of the Population: 1950, Vol. II, Part 36, Oklahoma Chapter B.

7. *Shelley v. Kraemer* (1948).

Lunch counter sit-in at Katz Drug Store, August 26, 1958, in Oklahoma City. Clara Luper and the NAACP Youth Council organized sit-ins with young children (courtesy of the Oklahoma State Historical Society).

PART III

Implications for the Analysis of Social Movements

Lunch counter sit-in on August 27, 1958, at John A. Brown's, a department store in downtown Oklahoma City (courtesy of the Oklahoma State Historical Society).

7

Current Debates in Theories of Social Movements

This chapter draws on Weber's notion of value-rational action to further conceptualize the way individuals become involved in social movements. Although this process is acknowledged as central to the study of social movements, understanding of the individual level of participation is fragmented. As the previous chapters suggest, it is more appropriate to reframe these segments in terms of the intersection of private troubles and public issues (Mills 1959). Building on discussions from previous chapters, this chapter illustrates how present formulations of the individual/structural level dichotomy are not in explicit dialogue with the theories—or with each other. Second, it allows us to take a fresh perspective on current controversies in the field by drawing specifically on Blumer's (1986) concept that "joint action" to capture separate lines of individual action can coalesce, eventually merging into longer "strips of action" (Goffman 1956). This approach complicates notions of agency and identity while offering more specificity about how these processes operate within social movements.

Race and the Sociological Imagination

In his 1963 presidential address to the American Sociological Association, President Everett C. Hughes pondered what was new to say about race relations and what could be learned from studying them (Hughes 1963, 879). Hughes's remarks were delivered during a year of escalating racial violence, starting with the mass mobilization in Birmingham in April, the march on Washington, DC, in August, and the deadly bombing of the Sixteenth Street Baptist Church in Birmingham, Alabama, in September, which resulted in the killing of four innocent children. What troubled Hughes was the failure of social scientists—and sociologists in particular—to "not foresee the explosion of collective action" that erupted seemingly without warning in the late 1950s and early 1960s (879). In his search for answers to the current race problem, Hughes urged sociologists to invoke their sociological imaginations by being more attentive to what was happening in the world around them, to not isolate and define things like race relations as a "peculiar problem" affecting only African Americans. Rather, he thought it important to explore a multiplicity of casual factors in the broader society itself, from both sides of the color line. By just focusing on those causing the racial unrest, Hughes argued that sociologists would lose sight of the broader social processes involved in how some disaffected individuals are able to make their grievances heard whiles others are not, as had been the case with the civil rights movement. Why *are* some individuals able to articulate their dissatisfaction with the status quo? In Hughes's judgment this question could only be adequately answered through activation of their sociological imaginations, defined by C. Wright Mills as being able "to understand the larger historical scene in terms of its meaning for the inner life and the external career of a variety of individuals," thus enabling them to grasp how "the personal uneasiness of individuals is focused upon explicit troubles and the indifference of publics is transformed into involvement with pubic issues" (Mills 1959, 5).

"The Personal Is Political"

How do personal troubles become public issues? Though Mills was asking this as a general question, one way to study this problem is to consider how individuals come to act as agents in collective action and social movements. As a scholar of the civil rights movement, I am interested in understanding how individual actors become involved in collective action. In the course of personal interviews with people supporting and opposing school desegregation in Topeka, Kansas (Chapters Four and Five), it became obvious that their agency was not easily explained using the existing literature. In social movements literature, the issue of agency has been shunted to the side in favor of studying structural and organizational processes as expressed in the resource mobilization and political process models. Many theorists prioritize structures of power, economics, formal organizations, and social networks. This approach has dominated social movement theory for the past several decades (most notably McAdam 1982; McCarthy and Zald 1977; Meyer 1993; Staggenborg 1991; Tarrow 1983; and Tilly 1978, 1995).

Recently, scholars have become interested in learning more about how "individual social psychological processes" are related "to collective processes" (Johnston and Klandermans 1996, 11), by considering how culture—ideas, ideology, language—figures in mobilizations in addition to structural issues. Interest in culture has led scholars to draw from the vocabulary of symbolic interactionism, focusing on "identities, meanings, and emotions" (Kurzmann 1996; Morris 1984; Polletta 1997; Snow and Benford 1992). Goffman (1974) is particularly important since his idea of "framing" is frequently used as a way to focus on human agency and interpretation (e.g., Snow and Benford 1992), which has increased our understanding of motivations for mobilization, that is, injustice, agency, and identity.

However, one shortcoming of the framing perspective, much like resource mobilization approaches its critiques, is that the question of culture is usually considered from a "traditional social movement" perspective or factors located within social movements (i.e., movement-centric) rather than including a contextual understanding of the broader society (Williams 2004, 94-95).

Beginning with the broader conceptualization of culture discussed in Chapter Five, I propose to better understand how personal troubles become public issues resulting in collective action and/or social movements. How can linkages of agency and structure in social movements be better understood through the insertion of culture? Why is culture another important domain of society to be considered in conjunction with other social structures arising from political and economic institutions when studying social movements?

As discussed in Chapter Five, the inclusion of "culture" is an important dimension of current social movement research and reflects the overall "cultural turn" sociology took in the United States beginning in the 1980s (91). The interest in culture is also reflected in the emergence of the "new social movement" approach of the mid-1980s that focused on such cultural issues as identity and initially seemed a promising way to consider the role of agency in collective action. The interest in incorporating culture into the study of social movements was partially a response to the emergence and dominance of "new" social movements that focused on moral issues—such as the Greens in Europe—replacing "old" labor and civil rights movements whose aims were primarily material interests associated with changing political and economic institutions.

Culture and Social Movements

The inclusion of "culture" is an important dimension of current social movement research and reflects the overall "cultural turn" sociology took in the United States, beginning in the 1980s (91). The interest in culture is also reflected in the emergence of the "new social movement" approach in the mid-1980s that focused on such cultural issues as identity and initially seemed a promising way to consider the role of agency in collective action. The interest in incorporating culture into the study of social movements was partially a response to the emergence and dominance of "new" social movements that focused on moral issues—such as the Greens in Europe—replacing "old" labor and civil rights movements whose aims were primarily material interests associated with changing political and economic institutions. In the United States, as Williams points out, social movement scholars "focused on the ways in which movements have used symbols, language, discourse, identity, and other dimensions of culture to recruit, retain, mobilize, and motivate members" (93).

Williams argues for two analytical shifts to begin studying movements as (1) part of "a larger cultural array in which the movement is but one set of actors or meaning-systems"; and (2) to focus on other meaning systems such as symbols, languages, and rituals instead of mainly privileging political and economic ones. In this way the contributions of individuals are counted as well as larger-scale structural changes and modifications. Williams proposes a better way to understand social movements by delineating how the boundaries of "available cultural repertories" resonate with "existing rhetoric or framings" such as the rights of individuals or "individual rights" (used by the pro-choice movement, gays, and lesbian); "individual duties" or the primacy of the public good over individual claims; and "collective duties" as found in environmental movements. Though Williams is sensitive to the importance of ideas, language, and discourse to social movements, his notion of the "cultural environment" still does not overcome the agency/structure dichotomy, since it emphasizes the importance of external factors (cultural systems of ideology). His argument goes a long way toward fleshing out the role of culture in social structure, but it does not really help us understand how individual agency converts private problems into public issues in some cases but not in others.

Goodwin and Jasper (2004) argue that the best way to resolve the divisions between agency and structure is to merge cultural/constructionist concepts into structural explanations. Such a move would also bring in the relevance of emotions along with agency and culture to the study of social movements. But this approach does not eliminate the central problem of the political process model, which synthesizes theory directed toward an abstract universality, often overlooking the significance of unique or unusual events. But emphasis on the cultural aspects of social movements runs the risk of prioritizing the cultural context over structure. So how can social movement scholars ever hope to overcome this dualism?

Agency, Structure, and Social Theory

In writing generally about the problem of delineating agency in social theory, Margaret Archer (1996, xv) argues that existing structural and cultural models conflate agency by "elid[ing] the 'parts' and the 'people.'" Archer also argues that when these two levels of analysis are conflated it "withdraws any autonomy or independence from one of them, if not from both." We are left then with either monolithic configuration of social structure and culture that are "simply formed and transformed by some untrammeled dominant group . . . placed at the mercy of capricious renegotiation by unconstrained agency" or agents are simply reduced to oversocialized individuals.

Archer also rejects conceptualizing agency and structure as being tightly constitutive—the fallacy of the "central conflation"—and proposes instead to focus on the "interplay" between agency and structure. In this way, agency or the properties of interaction are kept analytically separate from the properties of structure. Archer terms this approach as analytical dualism, not to be confused with "philosophical dualism," which refers to separate entities. Instead, analytical dualism deals with only "analytically separable ones and ones which it is theoretically useful to treat separately" (xiv–xvi). Assuming that neither agency nor structure is totally coherent or conflictual, this approach emphasizes where they intersect, their interplay, in terms of beginning to distinguish "the orderly or conflictual relations pertaining between groups of actors (the degree of social interaction), from the orderly or contradictory relations prevailing between parts of the social structure (the degree of system integration)" (xvi). In this way, there is a distinction made between the logical consistency, or ideas, of a cultural system and the causal consensus, or influence, of ideas on people (socio-cultural interaction).

By focusing on the interplay between agency and structure, without conflating them to the top, bottom, or middle, we can begin to unravel which systemic relations impinge upon agency (socio-cultural interaction) as well as which social relations affect how agents might respond to and react back on the cultural system. Analysis of agency leading to collective action can begin by "examining the effects of holding ideas with particular logical relations (of contradiction or complementary to others)—not with the (socio-cultural) reasons for these being held" (xxii).

For example, the civil rights movement was a social movement that challenged racial segregation. In the literature on the civil rights movement, racial segregation is conceived as a coherent pattern of social interaction denying its complexity as a cultural system of beliefs, ideology, norms, and language; it lumps people as a homogenous whole lacking individual agency. However, in border states like Kansas, racial segregation was limited to elementary schools in four cities. As a cultural system, segregation was diffused and did not permeate the race relations as it did in the Deep South. Challenges to segregation are better understood by not concentrating solely on the structure of social action relationships as they coalesce in terms of institutions (organizations) and groups. One way to consider this is to draw on Blumer's concept of "joint action" to better capture how separate lines of action can coalesce, merging into "strips of action" (Goffman). This works to sensitize us to how "individuals may orient their action on different premises," leaving open the possibility that even commonly defined joint actions can lead to a variety of courses or outcomes.

By conceptualizing the ways in which individuals join others to formulate collective action as dynamic rather than static, we arrive at the definition of group actions as being created through the process of the building up of joint actions or strips of action. Thus, there are potentially a vast number of individual social actions occurring at any given moment that might coalesce into collective action, eventually formulating a social movement. However, it is also important to be sensitive to how social action has an historical dimension or career limited by its ability to resonate with the existing cultural system at any given moment.

Preexisting Protest Traditions

Civil rights activism has numerous manifestations throughout the United States prior to *Brown* in 1954. Preexisting protest traditions include boycotts against Jim Crow streetcars between 1900 and 1906 (Barnes 1983; Meier and Rudwick 1976). Between 1929 and 1941, northern African Americans organized "don't buy where you can't work" campaigns, boycotting white restaurants, grocery stores, clothing stores, and other stores that refused to hire blacks. Mass-based protest tactics included the mass march planned for Washington, DC, in 1941 (the March on Washington Movement); lunch counter sit-ins staged by CORE (Congress of Racial Equality, which emerged from the earlier FOR—For Racial Equality) that same year in Chicago; and the first Freedom Ride in 1947 (Blumberg 1984, 1–36; Dalifume 1968; Meier 1963; Meier and Rudwick 1969; Patterson 2001, 1–8).

In the early twentieth century, racial inequality was more likely to be addressed through organizations, such as women's benevolence associations as discussed in Chapter Three. The first national organization targeting racial equality—the National Association for the Advancement of Colored People—was organized in 1909-1910. The emergence of a black protest literature emerged with the Harlem Renaissance of the 1920s.

These earlier manifestations of protest point to the presence of black resistance and an insurgent ideology long before the 1950s. Documents about the continuity of black protest in the nineteenth century include Harding's (1981) study of protests and insurrections initiated during slavery and Frederickson's (1995) contribution to our understanding of radical liberation ideologies and their historical role in black protest traditions. Since we are concerned with early civil rights protest in the decades preceding *Brown,* we leave to others the linking of these earlier slave insurrections and our understanding the complex rule of black liberation ideology in civil rights activism.

As discussed in previous chapters, recent scholarship on the origins of the civil rights movement provides insights into how national organizations brought change into local communities (Lawson 1991). Writers such as McAdam (1982) and Tarrow (1994) emphasize the structural prerequisites to civil rights protest, focusing on the importance of the development of an internal political opportunity structure in the early twentieth century brought about by the mass migration of blacks to the northern cities and the emerging political power of the Northern black vote. In particular, McAdam argues that these political opportunities permitted the groundwork for the new national political insurgency that was to follow in the 1950s and 1960s. An important external political opportunity structure and is related to America's role in Cold War politics emphasizing freedom and democracy; this pressured Americans to reevaluate their own racial practices within their own borders.

Because the Master Narrative uses watershed moments, or Big Events, to demarcate the modern civil rights movement from its antecedents, it tends to overlook the local context. One concern here is how local contexts are an important way to study the "internal processes of social movements" and "decisive shapers of reform" (Carson 1986, 19-20). Also problematic is the "view of activists only as harbingers of change—colorful, politically impotent, socially isolated idealists and malcontents who play only fleeting roles in the drama of American political history" (29-30).

This book has focused on local initiatives in areas not in the South. Though Morris (1984, xi) acknowledges the importance of a "preexisting protest tradition," in arguing that the "demands of the black masses" changed the nature of black protest to direct action, he leaves unanswered certain questions about how these demands come about in the first place. What factors contributed to the appearance of direct action protest associated with the modern civil rights movement? By focusing on the public aspects of the protests in Baton Rouge, Louisiana (1953), and Montgomery, Alabama (1955), Morris prioritizes the sudden appearance of mass mobilizations as being characteristic of civil rights protest. His discussion of pre-*Brown* (1954) civil rights protest is examined with post-*Brown* civil rights protest in mind. If there were not dramatic mass marches and boycotts, then it was not "civil rights" protest; it was coded as something else if it was noticed at all.

Turner and Killian (1972, 289) argue that without the use and cultivation of power to influence persons and institutions outside a social movement, it is impossible to bring about social change. Since having the adequate power to carry out civil rights protest varies according to the situation (historical and/or geographical), it is easy to overlook failed attempts or ones that utilize diverse tactics.

The Historical Situation

The Border Campaign demonstrates how useful it is to focus on how people in specific historical situations attempt to cultivate power through the selection of "the strategies for the exercise of the power at its disposal" (289). The historical situation is also important because it helps us understand how a group selects its "main power objective" and its "strategies" of protest. In the Midwest, many times groups favored strategies aimed at improving the immediate situation, such as strengthening segregated institutions. When viewed in terms of the Master Narrative, they appear to be aimed toward maintaining the racial status quo rather than practical strategies designed to deal with the situation at hand. The later mass mobilization era of the civil rights movement was able to displace the significance of these types of strategies with ones that sought change. The literature on the civil rights movement has emphasized the importance of the cultivation and use of power, causing its values to be overlooked or forgotten. In episodes of forgotten civil rights activism, values are important to understanding the principal strategies in the exercise of power.

In order to appreciate the heterogeneity of forgotten civil rights protest, and the agency embedded in it, it is also important to distinguish between organizational structures and social actions. As Lofland (1996, 9) points out, it is easy to "conflate aspects of organizations and their resources with aspects of forms of *action*." By distinguishing between *organizations* and *actions* in terms of their bargaining tactics, we conceive of a protest continuum ranging from polite persuasion to violent disruptions. This distinction between different dimensions of collective behavior in forgotten civil rights protest brings to light the relevance of loosening the coupling of organization and action as suggested by Lofland (258). This gives us a clearer conception of what is involved, by contrast, in the tight coupling of organizational form and action predominant in the mass mobilizations in Montgomery and Birmingham.

The Border Campaign focuses on the polite/persuasion end of the continuum as being more characteristic of forgotten civil rights protest before the 1954 *Brown* decision. Given the dominance of racial segregation, either *de jure* or *de facto,* it is not surprising that the tactics of polite/persuasion were more likely to be used; further, this type of civil rights protest can be distinguished from the mass mobilizations type of civil rights protest more likely to incorporate some form of violence, characteristic after there was no longer a legal sanction for segregation after 1955.

As the civil rights movement matured after 1960, there was a shift in how the authorities define protest, choosing to define public gatherings as needing intervention, that is, needing to be stopped or interfered with. For example, at the first sit-in staged in 1958 in Wichita, Kansas, participant Ronald Walters remembered that when the police arrived "they looked around, and an officer said, 'I don't see any disturbance taking place'" (1993, 22). The Wichita sit-ins, like the ones in Oklahoma City, were carried out within the parameters of the border state ideal of consensus and cohesiveness consistent with America's broad democratic values. This definition of the situation would change rapidly as civil rights activism became more radical, particularly by the time sit-ins were staged in the early 1960s.

Lofland reminds us it is "important to "sharpen our perception of some basic units of human association or organization, irrespective of their relevance to collective behavior." Turning to Goffman, we can break this down even further, to understand better the dramaturgical implications of early civil rights protest by studying segregation as an interaction order or a type of organizational behavior. Due to the lack of institutional and structural resources provided in mass mobilizations, it is important to look at the structure of social interactions and how segregation was organizationally, structurally, and socially sustained in order to fully understand how it all became unraveled. Although studies of the mass mobilization era provide us with a wide variety of empirical evidence to study the dynamics and strategies or protest, it does not help us understand this earlier period—because we need to shift focus to the structure of maintenance rather than the structure of change. Political opportunities and local movement center models only provide a partial picture of how this change came about.

The types of civil rights protest that African Americans participated in the 1880s was very different from that of the 1950s. In the 1880s, particularly in Topeka, Kansas, African Americans were protesting the lack of local control over their segregated schools and demanded that teachers of their own race be hired instead of whites (see Chapter Two).

In the 1950s, African Americans were challenging the entire institution of school segregation (see Chapter Five). Though the actions in the 1880s and the 1950s were fundamentally different, since one reinforced segregated schools and the other was a direct challenge to it, both types of actions qualify as "protest." By focusing on the material goal of desegregation, sociologists have studied the civil rights movement by its outcomes rather than its motivating factors. Since the outcome of protest in the nineteenth century reinforced segregation, the significance of such actions has been overlooked in the overall historical understanding of the civil rights movement, which resulted in desegregation.

By analyzing collective action in relationship to its historical context and not exclusively by its goals discloses something previously unknown about the role of agency in civil rights protest, as well as protest in general. Outcomes change and are specifically related to local and historical contexts. By generalizing the outcomes, sociologists have limited their understanding of the origins of the civil rights movement to those collective actions specifically directed against segregation.

Using a continuum, the principal strategies used in the exercise of power are "persuasion, bargaining and coercion" (Turner and Killian 1972, 291). These different types of strategies "are distinguished by the manner in which the movement attempts to influence the actions of the target group." Though there is overlap between these different types, in forgotten civil rights activism, its value orientation toward racial exclusion drives its power orientation toward "persuasion." Turner and Killian define persuasion as "the use of strictly symbolic manipulation without substantial rewards or punishments under the control of the movement. The basic procedure of persuasion is to identify the proposed course of action with values held by the target group" (292). If the target groups' dominant values are racial separation, rather than racial equality, it is easy to see why they are now forgotten. But what about the time and place when this decision was made? Did it make more sense to select tactics aimed at modifications to segregation rather than its abolishment?

Civil Rights Leadership and Collective Action

In previous chapters on how individuals became involved in civil rights struggles, it was found that prevailing theories of leadership did not always adequately explain the ways in which civil rights collective action developed in the Midwest. According to the Master Narrative of the civil rights movement, the Southern mass mobilizations of the late 1950s and early 1960s were orchestrated by charismatic leaders such as the Reverend Martin Luther King, Jr., and sustained by formal organizations such as the Southern Leadership Conference (SLC). The Master Narrative does not provide an adequate benchmark to measure the actions and tactics utilized in places like Topeka, Kansas, or Guthrie, Oklahoma (Chapter Three). These civil rights struggles employed a heterogeneous type of collective action, one that often used nonpolitical, informal leadership and activism. Briefly defined, nonpolitical informal leadership and activism is conceptualized as not being closely associated with formal organizations and/or group protests.

The actions of the nonpolitical, informal leaders and activists discussed in this book undertook private negotiations rather than public ones and engaged in smaller protests rather than mass mobilizations. Their actions were much more diffuse and private. The absence of stringent Jim Crow laws made it difficult to organize public tactics (mass mobilizations) in 1940s Kansas and turn-of-the-century Oklahoma. A more contemporary example of this type of protest emerged recently among antiabortion activists in Wichita, Kansas, after the morning-after pill was approved: public protests in front of abortion clinics were no longer as effective. Women now had more private avenues to secure an abortion and no longer needed to submit to the public humiliation of having to walk into an abortion clinic.[1] The lack of a collective target meant that antiabortion activists now had a wider array of potential objectives including pharmacies, pharmaceutical companies, and numerous physicians. The public face of protests in front of abortion clinics had been replaced by the many private spaces now available to quietly secure an abortion. Similarly, the absence of pervasive Jim Crow laws limited the size and scope of any given protest in border states.

As a way to capture the more diffuse tactics of individuals and the smaller scale of the protests in the Midwest, the Border Campaign uses the concept "career activist" to include leadership characteristics without claiming to be exclusively related to leadership (Van Delinder 1996). It captures the heterogeneous actions and contributions of informal leadership and individual activism that is overlooked by the Master Narrative. It is based on Weber's typology of value-rational action and includes actions of individuals who act without any formal organizational affiliation. Their agency is guided through the rationality of their values or commitment to an ideal, such as social justice or civil rights.

The concept "career activist," introduced in Chapter Four, also helps to explain the type of collective action that is sustained more by individual interventions than the exclusive resources of a formal organization or leader. A career activist tends to be a self-starter whose initial participation in a protest is based on an internal value-rational commitment rather than commitment to an organization, which can also be characterized as nonorganizational actions. A career activist is a person who exhibits leadership qualities in trying to address immediate problems rather than attempting to change the entire system. It was this value-rational commitment rather than formal leadership or organizational affiliation that brought several individuals into protest and subsequent leadership-like roles in the early civil rights movement. In some cases, formal leadership in an organization sustained their activism once the issues that created the protest were resolved. Other times, if they became organizationally affiliated, their activism tended not to be confined to what was officially sanctioned by the protest organization.

A career activist can also function as an intermediary leader, which helps to explain how leadership can vary in relationship to the social context of the action. The early civil rights movement in the United States was led by individuals who could not be characterized as leaders in the traditional sense but made significant contributions to successful protest episodes. These career activists represent a wide spectrum of race, class, and gender, thus focusing on the problem of how difficult it is to distinguish between a person's biography and their leadership roles.

In general, career activists provide a way to better understand the interplay between agency and structure in social movements. As discussed previously, the framing model does focus on human agency by asking how "individual social psychological processes" are linked "to collective processes" (Johnston and Klandermans 1996, 11). Though this approach has increased our understanding of identities and has drawn people to social movements, this perspective still conflates agency and structure by either prioritizing one over the other, instead of examining how they interact. The fallacy of conflation is less likely to occur if attention is focused on the intersection between the social interactions between and in groups of actors (the degree of social interaction) rather than dichotomizing them as either individual or collective (Archer 1996). In addition, Archer also suggests that it is important to consider how these social interactions are shaped by the broad range of ideas, beliefs, and values embedded in any given cultural system (1996). Instead of collapsing agency into structure, this approach broadens our conceptualization of agency to include a multiplicity of actions, individual and collective, that are shaped by the predominate configuration of any given cultural system. In this way, actions that fall in between these two levels, that is, career activists, are not swept into a single category: they stand on their own.

As discussed above, in social movements there are people who will continually move in and out of institutional community structures; their actions, though not completely ignored, are often oversimplified or even discounted as significant.

Postmodern Social Action and the Case of the Career Activist

New social movement literature argues that it breaks new ground in discussing "postmaterial values" by separating movement objectives from material and/or political gains (Stephen 1995). It also suggests that new social movements are more "expressive" and "less political," separating them from earlier forms of social movements, such as the type of actions associated with the Master Narrative of the civil rights movement. Harper (1993) suggests a similar argument by distinguishing between "instrumental" and "expressive" movements. "Instrumental" being means-end or goal oriented, aimed at changing the political structure, while "expressive" movements are directed toward changing the individual. However new this theoretical orientation is, it still confines the study of social movements to being generated by goals—whether they are common/general or single/individual.

By incorporating Weber's conceptualization of value-rational action into career activists, suggests a better way to understand the contribution of individuals to social action and social movements. This approach also suggests a way to consider social movements as being driven by something other than an objective goal. The career activists' cases discussed in this chapter provide a way to link the agency of individuals to social action and social movements while considering social movements as something other than exclusively goal driven. Finally, we suggest that both old and new social movements combine elements of many types of social action. The career activist concept provides a lens by which to study slices of social action without collapsing it into preexisting categories of leadership or organization, thus expanding our knowledge and understanding of how social action of one individual coalesces into the actions of many.

By considering this broad dimension of actions through career activists allows us to see how all social movements are a mixture of actions; what is emphasized is that which is singled out and "labeled" as one type or another. In moving forward from the civil rights era of mass mobilization to one of numerous smaller mobilizations that are new only in the sense that the type of social actions they incorporate are different than those used in an earlier period. They are not new to our understanding of social action—which dates back to Weber. Like Weber, though, we are struggling to understand events in our own time, their connection to the past as well as to the future. The next chapter discusses future directions of social movement research given what we have learned so far about forgotten civil rights activism.

In drawing out the implications of this study for the analysis of social movements, let us not forget the importance of a broad methodology— such as the Web and Part/Whole Approach to the scientific method—that can enable us to dig deeply into their complexity. In particular, such a methodology is broad enough to encompass both the Master Narrative and the Border Campaign. We revere Mills's concept of "the sociological imagination" because of its breadth, yet such reverence will not carry the day when it comes to our efforts to invoke that breadth in the analysis of any given social movement. What we require are procedures that social scientists can bring to bear on their analyses, procedures that follow the ideal of the scientific method for opening up to the range of phenomena relevant to a given problem. I believe that this approach—building on Mills's visionary orientation—has proven to be useful in the foregoing analysis. And I believe that it will prove to be useful not only for other research on social movements but also for social science research in general.

Notes

1. In the early 1990s, Wichita, Kansas, was the site of intense anti-abortion protests organized by Operation Rescue. See "Target Wichita," *Newsweek,* August 19, 1991, vol. 118: 18; "Bloody Kansas," *Commonwealth,* September 27, 1991, 118: 532-33. The protests subsided after concerted efforts by pro-choice forces; see "It Ain't Kansas" *Progressive,* August 1992, 56: 3-4, and the approval of the morning-after pill a few years later.

8

Conclusion

This final chapter first summarizes the general purpose and logic of the Border Campaign and reviews in detail four contrasting tendencies opposed to the Master Narrative: career activist, diffuse location of collective action, diverse targets of collective action, and value-rational agency. These four contrasts are further explored in terms of its relationship to future directions for social movement research. The next section of this chapter turns from conceptualization to explanation. It presents hypotheses based on the differences observed between the cases of this study and the Southern campaigns that followed the *Brown* decision, particularly in Birmingham, Alabama. This is followed by a section that discusses directions for further research. This chapter concludes with some final, broader observations about Border Campaigns.

Many of the campaigns discussed here occurred in relative obscurity, before the Southern direct-action campaigns of the 1950s and 1960s. This research seeks to single out, describe, and conceptualize characteristic actions of forgotten civil rights activism. Many challenges to segregation were unlike the mass-mobilization campaigns characteristic of the Master Narrative. They did not mount mass marches or mass boycotts, much like the spectacular direct action seen in Montgomery and Birmingham. Intense national media attention was not focused on the activists in Wichita, Kansas, and Oklahoma City who staged some of the first sit-ins. In Topeka, the undeniable importance of *Brown*, as a case, and the absence of public drama has left the significance of its local initiatives less obvious. Yet, without some locality, there would not have been a *Brown* case. This book has shown that the activism in Kansas and Oklahoma were initiated locally and that the resulting changes in race relations were significant in local terms. Sociological understanding of these modest beginnings prior to a national movement is, therefore, also important.

The Border Campaign ideal type is used to describe the diverse collective action in Kansas and Oklahoma in a systematic manner without losing their distinctive characters as in the Master Narrative. This approach included searching for the differences between the concrete events themselves and the cultural significance attributed to them. The Master Narrative tends to presuppose that all actions challenging the color line were proactive challenges to segregation. The intent of the Border Campaign was not to search for an inventory of causes but to develop a conception of the underlying logic of an ideal type that represented tendencies decisive in these sometimes-disparate challenges to segregation.

The Border Campaign ideal type was developed to clarify how early civil rights episodes or forgotten civil rights activism compared with and differed from direct-action desegregation campaigns in the South from 1955–1965. The Southern campaigns were typified by the Master Narrative. Supplementary comparisons and contrasts were found in the literature and in the history of prior legal challenges to segregation in Kansas and Oklahoma. In Kansas, both the South Park and Topeka campaigns were oriented toward obtaining the collective good of desegregated schools for African Americans. The public elementary schools were legally segregated in Topeka and were illegally segregated in South Park. The permissive segregation statutes in Kansas reflected the ambivalent border-state mix of racially exclusive and inclusive institutions and ideologies. This context for collective action was significantly different from the segregationist hegemony characteristic of the mid-1950s American South. In the South, the hegemonic cultural context of color line practices tended to suppress even discussion and symbolic expressions of integration (Harding 1984). In Kansas, "free state" culture and segregationist practices coexisted, notably in the arbitrary segregation of *some* public schools. In Oklahoma, segregation was more hegemonic than in Kansas but with some of the ambivalence of the Midwest and the Frontier. All these differences contributed to the characteristics of collective action oriented toward challenging the color line in specific geographic regions.

The Border Campaign Type

The shortcomings of the Master Narrative led to the development of an ideal type methodology to conceptualize what was distinctive about collective actions so different from those undertaken later in the South. The development of the ideal type was aided by Marwell and Oliver's (1984) conceptualization of collective campaigns as discrete units of collective action arising in response primarily to local issues.

The construction of the Border Campaign type was added by new primary data collected about how local level issues were addressed prior to the national push toward desegregation that occurred after the 1954 *Brown* decision, which is the focus of the Master Narrative.

The literature assessment indicated that among sociologists, Morris's (1984) study is one of the most sophisticated sociological conceptualization of local manifestations of the civil rights movement. He found existing indigenous formal and informal organizations to be essential in Baton Rouge, Montgomery, and other mass campaigns of the civil rights movement. Thus, Morris's perspective highlights formal and informal organization as the primary carriers of Southern mass-mobilization campaigns. It emphasizes formal leadership as the primary source of direction and cohesion in these campaigns, and his study is organized around these points. In the early civil rights struggles considered in this book, the collective action was not organizationally directed. The action was not primarily carried through formal or informal organization, nor was formal leadership particularly illuminating as a source of direction and cohesion. The diffuse types of action encountered contrasted in several significant ways with the predominance of organizational mobilization and control documented in Southern civil rights campaigns.

The Border Campaign type was developed to more adequately conceptualize and highlight tendencies not captured by the Master Narrative. The Border Campaign type's *conceptual* purpose is to identify and relate tendencies important for the pre- and post-*Brown* campaigns but not anticipated by the Master Narrative. The contrast is not made to set up supposedly mutually exclusive categories into which local campaigns can be sorted. The contrasting concepts of the Master Narrative and the Border Campaign type can be thought of as opposing endpoints of several continua along which local campaigns of the civil rights movement can be placed for comparison.

The contrasts provided by the Border Campaign type are suggested by the following concepts: campaign, career activist, diffuse location of collective action, targets of collective action within the educational domain, and value-rational agency. The uses of these concepts for understanding the challenges to segregation discussed in this book are summarized in the following paragraphs.

Campaign

Marwell and Oliver (1984) refers to collective action directed toward social change by pursuing a collective good. It is the preferred unit of analysis for local aspects of a social movement because it calls for the examination of both organizational and nonorganizational elements, as well as the dynamics of their interaction (Oliver 1989). It is more open than organizational units of analysis—even complex and sophisticated ones like local movement center—in comparison to the multiplicity of actions likely to constitute a social movement (Marwell and Oliver 1984; Turner and Killian 1987). Rather than as a category used to make mutually exclusive classifications or to explain a general class of collective actions, I have used "campaign" as a reference point to sensitize me to variations in the range of collective actions oriented to a collective good.

Oliver (1989) suggests that campaigns are constituted by the nonorganizational influences that flow between loosely coupled actions. The Master Narrative, in contrast, brings into focus a narrower range of actions that are presumed to be interrelated by organizational controls and institutionalized charismatic leadership. Actual concrete local campaigns seem likely to fall at varying points between these extremes by combining different degrees of nonorganizational influences and organizational control of their activities. The South Park and Topeka collective actions both tend toward the nonorganizational interplay of actions characteristic of Border Campaigns rather than organizational control of the Master Narrative.

In Kansas, the campaign in Topeka was more complex than the one in South Park. It was a challenge to a long-standing, legally sanctioned practice of segregation as opposed to the informal, illegal segregation in South Park. The Topeka NAACP branch had been established in 1914 and had a modest tradition of participating in the resolution of Topeka's race relations issues. The organizational resources of a local chapter of the NAACP were more important in the Topeka campaign than in South Park. The role of the Topeka chapter, however, was primarily as a meeting point of otherwise scattered people and resources. It was not the disciplined controller of resources and participants as the Master Narrative suggests church organizations were in the South. The Topeka chapter functioned in the campaign more as a linkage point for activists than bureaucratic system of imperative coordination (Perrow 1986, 20–41).

The Topeka campaign compares at least in one way with those in the South. Just as in the Montgomery, Alabama, campaign, for example, activists named a new organization that fronted for the involvements of established organizations. At times, local African Americans found it useful to form an adjunct "citizen's committee" to attend meetings with school boards or other dominant-community officials rather than present themselves as the local chapter of the NAACP.

Career Activist

Career activist conceptualizes a tendency observed in early civil rights struggles for persistent, committed individuals to make decisive contributions to a campaign of collective action. It reflects the capacity of some individuals to be self-starting, self-directing, and self-sustaining in their activism, rather than either the formal leaders or the mobilized followers of an organization. Career activists tend to inject themselves into campaigns through their own value-rational agency rather than be drawn in by organizational affiliation. The career of their activism tends to extend beyond any particular campaign. Although conceptually their actions are characterized as nonorganizational, career activists may cooperate with organizations during a campaign. However, the tendency is for career activists to attempt to utilize organizations (even to the point of attempting to transform them), rather than be controlled by them. Career activism continues outside of and beyond the affiliation with an organization and tends to be directed by personal value-rational agency.

This emphasis contrasts with the representation of the Master Narrative that the formal leaders and mobilized members of organizations are central to local campaigns. The contrast is made not to completely dismiss the Master Narrative's conclusions, but to indicate the need to also conceptualize and explain nonorganizational actions. In the campaigns studied here, individuals often acted in consequential ways apart from organizations. Career activist Esther Brown sometimes appeared to be working inside the local NAACP (a bi-racial organization) when she used that organization's resources and membership networks to raise funds, obtain legal advice, and secure the services of civil rights attorneys. Typically, however, Esther Brown was out ahead of established organizations. She made persistent contributions to desegregation campaigns that did not depend on and were certainly not controlled by a local movement center. Often, perhaps, careers of activism are initiated by organizations or inspired by leaders. In South Park and Topeka this was not the typical pattern. The local branch of the NAACP in South Park was organized *after* the campaign was initiated by nonorganizational activists in South Park. The local NAACP branch was not a mobilizer of the campaign; it was a result of the campaign. The campaign itself was the creation of Alfonso Webb, Esther Brown, and other key activists. This reversal of the causal ordering from collective action to organization raises an issue about conventional understandings of Southern mass-mobilization campaigns.

Social Domains

Border Campaign and the Master Narrative identify contrasting tendencies in both the *location* of collective action and its *targets*. The Master Narrative points to the preponderant contributions of African American churches in southern mass-mobilization campaigns. The Border Campaign, in contrast, identifies a tendency for *diffuse location* of collective action within the social domains of a community. Collective action tends to be located among several social domains, rather than concentrated in one.

The Master Narrative envisions collective action as carried by organizations and networks within a single social domain, religion. Many of the struggles studied departed in various degrees from the single-domain pattern described by the Master Narrative.

Attention to the intersection of a struggle with the social domains of its community also raises a second issue, the location within social domains of *targets*. Collective action tended to target public accommodations in the mass campaigns in the Master Narrative, but the social-domain location of public accommodations as targets are ambiguous. Usually, profit-making firms are challenged, but often they are publicly regulated or of general significance for local economies. Significantly, Morris (1984) indicates that the southern phase of the civil rights movement based on indigenous resources and organizations faltered somewhat when it shifted to target voter registration in the political domain.

Some of the campaigns target the domain of education. Both Topeka and South Park targeted the social domain of education, but Topeka and Oklahoma City also incorporated actions targeting public facilities access and political representation in city government. By the late 1940s, activists in the Topeka campaign shifted social domain targets as social action directed toward challenging public accommodations was switched toward education. In Oklahoma City, the domain of public accommodation was targeted after the schools were nominally integrated in 1958.

This contrast with Southern campaigns suggests that some tendencies identified by the Master Narrative were heavily conditioned by the targeted social domain. For example, the targeting of public transportation in Southern campaigns tended to require the mass membership and coordination abilities of bureaucratic organizations, leading to the dependence of those campaigns on organizational control through local movement centers. The targeting of the educational domain in Topeka through the leverage of the legal system required only the persistent coordinated activism of a relative handful of lawyers and plaintiffs, thus not requiring or exhibiting organization control of a mass mobilization.

Underlying Logic

An *underlying logic* interrelates the concepts of ideal types (Kalberg 1994, 81). Such logic attempts to conceptualize the principle that makes it consistent with the conceptualized tendencies of an ideal type to cluster empirically. *Value-rational agency* is the underlying logic of the Border Campaign. The term value-rational agency was used to convey both Weber's (1968, 24–25) concept of "value-rational social action"[1] and the significance of agency—individuals attempting to bring about social change. Organizational control is the underlying logic of the Master Narrative. Both logics are selective and incomplete attempts to see why certain tendencies of campaigns might cluster together. Organizational control is an underlying rationale as to why organization, formal leadership, and location action in the religious domain would cluster in the Master Narrative. There is also a tendency for the Master Narrative to consider agency in terms of methodological individualism, an admitted shortcoming by McAdam, Tarrow, and Tilly (2001, 12–13). Value-rational agency is an underlying rationale for why campaigns of loosely coupled actions, career activism, and diffuse social locations of collective action tend to cluster together in the struggles discussed in this book. Value-rational agency overcomes recent critiques of the cultural approach in social movements by *not* conflating cultural meanings in giving "causal power to norms, values, beliefs and symbols that individuals experience and absorb from outside themselves" (22). This value-rational understanding of agency recaptures the overlooked (important and interesting) contributions of individuals to collective action. This raises the issue of whether the concepts developed in this study can contribute to explanations of collective action.

Hypothesized Causes and Effects of Border Campaign Tendencies

The Border Campaign type's usefulness in studying pre–mass mobilization collective action depends in part on its use as an explanation of contrasts with the Master Narrative. According to Kalberg (1994, 81–84), the explanatory objective of Weber's comparative methodology is the "causal explanation of cases or developments." Explanation was a secondary objective of this study. Nevertheless, it is possible to form some hypotheses about the causes and consequences of collective action that exhibits the tendencies of the Border Campaign type.

First, border states seem particularly conducive to campaigns to establish civil rights because they are on the overlapping edges of Northern and Southern race relations. It is in a cultural rather than geographic sense that Kansas and Oklahoma are termed border states. Kansas's mixture of patterns of racial exclusion and inclusion indicates a lack of hegemony, while Oklahoma's stronger hegemony was tempered by competing Frontier and Western ideologies favoring inclusion. Hypothetically, these conditions at overlapping borders of contradictory cultural practices connect with the tendencies for local campaigns to exhibit the characteristics conceptualized by the Border Campaign type.

The tendencies summarized in the Border Campaign type are likely to be characteristic of "early" collective action antecedent to a mass phase of a movement. This happens both because inconsistent segregation experiences are more provocative, and either the absence of or competition with hegemony permits discourses advocating integration and actions modeling it. Such early, locally generated campaigns are likely to attract relatively low levels of public attention and mobilized resources. Similarly, campaigns in border states are less likely to require them. They face a divided and culturally ambivalent dominant community.

Most times, as in South Park and Guthrie, Border Campaigns would seem to be short-lived and limited to local effects, not impacting a broader social movement. Sometimes, in rare instances, inauspicious local campaigns contribute to major social movements, as happened with *Brown*. Also, after a major movement is under way, the Border Campaign type is likely to bring into focus collective action on the margins of mass movements, rather than such larger mobilizations as Montgomery and Birmingham. Collective actions with tendencies conceptualized by the concepts of the Border Campaign type are likely to be present but are unlikely to be recognized within "mature" social movements, coexisting with actions mounted by local movement centers. The likely consequence of such social actions is to demand concessions in culturally ambivalent contexts, for example, affirmative action in already integrated social domains.

Conversely, it seems likely that there is an affinity between mass-mobilization tactics and social domains that have large-membership bureaucratic organizations to carry the action. In the absence of mass mobilization for boycotts and demonstrations, campaigns do not have the same need for large bureaucratic mobilizing organizations and may sometimes mount a modest local campaign of petition, pressure, or litigation, drawing resources and participants selectively from throughout a community. The Border Campaign type offers a conceptualization with which to analyze campaigns that do not mount mass mobilizations.

There are also likely consequences of campaigns with Border Campaign tendencies. Lack of maturity, in the sense of well-defined goals and targets, is suggested in the Topeka and South Park data, by the tentativeness of the campaigns. The action stopped and restarted, and the campaigns fluidly shifted goals. Initially in Topeka, the actions of the local NAACP chapter were directed toward public accommodations; they shifted to target segregated schools. Still later in Topeka there was a decisive shift in the legal basis of the challenge to segregation precipitated by the entry of the national NAACP Legal Defense Fund attorneys into the campaign.

There was a definite goal shift in South Park from equalization (or improvement) of African American schools to desegregation. There is no mistaking that this shift occurred in the South Park campaign, but the exact timing and reasons for the shift are still not clear. Both timing and cause of a similar shift from improvement (justified as equalization) of African American schools to desegregation (justified by inherent inequality of segregation) are very clear in the southern school desegregation cases in Summerton, South Carolina, and Farmville, Virginia.[2] Each of these local campaigns was persuaded to shift to desegregation goals as a requirement for legal assistance from national NAACP Legal Defense Fund attorneys. The processes of goal succession (Perrow 1986) in such campaigns offers an interesting set of questions for future research.

Directions for Research: Montgomery and Birmingham Reconsidered

This section discusses the general importance of further research using the concepts developed for this study. To assess the generality of the conceptual framework developed in this study, this framework can be applied to other campaigns on the margins of social movements by comparing and contrasting cases (rather than at once proposing a general categorical explanation). This section also discusses the importance of the local context in shaping the unique actions of individuals who acted without organizational affiliation and could not be characterized as formal leaders, yet made significant contributions to protest. The contrast of informal leadership practices with formal, organizationally affiliated leadership heightens our awareness of individual activism that carried early civil rights protest forward. These actions have been obscured due to subsuming them under formal leadership categories. Future directions of study are suggested for understanding the significance of informal leadership and individual activism to social movements in general. Next is a discussion of the implications of these tentative conclusions for further research by briefly reexamining the 1955–1956 Montgomery Bus Boycott and Birmingham, Alabama, in the spring of 1963.

"The Black Women Did It": Women Who "Started" the Montgomery Bus Boycott

Overlaps in membership between the NAACP and the local African American churches are underplayed by the Master Narrative, which emphasizes formal and indigenous organizations. Its masculine logic of leadership also obscures the nature of women's social relationships and networks of communication in collective action (Freeman 1983). When analyzed in terms of human networks, as the Border Campaign does, the boundaries between gendered leadership roles become more fluid and take on a different significance. For example, the Montgomery Improvement Association was formed during the Montgomery Bus Boycott in 1956, but this organization was carved out of the overlapping membership from three organizations: Dexter Avenue Baptist Church, the local chapter of the NAACP, and the Montgomery Women's Council.

The emergence of this organization predated the arrival of Dr. Martin Luther King, Jr., in Montgomery, Alabama, by ten years. Reverend Vernon

Johns had orchestrated an (albeit ill-fated) antisegregation campaign out of the same church. Under Johns's leadership, blacks in Montgomery had participated in boycotts, sit-ins, and other peaceful demonstrations (Branch 1988). Johns's leadership of these numerous, short-lived protests is best captured by the term career activist. Like other career activists discussed in this book, Johns's activism was concerned with the immediacy of racial segregation. He constantly challenged segregation, trying to create a better reality. The response of the white community to Johns's activism was forceful, prompting Johns to be removed from his pulpit by the church deacons in 1955. However, the collective action did not cease with his departure from Montgomery; rather once he left, the remaining activists redirected the activities of what had been perceived as solely those of the Dexter congregation into the Montgomery Improvement Association (MIA). To the rest of the black community and the white community, the perception was that a new organization had suddenly emerged (Garrow 1985).

Like Reverend Johns, JoAnn Robinson laid the groundwork for the Montgomery Bus Boycott in the late 1940s. She arrived in Montgomery, Alabama, in 1949, assuming a position as an English teacher at segregated Alabama State College. She also became a member of Dexter Avenue Baptist Church and joined the Women's Political Council (WPC), a professional civic group. Robinson's membership in these two organizations would draw her into community activism. For example, after a humiliating experience with Montgomery's segregated bus seating in December 1949 led her to make up her "mind that whatever I could add to that organization that would help to bring that practice down, I would do it" (Robinson 1987, xiv). For the next five years, she and her WPC colleagues pursued the desegregation of Montgomery's buses through behind-the-scenes negotiations with the mayor and the city commission.

Their attempts at bargaining and negotiations were not very successful. After receiving thirty complaints against the bus company in 1953, the WPC stepped up their efforts to do something about Montgomery's city bus system and their uncivil treatment of black customers. Robinson wrote a letter to Montgomery Mayor Gayle on May 21, 1954, requesting that the Montgomery Bus Company treat black customers with more respect. Robinson reminded Mayor Gayle that "three-fourths of the riders" are black, and if they decided to boycott the buses, it would bankrupt the bus company. Up until early December 1955, when the citywide bus boycott actually began, Robinson and the WPC worked to lay the groundwork for the eventually successful protest. Robinson recalled, "(w)e women prepared the notices calling riders off the buses. We distributed those notices, and then, when the ministers took over, we worked with them until the very end" (Robinson 1987, 10). Robinson goes on to state that she "kept a low profile and stayed as much as possible in the background" due to her "deep respect for Dr. Trenholm, for Alabama State College, and for its faculty and student body" (10).

As it became clear that negotiations and letter-writing campaigns were not effective, Robinson and the WPC next focused their efforts on how to best implement and sustain a bus boycott. By the time the boycott started in 1955, the WPC had organized itself into three chapters that covered three different sections of the city (24; Garrow 1985). Robinson said that the WPC had in place "one of the best communication systems needed for operation of the boycott" (Robinson 1987, 24). "Each group played a part in the distribution of the notices that called riders off city transportation lines" (24). When Rosa Parks was arrested the evening of December 1, 1955, the WPC was ready for the boycott. "On paper, the WPC had already planned for fifty thousand notices calling people to boycott the buses; only the specifics of time and place had to be added. And as tempers flared and emotions ran high, the women became active." It was the only organization out of sixty-eight black organizations in Montgomery that was ready for the next step (39).

Robinson first heard about Parks's arrest in the early evening of December 1, and Robinson immediately implemented the printing and distribution of leaflets announcing a boycott (46). The morning of December 2, 1955, Robinson's WPC boycott leaflets were delivered to an already scheduled interdenominational meeting of black clergy (50). The evening of December 2 turned into the first mass meeting related to the boycott, making the black clergy visible and the women invisible. Though Robinson continued to help coordinate the boycott, her informal leadership and individual activism were obscured by the formal leadership of the all-male black clergy and the formal MIA organization, which became dominant during the boycott (14).

Although Dr. Martin Luther King, Jr., was later the acknowledged leader of the 1955–1956 Montgomery Bus Boycott, the Master Narrative ignores how ten years of prior activism by Dexter Avenue Baptist Church members was developed under Reverend Vernon Johns's leadership (Branch 1988). This perspective also does not attach much significance to the career activism of women like JoAnn Robinson who used their civic and professional groups to work quietly behind the scenes long before and after the MIA came into existence. Also overlooked are the types of actions of another local community activist, E. D. Nixon, a longtime member of the Brotherhood of Sleeping Car Porters. Nixon had learned leadership and organizational tactics that were employed by union organizers, which he admittedly adapted to the Montgomery Bus Boycott (Branch 1988). The Master Narrative does not understand these nonorganizational elements whose existence and significance are now captured by the Border Campaign.

The hegemonic ideology of Southern segregation did not work to unite the black community in Montgomery. According to Weems (1995, 73) "in pre-boycott Black Montgomery ... [f]actionalism had retarded the effectiveness of the leadership class. The middle class appeared self-absorbed and apathetic. Moreover, the working class seemed passive and resigned to second-class citizenship." Weems argues that an important but less dramatic factor in facilitating the boycott was the growing resentment against the daily humiliations blacks faced on the city buses. "While Black bus riders accounted for nearly seventy percent of Montgomery bus line's receipts, the company employed no African American drivers (74). Though the Master Narrative places particular emphasis on the internal cohesion of the black community to undertake mass mobilizations, closer examination of the local situation brings into focus how the promise of economic empowerment was a motivation for action. Even though African Americans could not directly strike out against white oppression, they could indirectly hit back by participating in a consumer boycott. As Weems points out, the significance of consumer boycotts has been shunted to the side, "[m]inimizing the central role of African American economic retribution" (72). The Montgomery Bus Boycott of 1955–1956 and other boycotts against segregated public transportation companies had historical precedence in the streetcar boycotts half a century earlier. Boycotts presented an immediate, tangible, and less dangerous way to subvert white dominance. Inclusion of these diverse actions uncovered by the Border Campaign, combined with the other factors the Master Narrative emphasizes, provides a more comprehensive explanation and understanding of this significant civil rights episode.

Birmingham, Alabama: Obscure Beginnings, 1956–1962

We turn now to a discussion of Birmingham, Alabama, signaling a new phase in nonviolent protest that was much more confrontational than previous struggles. A relatively large city of almost three hundred thousand in 1963, Birmingham was "thoroughly segregated" with a violent history, earning it the nickname "Bombingham" (Morris 1984, 68). For example, between 1957 and 1963 several bombs were thrown into the homes of prominent African Americans, including Rev. E. D. King, who was the brother of Rev. Martin Luther King, Jr. Arthur Shores, one of two black attorneys allowed to practice law in the State of Alabama, reported his house being bombed twice during this period. Though Shores did not think he was "an activist," his handling of several civil rights cases made him an obvious target.[3]

The timing of events in Birmingham demonstrates how much more quickly African Americans began to respond to white intransigence. For example, when Alabama outlawed the NAACP in 1956, African Americans replaced it with a more radical, indigenous organization—the Alabama Christian Movement for Human Rights (ACMHR). The ACMHR was organized at a mass meeting by Reverend Fred Shuttlesworth, a minister and former membership chairman of the then-outlawed NAACP (68). The ACMHR used the organizing logistics of the then-defunct Alabama NAACP to mobilize Birmingham blacks and build momentum for radical social change between 1956 and 1963.

Initially beginning by presenting a series of grievances that were ignored by the city government, the ACMHR filed a lawsuit against Birmingham's personnel board for not allowing blacks to take the civil service exam as an initial step to be hired as police officers. Though the city quickly allowed blacks to take the exams, none of them were hired. In December 1956, just one year after the Montgomery Bus Boycott had started, Shuttlesworth's house was bombed after several hundred blacks rode the city buses in an attempt to test the Supreme Court's ruling on the Montgomery case. The ACMHR quickly filed a lawsuit in federal court (70). A few months later, in 1957, Shuttlesworth and several others from ACMHR were chased by a white mob when they tried to integrate the railroad station. Attempts to enroll their children in an all-white school resulted in more violence. Another lawsuit was quickly filed against the board of education.

Between 1956 and 1962 there was continuous pressure by Shuttlesworth and the ACMHR to desegregate Birmingham. In the spring of 1962, a highly successful economic boycott of downtown businesses set the stage for the eventual dramatic confrontations the following spring, accompanied by the arrival of Rev. Martin Luther King, Jr. Despite the unfailing efforts of Shuttlesworth and the ACMHR, Morris (254) argues that as in Montgomery, efforts to unite the black community failed until the arrival of a charismatic leader, Rev. King.: "Dr. King's stature as a charismatic leader helped to bring about internal cohesion in Birmingham" (255). Once again the Master Narrative's emphasis on formal leadership obscures the several years of previous activism carried out by Shuttlesworth and the ACMHR. A contrasting interpretation is provided by the Border Campaign in how the pre-1963 activism follows a similar pattern of negotiation, legal redress, and direct action found in many other places like Montgomery, as well as the border state civil rights cases discussed in this book.

What is interesting about Birmingham is how its pattern of protest is speeded up by the quick succession of each stage. In Montgomery, negotiations went on several years before the bus boycott, and in Oklahoma City, Clara Luper spent six years negotiating with the city *after* the first sit-ins were staged in 1959. Given its particular historical situation in Birmingham, there is urgency for immediate change that is lacking in the border states. For example, the timing of the Oklahoma City sit-ins was much slower; they were preceded and succeeded by negotiations. The sit-ins were also aided by a movement by white elites to the restructure the municipal government. The Border Campaign highlights the importance of these informal, off-the-record assemblies of business leaders who influenced the public policymaking behind the scenes in places like Topeka and Oklahoma City.

Recent studies on Birmingham reveal the importance of Shuttlesworth's campaign between 1956 and 1962 to create equal employment opportunities for African Americans (Eskew 1997; Wilson 2000). There was also a considerable effort by white elites to open a dialogue with the African American community, as well as efforts to remove "Bull" Connor from office before the violent May 1963 demonstrations (Eskew 1997, 5-6; McWhorter 2001). Though King declared Birmingham a "national victory," in terms of the local issues and grievances, the victory failed as the demonstrations ended before negotiations were finished for what Shuttlesworth had spent several years working toward: equal opportunities for employment (Eskew 1997). "What the white people had tried to do so for long, neutralize Shuttlesworth, had just been achieved in the name of freedom." King's "national victory" obscures what a hollow victory it really was for Shuttlesworth's efforts: "The settlement called for promoting only one black employee, total, in all the downtown stores—not one in each store, as the Movement was interpreting it" (McWhorter 2001, 441–442).

The emphasis on spectacular events like what happened in Birmingham not only obscures antecedent actions, but also obscures what has been left unfinished in the civil rights movement. The Master Narrative's stationary conceptualization of events objectifies them, rendering them static and one-dimensional. This makes it difficult to comprehend the ways in which social action ebbs and flows. In severing events from their local situation and historical contexts, the Master Narrative deflects attention away from a better understanding of the early civil rights movement itself. The Border Campaign's ability to capture disparate actions not only provides a more complete understanding of the specifics of the local situation, its subjectivism overcomes the linear bias of social movements. The problems underlying racial segregation did not immediately dissolve after significant court cases and legislation. Though the Master Narrative characterizes the civil rights movement as moving toward the goal of desegregation, it shunts aside those actions aimed at more intermediate ends. This emphasis on desegregation leaves its aftermath undertheorized. There is a tendency to examine events in contemporary society as unrelated or cut off from the mass mobilization era. The Border Campaign helps to link these seemingly unconnected periods together and better understand the relationship between social problems and collective action (Piven and Cloward 1979).

The problem of the Master Narrative's selectivity is best illustrated by examining the aftermath of the *Brown* decision in Topeka, Kansas. The symbolic importance of the landmark court case has overshadowed enduring tensions revolving around school desegregation. As was the case in the early 1920s, real estate speculators played a significant role in continuing segregation by enticing white Topekans to move to the suburbs and thus outside the school district. This scenario has been played out in many cities throughout the United States since 1954 (Jacobs 1999), but it is illustrative to return here to Topeka to examine this phenomenon in terms of a familiar local context.

What Happened to *Brown*?

Brown was not literally the cause of the civil rights movement, but it served as a legal justification to pursue racial equality on many different fronts. On June 28, 2007, the United States Supreme Court ordered in a 5-4 decision that using race to assign students to schools is unconstitutional (Rosen 2007). The majority opinion, authored by Chief Justice John Roberts, struck down public school choice plans in Seattle, Washington, and Louisville, Kentucky.[4] But as Justice Breyer remarked in his dissent, Chief Justice Roberts's idea of a colorblind society gives all races equal weight and "indeed the history books do not tell stories of white children struggling to attend black schools." As an aside, Justice Breyer added, "I have long adhered to the view that a decision to exclude a member of a minority because of his race is fundamentally different from a decision to include a member of a minority for that reason" (Breyer 2007, 2, fn3).

Justice Breyer's words speak to the heart of the problem of any pluralistic society: how to redress past injustices related to racial stigma toward one group without creating another type of inequity for another. This dilemma demonstrates the continuing significance of the 1954 *Brown* decision. The effort to reverse discrimination through affirmative action programs such as those aimed at specific minority groups "causes real injustice to particular individuals" (Walzer 1997, 59). As an immigrant society, the United States is comprised of various ethnic and religious groups over which the "state claims jurisdictional rights, regarding all its citizens as individuals rather than as members of groups" (31). Using racial criteria to make school assignments based on group membership, in this case a racial group goes against the notion of individual rights. Because the 2007 majority opinion makes the "distinction between *de jure* segregation (caused by school systems) and *de facto* segregation (caused, e.g., by housing patterns or generalized societal discrimination)," the court is working to "rule out categorically all local efforts to use means [to integrate] that are 'conscious of the race of individuals'" (Breyer 2007, 6). Ignoring the significance of the local situation overlooks the unique ways school districts have tried to create a diverse society in the fifty years since African Americans successfully petitioned to be admitted to their neighborhood schools. Today, because of residential housing patterns and school board policies, neighborhoods are as much segregated by social class as they are by race. In examining the histories of earlier school segregation, whether in Seattle, Louisville, or even Topeka, it is clear that "*de jure* discrimination can be present even in the absence of racially explicit laws" (Breyer, 19).

For example, the explicitly racial *de jure* segregation in Topeka, Kansas, which existed before the 1954 *Brown* decision, was replaced with another type of *de jure* discrimination created through school redistricting and convoluted attendance boundaries. Real estate developers riding the post-war housing boom urged white homeowners to buy new houses in the suburbs. Although Seattle, Washington, never had state statutes like Kansas's pre-*Brown* racial segregation, it nevertheless developed a system of racial segregation. After World War II, blacks moved into the central city, and whites headed to northern suburbs; while in Topeka whites headed west, and blacks stayed in the eastern portion of the city trapped by an eroding infrastructure. "Although black students made up about three percent of the total Seattle population in the mid-1950s, nearly all black children attended schools where a majority of the population was minority ... [while] schools outside the central and southeastern sections of Seattle were virtually all white" (Breyer 2007, 6).

A similar demographic change happened in Topeka between 1950 and 1979 (see Figure 8.1). Like Seattle, Topeka witnessed the creation of an "alternative predominantly white school sub-system generally around the peripheral boundary but specifically concentrated in the southern and western portions of the Topeka school system...."[5] New schools built after 1959 would have pupil racial ratios that would be all or disproportionately white. Additionally, classroom additions and/or portable classrooms would also be primarily at disproportionately white schools.

Following a similar pattern found in Topeka, Louisville, Kentucky—the other city involved in the recent Supreme Court decision—did have a previous history of racial segregation, and after the 1954 *Brown* decision, the Louisville School District "created a geography-based student assignment plan" to ensure integration. This plan subsequently failed despite reported public school enrollments that were relatively equal in terms of white and black students. However, by 1972, fourteen of its nineteen middle schools and high schools were "close to totally black or white.... Twenty-one elementary schools were between roughly ninety and one hundred percent white" (Breyer 2007, 12–13).

Though the official end of segregation in 1954 met with far less hostility in Kansas than in Mississippi or South Carolina, it was still not welcoming to African Americans. News correspondent Carl T. Rowan had found Topeka to be a "pretty segregated city" when he lived there as a navy trainee during World War II. Returning to Kansas in 1953, he described his earlier experiences by observing, "Topeka was a paradox. There was no Jim Crow in some areas where you had expected it; segregation had deep roots where it was not expected."[6] The state's permissive segregation laws meant that overt segregation was strictly limited, while covert segregationist practices arose unrestrained. Rowan continued, "There was no segregation on city buses, or in any public transportation. But I was unable to go to a movie or into a restaurant with white navy buddies. Hotels, bowling alleys and other public recreation facilities were closed to Negroes."

A decade later and just a few months before the first *Brown* decision, Rowan still found it difficult to find a restaurant willing to serve him and his companion, attorney Charles Scott, the original lawyer involved in the *Brown* case. Despite the legal demise of segregation, informal segregation was still intact. Rowan and Scott were asked by one restaurant owner to eat in the kitchen, not because of any law requiring racial separation, but simply because it was his "policy." As an attorney, Scott understood that segregation laws were much easier to remove than it was to confront and change the informal racial practices comprising the embarrassing day-to-day lived reality of racial segregation. "And it stems from Jim Crow schools," Scott declared to Rowan as they left one restaurant without being served, "because when segregation is part of the pattern of learning it permeates every area of life."

After the *Brown* decision, the number of African American teachers slowly dwindled. In 1953, Topeka had 27 African American teachers who taught 779 students. By 1956, the number of African American pupils had increased to 898, but the number of full-time teachers had declined to 21: desegregation of students did not result in integration of black teachers.[7] The decline in employment of black teachers after integration is a largely unacknowledged fact of desegregation.

Post-*Brown* Challenges in Topeka

Topeka had one high school, Topeka Senior High School, until 1958.[8] A year later its racial balance dramatically changed when Highland Park Senior High School was created through annexation. By 1960, 87.2 percent of the black students in the Topeka school system were being assigned to Topeka Senior High School in "East" Topeka, while whites were being predominately assigned to Highland Park, in "West" Topeka. The year before Topeka West High School opened, the original Topeka High School was approximately 11 percent black and Highland Park was 5.1 percent black. One year later, 83.2 percent of all black students were now being

164

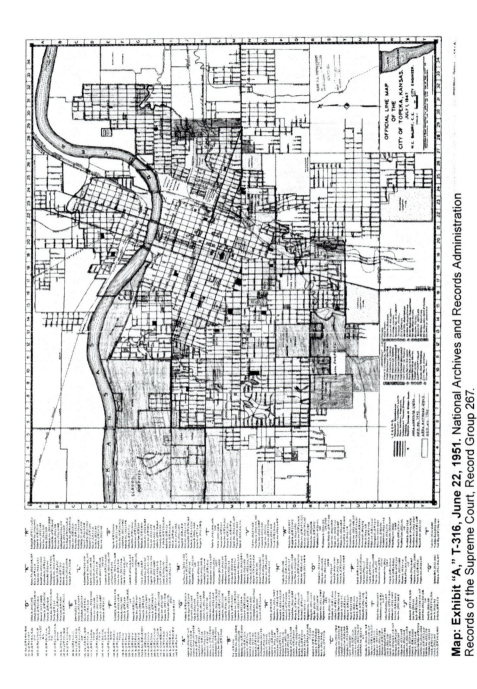

Map: Exhibit "A," T-316, June 22, 1951. National Archives and Records Administration Records of the Supreme Court, Record Group 267.

Figure 8.1 Westward Expansion of Topeka, Kansas, in 1950.

As the city expanded south and west by incorporating outlying areas, school segregation challenges came from Mission Township, which included Lohman Hill School (Reynolds 1902–1903), and the Randolph School (Wright, Rich, and Foster 1924–1929). The city of Topeka expanded westward rather than northward because of the Kansas River and its floodplain. The majority of the African American population was concentrated in the northern area of Topeka on both sides of the Kansas River. This area included parts of the townships of Topeka City, Topeka, and Soldier. By 1940, there were fewer than fifty African Americans living south and west of Topeka in Mission Township (and fewer than ten living in Menoken, Silver Lake, and Tecumseh townships, which were further south and west).

Sources:
U.S. Department of Commerce. Bureau of Census. Tenth Census of the United States, 1880. Vol. I. Washington, D.C.: Government Printing Office, 1883.
_____. Eleventh Census of the United States, 1890. Vol. I. Washington, D.C.: Government Printing Office, 1893.
_____. Twelfth Census of the United States, 1900. Part 1. Washington, D.C.: Government Printing Office, 1901.
_____. Thirteenth Census of the United States, 1910. Vol. I. Washington, D.C.: Government Printing Office, 1911.
_____. Fourteenth Census of the United States, 1920. Vol. I. Washington, D.C.: Government Printing Office, 1921.
_____. Fifteenth Census of the United States, 1930. Vol. I. Washington, D.C.: Government Printing Office, 1931.
_____. Sixteenth Census of the United States, 1940. Vol. I. Washington, D.C.: Government Printing Office, 1941.
_____. Seventeenth Census of the United States, 1950. Vol. I. Washington, D.C.: Government Printing Office, 1951.

assigned to Topeka High, while Highland Park and Topeka West were predominately white.

Though the 1960 U.S. Census data indicates that the largest concentration of Topeka's black population with school-age children resided midway between Topeka High and Highland Park, new schools were being built only in the western area of the city. A simple change in the attendance boundary when Highland Park was annexed would have brought its minority enrollment to 50 percent.[9] It would have also alleviated overcrowding at Topeka High, since Highland Park had 497 empty seats. Instead, the school board designated a third high school (Topeka West) to be built at the western fringe of the growing city, assigning to it two black children and 702 white children.[10]

In the post-*Brown* era, the school board argued that since the junior high schools were desegregated before *Brown* in the early 1940s, and the high school was never segregated, they were not considered to be part of the original court order.[11] The school board also argued that the original *Brown* decision had targeted legal or *de jure* segregation, and it did not apply to *de facto* segregation or the type of segregation that was the "natural" outgrowth of an individual's choice and their financial resources allowing them to live in any given neighborhood. The overt racism of segregation was being replaced by more covert attempts to relegate African Americans to inferior and substandard schools. Because the school board had designed and built schools with the effect of limiting access to its newer facilities to only those residing in Topeka's western suburbs, most African Americans in Topeka were relegated to East Topeka's rapidly aging and increasingly inferior schools.

The *Brown* case was reactivated in 1979. The original lead plaintiff, Linda Brown, now an adult, along with other African American parents and their children, argued that the Topeka School Board and its successor U.S.D. No. 501 had failed to desegregate within the mandates of *Brown* and *Brown II*. Between September 10, 1973, and September 7, 1979, four separate cases were filed in the federal district court of Kansas raising questions as to whether the Topeka Board of Education and U.S.D. No. 501 had complied with the mandates of *Brown* and *Brown II*.[12]

Not only were African Americans geographically bound to attend inferior schools, they were also now economically limited by not having the financial resources to purchase homes that automatically provided them access to newer and better schools. By the 1970s, Topeka was more spatially and economically segregated than it was prior to *Brown*.[13] In October 1986, the reactivated *Brown* was tried in the District Court of the District of Kansas. Six months later the plaintiffs appealed to the Court of Appeals for the Tenth Circuit when the court decided that there was not enough evidence of purposeful discrimination found. On December

11, 1989, the Court of Appeals voted to reverse the findings of the lower court. The school district appealed to the U.S. Supreme Court, but on April 20, 1992, the U.S. Supreme Court sent the case back to the Court of Appeals for further consideration. The appellate court reaffirmed its earlier decision and denied rehearing on January 28, 1993. A few months later on June 21, 1994, the Supreme Court declined to consider the matter further. Finally, on July 25, 1994, the District Court approved the school district's third desegregation proposal, but the school district continued to be subject to the court's jurisdiction.

Comparisons with detailed narrative accounts of the mass-mobilization campaigns in the Master Narrative suggest a great deal of potential for research that links changes in responses to the color line with trends in education, migration, and urban expansion along cultural borders. Topeka's urban growth triggered reconfigurations of its mixed segregationist and integrationist color line practices during the late nineteenth and early twentieth centuries. Changes in the social domain of education affected color line practices when junior high schools were introduced. A reconfiguration of the color line related to their segregation occurred in Coffeyville in 1924 and in Topeka in 1941. The effect of other demographic changes such as migration patterns and employment opportunities might illuminate changes in color line practices previously understudied.

The social domain target of public accommodations differed from action directed toward challenging segregation in education. Challenges to segregation of public facilities targets were swift and short-lived. Efforts to desegregate public facilities in many cases (for example, movie theaters) escalated and were resolved more quickly than challenges to segregated schools. The process of those campaigns took more time to evolve and the actions involved were diffuse. Desegregation campaigns should be studied for variations in pace and tactics that might stem from the type of target challenged.

The desegregation campaigns in Kansas and Oklahoma were also less public in nature, particularly initially, than those later in the civil rights movement. In the Southern direct-action phase of the civil rights movement, the mass boycotts were sustained and mass marches were conducted in the streets. Challenges occurred in Kansas and Oklahoma, but they were by comparison discrete and handled with less public display. African Americans in Topeka requested that the school board modify their schools. They did not mount a mass march to the board of education building or boycott the schools altogether. In South Park, Kansas, where the schools *were* boycotted, the community involved was so small that it was barely noticeable outside its own borders. The effects of the boycott were less public and diffuse.

Significant behind-the-scenes elements of campaigns have been noted in Montgomery and Birmingham. Elsewhere, in the Knoxville,

Tennessee, sit-ins for example, a covert deal among representatives of protesters, downtown businesses, and city government almost achieved a quick and less extreme modification of the color line. The deal is probably known only because some businesses reneged and public claims of betrayal followed (Proudfoot 1962). Actions within campaigns not taken in public will be difficult to find and confirm, but they ought to be looked for and studied alongside more obvious and dramatic elements of campaigns.

Resistance to desegregation from African American teachers employed in segregated schools was found in Topeka in both *Graham* and *Brown* and opposition to a proposed school desegregation campaign in Wichita. In South Park, the teachers were active in the campaign, one even sacrificing her job with the school system. She and a former Walker teacher staffed for little pay an alternative school for the African American children. The African American parents in South Park initially were interested in securing a quality educational facility for their children. After a time they came to demand integration in the newly built South Park elementary school as their goal. Their allies in the Kansas City, Kansas, local NAACP chapter were interested in improving facilities available to African Americans but also maintaining some elements of the status quo of the color line, namely segregated schools. There was probably a convergence of interests between some African American elites in Kansas City, Kansas, and segregationist whites. They were proud of the excellent segregated institutions in that city, especially the segregated Sumner High School. State representative and plaintiffs' attorney William Towers saw a substantially enhanced Walker School as a satisfactory resolution to the South Park campaign. The activists in the South Park campaign went outside of the apparent wishes of the Kansas City, Kansas, NAACP in pushing for desegregation over equalization. These patterns suggest that desegregation of the social domain of education, which touches most of the lives and many of the other institutions of a community, will be viewed very differently from different social locations and interests. These heterogeneities should be studied for confirmation as well as to explore their effects on campaigns.

The effects of counter movements by white elites who see civil rights activism as an opportunity to bring about other political and economic changes is another important dimension to the Border Campaign. In Topeka, white elites seized the opportunity to remove school Superintendent Kenneth MacFarland and elect new school board members. In Oklahoma City, the sit-ins presented an opportunity for white elites to gain control of the city council and initiate a number of changes to the city government; some of these reforms included hiring a city manager to professionally manage the city. The establishment of a human relations commission facilitated better communication between the police and the

African American community as well as increasing overall awareness of racial issues in white citizens' minds (Saxe 1969, 183-185).

Finally, among the most important lines of research suggested by Border Campaigns is the further exploration of the interplay of local campaigns and national movements. Local campaigns were set in motion by local initiatives and are an aspect of the "indigenous perspective" (McAdam 1982; Morris 1984) consistent with the Border Campaign type. National agendas, such as the NAACP's school desegregation campaign, were built upon local issues and concerns. The Topeka campaign began as an attempt at school equalization that shifted to school desegregation once it became incorporated into national issues.

The Border Campaign helped search for "nuanced and complex answers to questions [about] the characteristics, causes and processes of the emerging civil rights movement" (Lofland 1993, 46). Many of the cases discussed here were both socially and historically situated before the mass mobilizations characteristic of the civil rights movement. Preliminary conceptualization of these earlier campaigns was necessary in order to not miss the subtleties of action orientations underlying them. This conceptualization was aided by not conflating collective action leading to the formation of the movement with a later type of "phenomenon that would crystallize into ... the civil rights movement" (46). The logic of this approach was to avoid oversimplification of these earlier collective actions and to not impose a preconceived deductive theory at the outset of the study.

Conclusion: Future Directions for Social Movement Research

What contributions does this study make toward understanding social movements? Like other historically important social phenomena, the civil rights movement has been extensively studied by both historians and sociologists. What new can be discovered on such well-trodden grounds? This study has uncovered significant, unacknowledged social action that has been obscured by the historical, symbolic significance of events such as the *Brown* decision in Topeka, Kansas.

Although the famous school desegregation case bears the name *Brown v. Board of Education of Topeka, Kansas*, scholars of the civil rights movement have given insufficient attention to the events that led up to the court case. This lack of interest might be related to the fact that Topeka, Kansas, was not located in the Deep South and did not have the same history of violence in race relations as, for instance, a place like Birmingham, Alabama. There were no spectacular events, such as bombings, race riots, mass marches, or boycotts that characterized the mass mobilizations in the South. Scholars of the civil rights movement have tended to view the *Brown* case more symbolically in relationship to the history of civil rights movement and school desegregation, rather than as something that was a product of the Topeka campaign. Little acknowledgment has been given to the fact that Topeka is an actual place, with its own history of race relations. The local situation is also obscured in places like Montgomery and Birmingham.

One contribution of this study is to demonstrate how "big events" such as the landmark 1954 Supreme Court decision *Brown v. Board of Education of Topeka* overshadows the local situation. For example, actions taken by African Americans in Topeka to end segregation in their community have historically (or for symbolic purposes) been conceptualized as the actions of one person—Rev. Oliver Brown—trying to enroll his daughter in a neighborhood school that discriminated on the basis of race. Numerous individuals involved in the planning and execution of the case, twelve other plaintiffs, and other complementary activism have been obscured by the now-famous court case. It was not just the case that was a collective production. The precipitating attempt to enroll African American students in neighborhood schools reserved for whites was itself a collectively produced action, one of an extended number of attempts to desegregate life in this border-state capitol. A multiplicity of social actions in both the Kansas and Oklahoma campaigns have, in retrospect, become compressed into a unified "historical singularity:" the *Brown* case. The South Park and Topeka campaigns have been "historically remembered," if at all, as incidental precursors of the case. In fact, they originated the case and, indirectly, much of its crucial contribution to the development of the national civil rights movement. The sociological point is not that the civil rights movement would not have happened without these obscure campaigns, because there were several other roughly contemporaneous campaigns that may have served the national cause as well. Some of these, in fact, were combined into the *Brown* case before the U.S. Supreme Court. The point is that the precipitant of the case was not an *isolated* act of personal courage. It was many acts of personal courage interacting within a collective campaign.

This study has attempted to look clearly at "what happened" in Kansas and Oklahoma civil rights campaigns by looking beneath the distortions resulting from the historical significance of the national movement they foreshadowed and inspired. This strategy breaks the Kansas civil rights campaigns out from underneath the *Brown* decision to study them in their own right. This study has not sought to construct a new linear historical account, but rather has attempted to deepen the understanding of types of action occurring in Kansas that have been obscured by the historical singularity of *Brown*.

The historical patterns of challenges to the color line in Kansas can be viewed as a "genealogical" pattern. This recapturing of past events and actions provided a baseline for comparison with the Topeka campaign of the late 1940s and early 1950s. Discussion of past challenges to color line practices revealed discontinuities in action orientations, as well as those that have been carried forward as "social action legacies" (Kalberg 1994) influencing later campaigns. An important discontinuity of the South Park and Topeka campaigns with prior court cases challenging segregation in the Kansas Supreme Court was the shift from representation of individuals to African Americans as a class.

This study examines particular strands of the many social actions woven into a decisive historical pattern, in this instance the civil rights movement. Interweaving of such small strands is often how "history" is conceived. For example, precipitating events are credited with starting wars in United States history: John Brown's Raid on Harper's Ferry in 1859 (Civil War), the sinking of *Lusitanian* in 1914 (World War I), and the bombing of Pearl Harbor in 1941 (World War II). The multiplicity of actions and events prior to these important occurrences may become compressed into a narrow perspective of the precipitating cause. History is written by looking back. Awareness of outcomes induces a linear recounting of the prior social actions that "led" to such singular development as the civil rights movement.

This view of history is not necessarily incorrect. Social action may, in fact, not coalesce without a "singular event." Local civil rights protests did not become "the civil rights movement" without a multiplicity of social actions being made into a singular symbol toward which subsequent actions were oriented. On the other hand, as my study shows, the character and contexts of early desegregation campaigns were constructed before and independently of an awareness of the historical movement they fed into and helped to precipitate.

The problem of penetrating the complexity of the civil rights movement parallels the problem of understanding human behavior in general. Our most powerful tool for doing so is the scientific method. Unfortunately, practices throughout the social sciences generally have not followed the scientific ideal of opening up to the range of phenomena relevant to a given problem. In this book, I have used the Web and Part/Whole Approach to the scientific method in an effort to follow that ideal. This is my own effort to help fulfill what C. Wright Mills called "the promise of sociology." If indeed that effort has been fruitful, then this book suggests a direction for moving the practices of social scientists up to that promise. Given the threatening nature of contemporary social problems throughout the world, the time is long past due when we social scientists must learn to fulfill "the promise of sociology." If we do not learn to understand those problems, who will?

Notes

1. "[T]hat is, determined by a conscious belief in the value for its own sake of some ethical, aesthetic, religious, or other form of behavior, independently of its prospects of success" (Weber 1968, 24-25).

2. These were the campaigns that led to two of the cases that were grouped with *Brown* before the U.S. Supreme Court. The case in Farmville was called *Davis v. Prince Edward County, VA. Briggs v. Elliott* was the case in Summerton (Clarendon County), South Carolina.

3. Author interview with Arthur Shores, June 1989, Birmingham, Alabama.

4. *Parents Involved in Community Schools v. Seattle School District No. 1 Et al.,* 551 U.S. 2007. (Justice Breyer, dissenting). http://www.supremecourtus.gov/opinions/06pdf/05-908.pdf. Accessed July 23, 2007.

5. William D. Lamson, "Race and Schools in Topeka, Kansas," March 1, 1985, p. 164. Plaintiff's Exhibit 219, T-B16.

6. Carl T. Rowan, "Jim Crow's Last Stand: December 1953." In *Reporting Civil Rights* Part One: American Journalism 1941-1963. Library Classics of the United States, Inc., New York (2003), p. 165. Originally appeared in *Minneapolis Tribune*, November 29-December 8, 1953.

7. Anna Mary Murphy, "Negro Problem in Kansas—Negro Teachers Hit by Desegregation." *Topeka Capital,* January 29, 1956. Box 16, No. 293. Plaintiff's Exhibit 293, T-316.

8. As mentioned previously, Topeka's high school had always been integrated.

9. See Lamson, 228-232. By 1974, twenty years after *Brown*, Topeka's school system (now called U.S.D #501) still underutilized predominately black schools while white schools remained overcrowded. For example, there was a 15.1 percent black enrollment at the elementary level, but more than half of them (56.7 percent) were assigned to seven schools while nine of the remaining eleven had an average of 4.5 black children assigned to each of them.

10. This resulted in a suit filed on September 10, 1973, *Johnson v. Whittier.* T-5430, Plaintiffs Exhibit 78 *Brown v. Board*, T-316. The complaint noted that "equality of facilities than distribution of students, alleging that the children in West Topeka and South Topeka received vastly superior educational facilities and opportunities, including buildings, equipment, libraries, and faculties, that could be obtained by students in the areas of East Topeka and North Topeka, which contained higher percentages of minority students." Though *Johnson* failed to qualify as a class action suit, it did set off an investigation by the then-federal agency, the Department of Health, Education, and Welfare (HEW) into "the practices of the Topeka public schools regarding race discrimination." This investigation led HEW to prepare to cut off federal aid to Topeka schools for desegregation noncompliance to and scheduled an administrative hearing. This action also resulted in the filing of *U.S.D. 501 v. Weinberger*, No. 74-160-C5. Though on August 27, 1974, *Johnson* moved to consolidate with *Weinberger*, this motion was never decided. The *Weinberger* case was later dismissed after the Topeka school district's motion for a preliminary injunction was granted by Judge Templar who found that the district court, and not HEW, had jurisdiction over Topeka's school desegregation.

11. The school board argued they were in compliance with the original desegregation plan that was approved by the district court on October 28, 1955, and fully implemented by September 1, 1961. Additionally, the school board argued that the district court has "exclusive jurisdiction to determine whether or not the Topeka school system is in violation of the Final Order of Judgment and the court approved plan for desegregation." The HEW attorney disagreed, stressing, "that while the original plaintiffs in our case were attacking segregation at only the elementary school level, HEW was charged

with investigating discrimination in all its aspects at all levels of the public school system."
Meanwhile, two other class action suits related to illegal segregation were filed on August
8, 1979 (*Miller v. Board of Education*), and September 7, 1979 (*Chapman v. Board of
Education*).

12. Though these cases resulted in minor judgments, they did prompt an investigation by the Office of Civil Rights of the then–federal agency, Department of Health,
Education, and Welfare. HEW found that Topeka was not in compliance and brought further attention to the ways in which the Topeka Board of Education sought to circumvent
desegregation.

13. U.S. Bureau of the Census, Department of Commerce. *1970 Census of Population: General Social and Economic Characteristics*, PC (1)—C, U.S. Government Printing
Office, Washington, D.C., 1971. The 1970 census showed that in Topeka, Kansas, the mean
family income in the wealthy, predominately white West Hills area was triple that of the
predominately black southeast area: $19,909 to $6,886. This statistic is also reflected in
the 1970 median value of housing, $28,800 in West Hills to $9,550 in East Topeka. The
reopening of *Brown* in 1979 tried to prove that the resegregation of Topeka's schools was
not the "natural" consequence of individual choice, but rather the result of the deliberate
actions of U.S.D. 501 to segregate its more affluent citizens (primarily white) who had
fled to its western suburbs from the less affluent (primarily black) concentrated in East
Topeka.

Shoe department sit-in at John A. Brown's department store, March 1, 1961. Sit-ins continued in Oklahoma City for several years, targeting other areas of public consumption besides lunch counters (courtesy of the Oklahoma State Historical Society).

Bibliography

Abramowitz, Jack. 1950. "Accommodation and Militancy in Negro Life, 1876–1916." Unpublished Ph.D. dissertation. New York: Columbia University Press.

Adler, Frank J. 1972. *Roots in a Moving Stream.* Kansas City, MO: Spangler Press.

Allen, Maxine Bednar. 1959. *The History and Present Role of the Elementary School Administrator in School District 110, Johnson County, Kansas.* Master's Thesis, University of Kansas, Lawrence.

Archer, Margaret S. 1996. *Culture and Agency: The Place of Culture in Social Theory,* rev. ed. Cambridge, UK: University of Cambridge Press.

Athearn, Robert G. 1978. *In Search of Canaan: Black Migration to Kansas, 1879-1880.* Lawrence: University Press of Kansas.

Ayers, Edward L. 1993. *The Promise of the New South: Life after Reconstruction.* New York: Oxford University Press.

Barnes, Catherine A. 1983. *Journey from Jim Crow: The Desegregation of Southern Transit.* New York: Columbia University Press.

Berman, Daniel M. 1966. *It Is So Ordered: The Supreme Court Rules on School Segregation.* New York: W. W. Norton.

Bloom, Jack M. 1987. *Class, Race, and the Civil Rights Movement.* Bloomington: Indiana University Press.

Blumberg, Rhoda Lois. 1980. "Careers of Women Civil Rights Activists." *Journal of Sociology and Social Welfare* 7: 708-729.

———. 1984. *Civil Rights: The 1960s Freedom Struggle.* Boston: G. K. Hall.

———. 1990. "White Mothers as Civil Rights Activists: The Interweave of Family and Movement Roles." Pp. 166-179 in Guida West and Rhoda Lois Blumberg, eds., *Women and Social Protest.* New York: Oxford University Press.

Blumer, Herbert. 1986. *Symbolic Interactionism: Perspective and Method.* Berkeley: University of California Press.

Branch, Taylor. 1988. *Parting the Waters: America in the King Years, 1954-1963.* New York: Simon and Schuster.

Brinton, Crane. 1952. *The Anatomy of Revolution.* Englewood Cliffs, NJ: Prentice-Hall.

Buechler, Stephen. 1993. "Beyond Resource Mobilization? Emerging Trends in Social Movement Theory." *Sociological Quarterly* 34: 217-235.

Bunche, Ralph. 1940. "The Programs, Ideologies, Tactics, and Achievements of Negro Betterment and Interracial Organizations.," in *Black Protest Thought in the Twentieth Century,* 2nd edition, August Meier, Elliott Rudwick, and Francis L. Broderick, eds. Indianapolis: Bobbs-Merrill Company, pp. 122-131.

Carper, James C. 1978. "The Popular Ideology of Segregated Schooling: Attitudes toward the Education of Blacks in Kansas, 1854-1900." *Kansas History* 1: 254-265.

Carson, Clayborne. 1986. "Civil Rights Reform and the Black Freedom Struggle." Pp. 19-37 in Charles Eagle, ed., *The Civil Rights Movement in America.* Jackson: University Press of Mississippi.

Cashman, Sean Dennis. 1991. *African-Americans and the Quest for Civil Rights.* New York: New York University Press.

Chafé, William H. 1980. *Civilities and Civil Rights.* New York: Oxford University Press.

Colburn, David R. 1985. *Racial Change and Community Crisis: St. Augustine Florida, 1877-1980.* New York: Columbia University Press.

Cooper, Anna Julia. 1988 [1892]. *A Voice from the South.* New York: Oxford University Press.

Cox, Thomas. 1982. *Blacks in Topeka, Kansas, 1865-1915: A Social History.* Baton Rouge: Louisiana State University Press.

Crawford, Vicki L., Jacqueline Anne Rouse, and Barbara Woods, eds. 1990. *Women in the Civil Rights Movement: Trailblazers and Torchbearers, 1941-1965.* Bloomington: Indiana University Press.

D'Anjou, Leo. 1996. *Social Movements and Cultural Change: The First Abolition Campaign Revisited.* New York: Aldine de Gruyter.

Dailey, Jane, Glenda Elizabeth Gilmore, and Bryant Simon, eds. *Jumpin' Jim Crow: Southern Politics from Civil War to Civil Rights.* Princeton, NJ: Princeton University Press.

Dalifume, Richard M. 1968. "The 'Forgotten Years' of the Negro Revolution." *Journal of American History* LV: 90-106.

Davies, James Chowning, ed. 1971. *When Men Revolt and Why: A Reader in Political Violence and Revolution.* New York: Free Press.

DeFrange, Ann. 1998. "40th Anniversary of Protest Sit-Ins Marked with Pride." *Daily Oklahoman.* August 16, 1998.

Douglass, Frederick. 1881. "The Color Line." *North American Review* 132 (CXXXII) June, pp. 567-577.

Du Bois, W. E. B. [1901] 1969. *The Souls of Black Folk.* New York: New American Library.

Eagles, Charles W., ed. 1986. *The Civil Rights Movement in America.* Jackson: University Press of Mississippi.

Eick, Gretchen C. 2001. *Dissent in Wichita: The Civil Rights Movement in the Midwest, 1954-1972.* Urbana: University of Illinois Press.

Einwohner, Rachel, Jocelyn Hollander, and Toska Olson. 2000. "Engendering Social Movements: Cultural Images and Movement Dynamics." *Gender & Society* 14: 679-699.

Eskew, Glen. 1997. *But for Birmingham: The Local and National Movements in the Civil Rights Struggle.* Chapel Hill, NC: University of North Carolina Press.

Fairclough, Adam. 1995. *Race and Democracy: The Civil Rights Struggle in Louisiana, 1915-1972.* Athens: University of Georgia Press.

Farmer, James. 1965. "The Early Sit-Ins." Pp. 243-246 in Meier, Rudwick, and Broderick, *Black Protest Thought in the Twentieth Century.*

Ferree, Myra Marx, and Silke Roth. 1998. "Gender, Class, and the Interaction between Social Movements: A Strike of West Berlin Day Care Workers." *Gender & Society* 12: 626-648.

Finchum, Tanya D., and G. Allen Finchum. 2001. "Celebrating the Library Spirit: A Look Back at the Carnegie Libraries in Oklahoma." *Chronicles of Oklahoma* 79: 454-475.

Fischer, David Hackett. 1989. *Albion Seed: Four British Folkways in America.* New York: Oxford University Press.

———. 2004. *Washington's Crossing.* New York: Oxford University Press.

Foner, Eric, and John A. Garraty, eds. 1991. *The Reader's Companion to American History.* Boston: Houghton Mifflin.

Frank, Thomas. 2004. *What's the Matter with Kansas? How Conservatives Won the Heart of America.* New York: Metropolitan Books.

Franklin, John Hope 1974. *From Slavery to Freedom: A History of Negro Americans.* New York: Knopf.

Frazier, E. Franklin. 1957. *Black Bourgeoisie: Rise of New Middle Class.* New York: Free Press.

———. 1957. "The Negro Middle Class and Desegregation." *Social Problems* 4: 291-301.

Frederickson, George M. 1995. *Black Liberation: A Comparative History of Black Ideologies in the United States and South Africa.* New York: Oxford University.

Freeman, Jo. 1975. *The Politics of Women's Liberation.* New York: David McKay Company.

———. 1983. *Social Movements of the Sixties and Seventies.* New York: Longman.

Gamson, William. 1990. *The Strategy of Social Protest,* 2nd ed. Belmont: Wadsworth.

Garfinkel, Herbert. 1973. *When Negroes March.* New York: Atheneum.

Garrow, David J. 1985. "The Origins of the Montgomery Bus Boycott." *Southern Changes* 7: 21-27.

———. 1986. "Black Civil Rights during the Eisenhower Years," pp. 269-281 in David J. Garrow, ed., *We Shall Overcome: The Civil Rights Movement in the United States in the 1950s and 1960s.* Brooklyn: Carlson Publishing.

Garrow, David J., ed. 1989. *We Shall Overcome: The Civil Rights Movement in the United States in the 1950s and 1960s.* Brooklyn: Carlson Publishing.

Giddings, Paula. 1985. *When and Where I Enter: The Impact of Black Women on Race and Sex in America.* Toronto: Bantam Books.

Gleason, Eliza Valeria Atkins. 1941. *The Southern Negro and the Public Library: A Study of the Government and Administration of Public Library Service to Negroes in the South.* Chicago, Ill.: University of Chicago Press.

Goffman, Erving. 1956. "The Nature of Deference and Demeanor." *American Anthropologist* 58: 47-85.

———. 1974. *Frame Analysis: An Essay on the Organization of Experience.* New York: Harper and Row.

———. 1983. "The Interaction Order." *American Sociological Review* 48: 1–17.

Goodrich, D. 1991. *Bloody Dawn: The Story of the Lawrence Massacre.* Kent, OH: Kent State University Press.

Goodwin, Jeff, and James M. Jasper, eds. 2004. *Rethinking Social Movements: Structure, Meaning, and Emotion.* Lanham, MD: Rowman and Littlefield.

Graves, Carl. 1981. "The Right to Be Served: Oklahoma City's Lunch Counter Sit-Ins, 1958–1964." *Chronicles of Oklahoma* 59: 152–166.

Greenberg, Jack. 1994. *Crusaders in the Courts.* New York: Basic Books.

Gumprecht, Blake. 1996. "A Saloon on Every Corner: Whiskey Towns of Oklahoma Territory, 1889–1907." *Chronicles of Oklahoma* 74: 164–173.

Gusfield, Joseph R. 1981. "Social Movements and Social Change: Perspectives on Linearity and Fluidity." *Research in Social Movements, Conflict, and Change* 4: 317–339.

Haarsager, Sandra. 1997. *Organized Womanhood: Cultural Politics in the Pacific Northwest, 1840–1920.* Norman, OK: University Of Oklahoma Press.

Hale, Grace Elizabeth. 1998. *Making Whiteness: The Culture of Segregation in the South, 1890–1940.* New York: Vintage.

Hall, Jacquelyn Dowd. 2005. "The Long Civil Rights Movement and the Political Uses of the Past." *Journal of American History* 91: 1233–1263.

Harding, Susan. 1984. "Reconstructing Order through Action: Jim Crow and the Southern Civil Rights Movement," in Charles Bright and Susan Harding, eds. *Statemaking and Social Movements: Essays in History and Theory.* Ann Arbor: University of Michigan Press, pp. 378–402.

Harding, Vincent. 1981. *There Is a River: The Black Struggle for Freedom in America.* Orlando, FL: Harcourt, Brace & Company.

Henderson, Cheryl Brown. 2003. "Lucinda Todd and the Invisible Petitioners of *Brown v. Board of Education* of Topeka, Kansas." Pp. 312–327 in Quintard Taylor and Shirley Ann Wilson Moore, eds., *African American Women Confront the West: 1600–2000.* Norman: University of Oklahoma Press.

Horton, Judith C. 1914. *How It Happened.* Guthrie, OK: State Capital Publishing.

Hughes, Everett C. 1963. "Race Relations and the Sociological Imagination." *American Sociological Review* 28: 879–890.

Irons, Jenny. 1998. "The Shaping of Activist Recruitment and Participation: A Study of Women in the Mississippi Civil Rights Movement." *Gender & Society* 12: 692–709.

Jacobs, Gregory S. 1998. *Getting around* Brown: *Desegregation, Development, and the Columbus Public Schools.* Columbus, OH: Ohio State University Press.

Johnson, Guy. 1938. "Negro Racial Movements and Leadership in the United States." *American Journal of Sociology* 43: 57–71.

Johnston, Hank, and Bert Klandermans, eds. *Social Movements and Culture* Minneapolis: University of Minnesota Press, 1995.

Kalberg, Stephen. 1994. *Max Weber's Comparative Historical Sociology.* Chicago: University of Chicago Press.

Katz, Milton S., and Susan B. Tucker. 1995. "A Pioneer in Civil Rights: Esther Brown and the South Park Desegregation Case of 1948." *Kansas History* 18: 234-247.

Kerber, Linda K. 1988. "Separate Spheres, Female Worlds, Woman's Place: The Rhetoric of Women's History." *The Journal of American History,* Vol. 75, No. 1. (June), pp. 9-39.

Killian, Lewis. 1984. "Organization, Rationality and Spontaneity in the Civil Rights Movement." *American Sociological Review,* 49: 770-783.

Killian, Lewis M., and Charles U. Smith. 1960. "Negro Protest Leaders in a Southern Community." *Social Forces* 38: 253-257.

Klarman, Michael J. 1994. "*Brown,* Racial Change, and the Civil Rights Movement." *Virginia Law Review* 80: 7-150.

———. 2004. *From Jim Crow to Civil Rights: The Supreme Court and the Struggle for Racial Equality.* Oxford: Oxford University Press.

Kluger, Richard. 1975. *Simple Justice.* New York: Knopf.

Kurland, Philip B., and Gerhard Carpe, eds. 1975. *Landmark Briefs and Arguments of the Supreme Court of the United States: Constitutional Law, Brown v. Board of Education.* Volumes 49 and 49A. Arlington, VA: University Publications of America.

Kurzman, Charles. 1996. "Structural Opportunity and Perceived Opportunity in Social-Movement Theory: The Iranian Revolution of 1979," *American Sociological Review,* 61: 153-179.

Lawson, Steven F. 1991. "Freedom Then, Freedom Now: The Historiography of the Civil Rights Movement." *American Historical Review* 96: 456-471.

Lawson, Steven F., and Charles Payne. 1998. *Debating the Civil Rights Movement, 1945-1968,* introduction by James T. Patterson. Lanham, Md.: Rowman & Littlefield.

Lemert, Charles. 1997. *Social Things: An Introduction to the Sociological Life.* Lanham, MD: Rowman and Littlefield.

Lengermann, Patricia Madoo, and Jill Niebrugge-Brantley. 1998. *The Women Founders: Sociology and Social Theory, 1820-1930.* New York: McGraw-Hill.

Lofland, John. 1993. "Theory-Bashing and Answer-Improving in the Study of Social Movements." *American Sociologist* (Summer): 37-58.

———. 1996. *Social Movement Organizations: Guide to Research on Insurgent Realities.* New York: Walter de Gruyter.

Luper, Clara. 1979. *Behold the Walls.* Oklahoma City, OK: Jim Wire.

Maines, David R. 2001. *The Faultline of Consciousness: A View of Interactionism in Sociology.* New York: A. de Gruyter.

Malone, Cheryl Knott. 1996. *Accommodating Access "Colored" Carnegie Libraries, 1905-1925.* Thesis (Ph.D.), University of Texas at Austin, 1996.

Martin, Charles H. 1980. "Oklahoma's 'Scottsboro' Affair: The Jess Hollins Rape Case, 1931-1936." *South Atlantic Quarterly* (Spring): 174-188.

Marwell, Gerald, and Pamela Oliver. 1984. "Collective Action Theory and Social Movements Research." *Research in Social Movements, Conflict, and Change* 7: 1-28.

McAdam, Doug. 1982. *Political Process and the Development of Black Insurgency, 1930-1970.* Chicago: University of Chicago Press.

———. 1988. *Freedom Summer.* New York: Oxford University Press.

———. 1992. "Gender as a Mediator of the Activist Experience: The Case of Freedom Summer." *American Journal of Sociology* 97: 1211–1240.

McAdam, Doug, and Ronnelle Paulsen. 1993. "Specifying the Relationship between Social Ties and Activism." *American Journal of Sociology* 99: 640–667.

McAdam, Doug, Sidney Tarrow, and Charles Tilly. 2001. *Dynamics of Contention* Cambridge, UK: Cambridge University Press.

McCarthy, John D., and Mayer N. Zald. 1977. "Resource Mobilization and Social Movements: A Partial Theory." *American Journal of Sociology* 82: 1212–1241.

McWhorter, Diane. 2001. *Carry Me Home: Birmingham, Alabama—The Climatic Battle of the Civil Rights Revolution.* New York: Simon and Schuster.

Meier, August. 1962. "The Successful Sit-Ins in a Border City: A Study in Social Causation." *Journal of Intergroup Relations* 2: 230–237.

———. 1963. "Negro Protest Movements and Organizations," The Journal of Negro Education, Vol. 32, No. 4 (Autumn 1963): 437–450.

Meier, August, and Elliott Rudwick. 1969. "The Boycott Movement against Jim Crow Streetcars in the South, 1900–1906." *Journal of American History* 55: 756–775.

———. 1969 "How CORE Began." *Social Science Quarterly* 49: 789–799.

———. 1976. *Along the Color Line: Explorations in the Black Experience.* Urbana: University of Illinois Press.

Meyer, David S. 1993. "Protest Cycles and Political Process." *Political Research Quarterly* 46: 451–479.

Mills, C. Wright. 1959. *The Sociological Imagination.* London: Oxford University Press.

Moore, Shirley Ann Wilson and Quintard Taylor. 2003. "The West of African American Women, 1600–2000." Pp. 3–21 in Taylor and Moore, *African American Women Confront the West: 1600–2000.*

Morris, Aldon D. 1981. "The Black Southern Student Sit-In Movement: An Analysis of Internal Organization." *American Sociological Review* 46: 744–767.

———. 1984. *The Origins of the Civil Rights Movement: Black Communities Organizing for Change.* New York: Free Press.

———. 1993. "Birmingham Confrontation Reconsidered: An Analysis of the Dynamics and Tactics of Mobilization." *American Sociological Review* 58: 621–636.

———. 1999. "A Retrospective on the Civil Rights Movement: Political and Intellectual Landmarks." *Annual Review of Sociology* 25: 517–539.

———. 2000. "Reflections on Social Movement Theory: Criticisms and Proposals." *Contemporary Sociology* 29, no. 3: 445–454.

Muse, Benjamin. 1964. *Ten Years of Prelude.* Beaconsfield: Darwen Finlayson.

Norrell, Robert J. 1985. *Reaping the Whirlwind: The Civil Rights Movement in Tuskegee.* New York: Knopf.

Oberschall, Anthony. 1973. *Social Conflict and Social Movements.* Englewood Cliffs, NJ: Prentice-Hall.

———. 1989. "The 1960 Sit-Ins: Protest Diffusion and Movement Take-off." *Research in Social Movements, Conflict, and Change* 11: 31–53.

Oliver, Pamela. 1989. "Bringing the Crowd Back In: The Nonorganizational Elements of Social Movements." *Research in Social Movements, Conflicts, and Change* 11: 1-30.

Oppenheimer, Martin. 1963. "Current Negro Protest Activities and the Concept of Social Movement." *Phylon* 24: 154-159.

Orum, Anthony M. 1966. "A Reappraisal of the Social and Political Participation of Negroes." *American Journal of Sociology* 72: 32-46.

Painter, Nell I. 1986. *Exodusters: Black Migration to Kansas after Reconstruction.* Lawrence: University of Kansas Press.

Patterson, James T. 2001. Brown v. Board of Education: *A Civil Rights Milestone and Its Troubled Legacy.* New York: Oxford University Press.

Payne, Charles. 1995. *I've Got the Light of Freedom: The Organizing Tradition and the Mississippi Freedom Struggle.* Berkeley: University of California Press.

Payne, Charles M., and Adam Green, eds. 2003. *Time Longer Than Rope: A Century of African American Activism, 1850-1950.* New York: New York University Press.

Perrow, Charles. 1986. *Complex Organizations: A Critical Essay.* New York: Random House.

Phillips, Bernard. 2001. *Beyond Sociology's Tower of Babel: Reconstructing the Scientific Method.* New York: Aldine de Gruyter.

Phillips, Bernard, ed. 2007. *Understanding Terrorism: Building on the Sociological Imagination.* Boulder, CO: Paradigm Publishers.

Phillips, Bernard, and Louis C. Johnston. 2007. *The Invisible Crisis of Contemporary Society.* Boulder, CO: Paradigm Publishers.

Phillips, Bernard, Harold Kincaid, and Thomas J. Scheff, eds. 2002. *Toward a Sociological Imagination: Bridging Specialized Fields.* Lanham, MD: Rowman and Littlefield.

Pichardo, Nelson A. 1997. "New Social Movements: A Critical Review." *Annual Review of Sociology* 23: 411-430.

Piven, Frances Fox, and Richard A. Cloward. 1979. *Poor People's Movements: Why They Succeed, How They Fail.* New York: Vintage Books.

Polletta, Francesca. 1997. "Culture and Its Discontents: Recent Theorizing on the Cultural Dimensions of Protest." *Sociological Inquiry* 67: 431-450.

———. 2002. "Review of Dynamics of Contention." *Contemporary Sociology* 31: 580-582.

Proudfoot, Merrill. 1962. *Diary of a Sit-In.* New Haven, CT: College & University Press.

Reese, Linda Williams. 2003. "Clara Luper and the Civil Rights Movement in Oklahoma City, 1958-1964." Pp. 328-343 in Taylor and Moore, *African American Women Confront the West: 1600-2000.*

Roback, Jennifer. 1986. "The Political Economy of Segregation: The Case of Segregated Streetcars." *Journal of Economic History* 46: 893-917.

Robbins, Louise S. 1996. "Racism and Censorship in Cold War Oklahoma: The Case of Ruth W. Brown and the Bartlesville Public Library." *Southwestern Historical Quarterly* 100: 18-46.

———. 2000. *The Dismissal of Miss Ruth Brown: Civil Rights, Censorship, and the American Library.* Norman: University of Oklahoma Press.

Robinson, JoAnn Gibson. 1987. *The Montgomery Bus Boycott and the Women Who Started It.* Knoxville: University of Tennessee Press.

Robnett, Bernice. 1996. "African-American Women in the Civil Rights Movement, 1954-1965: Gender, Leadership, and Micro-Mobilization." *American Journal of Sociology* 101: 1661-1693.

Rosen, Jeffrey. 2007. "Can a Law Change a Society?" *New York Times,* Section 4.

Rowan, Carl T. 1993. *Dream Makers, Dream Breakers: The World of Justice Thurgood Marshall.* Boston, MA: Little Brown.

Rynbrandt, Linda. 1997. "The 'Ladies of the Club' and Caroline Bartlett Crane: Affiliation and Alienation in Progressive Social Reform." *Gender & Society* 11: 210-214.

Saxe, Allan. 1969. "Protest and Reform: The Desegregation of Oklahoma City." Unpublished dissertation, University of Oklahoma, Norman, Oklahoma.

Schultz, Debra. 2001. *Going South: Jewish Women in the Civil Rights Movement.* New York: New York University Press.

Schultz, Elizabeth. 1993. "Dreams Deferred: The Personal Narratives of Four Black Kansans." *American Studies* 34: 25-52.

Sitkoff, Harvard. 1981. *The Struggle for Black Equality, 1954-1980.* New York: Oxford.

Smith, Bob. 1965. *They Closed Our Public Schools: Prince Edward County, Virginia, 1951-1964.* Chapel Hill: University of North Carolina Press.

Smith, Heather J., and Thomas Kessler. 2004. "Group-Based Emotions and Intergroup Behavior." Pp. 292-313 in Larissa L. Tiedens and Colin W. Leach, eds., *The Social Life of Emotions.* New York: Cambridge University Press.

Snow, David, and Robert Benford. 1992. "Master Frames and Cycles of Protest." *Frontiers in Social Movement Theory,* A. D. Morris and C. M. Mueller, eds. New Haven, CT: Yale University Press, pp. 133-155.

Snow, David A., Sarah Anne Soule, and Hanspeter Kriesi. 2004. *The Blackwell Companion to Social Movements.* Malden, MA: Blackwell Publishing.

Speer, Hugh W. 1990. *Funny Things Happened on the Way to the Supreme Court—And Back.* Kansas City, MO: School of Education, University of Missouri-Kansas City.

Staggenborg, Suzanne. 1991. *The Pro-Choice Movement: Organization and Activism in the Abortion Conflict.* New York: Oxford University Press.

Stall, Susan, and Randy Stoecker. 1998. "Community Organizing or Organizing Community? Gender and the Crafts of Empowerment" *Gender & Society* 6: 729-756.

Stiefmiller, Helen. 2001. "Judith Carter Horton: Founder of the First African American Library in the Southwest," unpublished manuscript, Oklahoma Territorial Museum, in Guthrie, Oklahoma.

Stinchcombe, Arthur L. 1978. *Theoretical Methods in Social History.* New York: Academic Press.

Strong, Willa A. 1957. "The Origins, Development, and Current Status of the Oklahoma Federation of Colored Women's Clubs." Ph.D. dissertation, University of Oklahoma.

Swidler, Ann. 1986. "Culture in Action—Symbols and Strategies *American Sociological Review* 51 (2): 273-286.

Sztompka, Piotr. 1993. *The Sociology of Social Change*. Cambridge, MA: Blackwell.

Tarrow, Sidney. 1983. *Struggle, Politics, and Reform: Collective Action, Social Movements, and Cycles of Protest*. Ithaca, NY: Cornell University Press.

———. 1988. "National Politics and Collective Action: Recent Theory and Research in Western Europe and the United States." *Annual Review of Sociology* 14: 421–440.

———. 1994. *Power in Movement: Social Movements, Collective Action, and Politics*. New York/London: Cambridge University Press.

Taylor, Quintard. 1998. *In Search of the Racial Frontier: African Americans in the American West, 1528–1990*. New York: W. W. Norton.

Taylor, Quintard, and Shirley Ann Wilson Moore. 2003. *African American Women Confront the West: 1600–2000*. Norman: University of Oklahoma Press.

Tilly, Charles. 1978. *From Mobilization to Revolution*. Reading, MA: Addison-Wesley.

———. 1995. "To Explain Political Processes." *American Journal of Sociology* 100 (6): 1594–1610

Tocqueville, Alexis de. 1955. *The Old Regime and the French Revolution,* trans. Stuart Gilbert. New York: Doubleday.

Turner, Ralph H., and Lewis M. Killian. 1972. *Collective Behavior,* 2nd ed. Englewood Cliffs, NJ: Prentice-Hall.

———. 1987. *Collective Behavior,* 3rd ed. Englewood Cliffs, NJ: Prentice-Hall.

Tushnet, Mark V. 1988. *The NAACP's Legal Strategy against Segregated Education, 1925–1950*. Chapel Hill: University of North Carolina Press.

———. 1994. *Making Civil Rights Law: Thurgood Marshall and the Supreme Court, 1936–1961*. New York: Oxford University Press.

Van Delinder, Jean. 1992. "Albany and Birmingham: A Comparison of Two Movements." Unpublished master's paper, University of Kansas, Lawrence, Kansas.

———. 1996. *Border Campaigns*. Unpublished Ph.D. dissertation, University of Kansas, Lawrence, Kansas.

———. 2003. "Invisibility Blues: Gendered Radicalism in Oklahoma," Paper presented at the Annual Meeting of the American Sociological Association Annual Meeting, Atlanta, GA.

———. 2004. "*Brown v. Board of Education of Topeka:* A Landmark Case Unresolved Fifty Years Later." *Prologue* 36: 12–22.

Vander Zanden, James W. 1963. "The Non-Violent Resistance Movement against Segregation." *American Journal of Sociology* 68: 544–550.

Vandever, Elizabeth. 1971. *Brown v. Board of Education Topeka*. Unpublished dissertation. University of Kansas.

Van Slyck, Abigail Ayres. 1995. *Free to All: Carnegie Libraries & American Culture, 1890–1920*. Chicago: University of Chicago Press.

Wallace, Michelle. 1990. *Invisibility Blues: From Pop to Theory*. New York: Verso.

Walters, Ronald. 1993. "Standing Up in the Heart of America." *American Visions* 8: 20–23.

———. 1996. "The Great Plains Sit-in Movement, 1958–1960." *Great Plains Quarterly* 16 (Spring): 85–94.

Walzer, Michael. 1997. *On Toleration.* New Haven, CT: Yale University Press.

Webb, Clive. 2001. *Fight against Fear: Southern Jews and Black Civil Rights.* Athens: University of Georgia Press.

Weber, Max, 1949. *Max Weber on the Methodology of the Social Sciences,* 1st ed. Glencoe, Ill: Free Press.

———. [1905] 1958. *The Protestant Ethic and the Spirit of Capitalism,* translated by Talcott Parsons. New York: Scribner's.

———. 1978. *Economy and Society: An Outline of Interpretive Sociology,* edited by Guenther Roth and Claus Wittich; translated by Ephraim Fischoff [et al.]. Berkeley: University of California Press.

Weems, Robert E., Jr. 1995. "African-American Consumer Boycotts During the Civil Rights Era." *Western Journal of Black Studies* 19: 72-79.

———. 1998. *Desegregating the Dollar: African American Consumerism in the Twentieth Century.* New York: New York University Press.

Weiss, Nancy J. 1986. "Creative Tensions in the Leadership of the Civil Rights Movement." Pp. 39-64 in Eagle, *The Civil Rights Movement in America.*

Wesley, Charles Harris. 1984. *The History of the National Association of Colored Women's Clubs: A Legacy of Service.* Washington, DC: NACWC.

West, Guida, and Rhoda Lois Blumberg, eds. 1990. *Women and Social Protest.* New York: Oxford University Press.

White, Forrest R. 1994. "Brown Revisited." *Phi Delta Kappan* 76: 12-20.

White, Robert M. 1964. "The Tallahassee Sit-Ins and CORE: A Nonviolent Revolutionary Submovement." Unpublished diss., Florida State University.

Wigginton, Eliot. 1991. *Refuse to Stand Silently by: An Oral History of Grass Roots Social Activism in America, 1921-1964.* New York: Doubleday.

Williams, Franklin, and Earl Fultz. 1949. "The Merriam School Fight" *The Crisis* 49: 140-156.

Williams, Rhys H. 2004. "The Cultural Contexts of Collective Action: Constraints, Opportunities, and the Symbolic Life of Social Movements." Pp. 91-115 in David Snow, Sarah Soule, and Hanspeter Kriesi, eds., *The Blackwell Companion to Social Movements.* Malden, MA: Blackwell.

Wilson, Bobby M. 2000. *Race and Place in Birmingham: The Civil Rights and Neighborhood Movements.* Lanham, MD: Rowman and Littlefield.

Wilson, James Q. 1961. "The Strategy of Protest: Problems of Negro Civic Action." *Journal of Conflict Resolution* 5: 291-303.

Wilson, Paul E.. 1995. *A Time to Lose: Representing Kansas in* Brown v. Board of Education. Lawrence: University Press of Kansas.

Woods, Randall B. 1983. "Integration, Exclusion, or Segregation? The Color Line in Kansas, 1878-1900." *Western Historical Quarterly* 14 (April): 181-198.

Woodward, C. Vann. 1974. *The Strange Career of Jim Crow,* 3rd ed. New York: Oxford.

Zald, Mayer N., and John D. McCarthy, eds. 1987. *Social Movements in an Organizational Society.* New Brunswick, NJ: Transaction Books.

Index

About the Author

Jean Van Delinder is associate professor of sociology and director of women's studies, with affiliated appointments in American studies and Africana–African American studies, at the University of Oklahoma. Born and raised in Hibbing, Minnesota, Van Delinder attended the University of Minnesota, in Minneapolis, earning an undergraduate degree in humanities. She then earned her master's degree in American studies and a Ph.D. in sociology from the University of Kansas. Dr. Van Delinder also worked as a historical researcher, developing exhibits at the National Civil Rights Museum in Memphis, Tennessee, and as an oral history consultant for the Kansas City Museum, Kansas State Historical Society, Johnson County Historical Society, Kansas State Humanities Council, and the *Brown v. Board* National Historical Site in Topeka, Kansas.

Van Delinder's major area of study is focused on contemporary American race and ethnic relations. Her primary expertise is the sociology of the civil rights movement. In addition to published research on the civil rights movement, she has published articles on topics including Taylorism and Native American witchcraft. Her funded research has included studying diabetes risk factors in Native American women and developing a social marketing program targeting healthy eating behaviours for Native Americans in Oklahoma.